Multilateralism and Regional Security

Canadian Cataloguing in Publication Data

Main entry under title:

Multilateralism and regional security

Co-published by the Lester B. Pearson Canadian International Peacekeeping Training Centre, Nova Scotia.
ISBN 0-88911-729-2

1. Security, International. 2. International cooperation. I. Fortmann, Michel.
II. MacFarlane, S. N. (Stephen Neil), 1954-   . III. Roussel, Stéphane,
1964-   . IV. Queen's University (Kingston, Ont.). Centre for International
Relations. V. Lester B. Pearson Canadian International Peacekeeping
Training Centre.

JX1952.M84 1996   327.1'7   C96-931497-3

Printed in Canada by Brown Book Company Limited, Toronto, Ontario.

Edited by Michel Fortmann, S. Neil MacFarlane,
and Stéphane Roussel

Multilateralism and Regional Security

The Canadian Peacekeeping Press
1997

The Lester B. Pearson Canadian International Peacekeeping
Training Centre
President, Alex Morrison, MSC, CD, MA

The Pearson Peacekeeping Centre supports and enhances the Canadian contribution to international peace, security, and stability. The Centre conducts research and provides advanced training and educational programmes, and is a division of the Canadian Institute of Strategic Studies. The Canadian Peacekeeping Press is the publishing division of the Pearson Peacekeeping Centre.

The Centre (a division of the Canadian Institute of Strategic Studies), established by the Government of Canada in 1994, is funded, in part, by the Department of Foreign Affairs and International Trade and the Department of National Defence of Canada.

Le centre (une division de l'Institut canadien d'études stratégiques) à été établi par le Gouvernement du Canada en 1994. Le soutien financier de Centre provient, en partie, des ministères des Affaires étrangères et du commerce international et de la Défense nationale.

Canadian Peacekeeping Press publications include:

Facing the Future: Proceedings of the 1996 Canada-Japan Conference
on Modern Peacekeeping (1997)

Seeds of Freedom: Personal Reflections on the Dawning of Democracy (1996)

Analytic Approaches to the Study of Future Conflict (1996)

Pearson Paper #1: Peacekeeping and the Coming Anarchy (1996)

The Centre-Periphery Debate in International Security (1996)

Rapid Reaction Capabilities: Requirements and Prospects
Les capacités de réaction rapide de l'ONU: exigences et perspectives (1996)

The New Peacekeeping Partnership (1995)

For publications information, please contact:

James Kiras, Publications Manager
The Pearson Peacekeeping Centre
Cornwallis Park, PO Box 100
Clementsport, NS B0S 1E0 CANADA
Tel: (902) 638-8611 ext. 161 Fax: (902) 638-8576
Email: jkiras@ppc.cdnpeacekeeping.ns.ca Or visit the Pearson Peacekeeping Centre website:
http://www.cdnpeacekeeping.ns.ca

Contents

Preface

The potential of multilateralism as a mode of interstate relations was substantially constrained during the Cold War by the bipolar rivalry of the United States and the Soviet Union. The end of the Cold War and increasing cooperation between the United States and the Soviet Union within the context of the United Nations appeared to have brought new life to the discussion of multilateralism in international relations and to its potential as a means of ordering international affairs. The increased likelihood of unanimity among the permanent members of the Security Council ostensibly widened the area of cooperative endeavour in the realm of international security in particular, as was evident in the collaborative efforts to settle many regional conflicts such as those in Namibia, Angola, and Afghanistan. The activities of the United Nations in this sphere expanded substantially in the early 1990s. As many peacekeeping operations were mounted in 1988-95 as in the entire prior history of the United Nations.

The explosion of conflict management activitied of the United Nations, as well as the broadening of the concept of peacekeeping, stretched the capabilities of this universal organization. In consequence, the then-Secretary-General, Boutros Boutros-Ghali, suggested that more attention be given to the role of regional approaches to the management of threats to international peace and security. In his view, these organizations constituted an important and underutilized pool of capabilities that could be more effectively deployed to keep and to strengthen the peace. In his *Agenda for Peace,* he stressed the desirability of devolution of responsibilities for regional security for regional organizations, among them the Organization of American States (OAS) and the Organization for Security and Cooperation in Europe.

Since that time, significant security initiatives by regional organizations have proceeded in the former Yugoslavia, the former Soviet Union, Africa, and Latin America. These provide a basis for initial assessment of the merits of this devolution of responsibility. With these considerations in mind, the *Chaire d'études militaires et stratégiques* of the Université de Montréal, the *Centre d'études des politiques étrangrès et de sécurité* of the Université du Québec à Montréal, and the Centre for International Relations at Queen's University organized a conference on the subject of multilateralism and regional security in May 1995. In addition to providing a thorough airing of theoretical issues surrounding multilateralism in the post-Cold War era, the group placed particular emphasis on the experience of multilateralism in security matters in two regions — Latin America and Central and Eastern Europe. The papers delivered at that conference are brought together here.

The sponsors of the conference and volume are grateful to the Security and Defence Forum of the Department of National Defence (Canada) for its generous underwriting of this project and for its broader support of strategic studies in Canada. The editors would also like to thank Marilyn Banting, Alison MacArthur, and Valerie Jarus for the many varied aspects of preparation of the manuscript for publication.

S. Neil MacFarlane

Michel Fortmann
S. Neil MacFarlane
Stéphane Roussel

Multilateralism and the Future of Security Studies

The Problem

Among the myriad events that have caught our attention in the past years, one catastrophe that has received insufficient attention is the crisis of security studies. In the words of Ken Booth, strategic studies has "lost its real world context."[1] Not only has the strategist's world been revolutionized in practice; it was also fracturing in theory."[2] Familiar themes like deterrence, nuclear strategy, balance of power, and arms control, have either lost their original meaning or seemingly faded into irrelevance.

For example, what does power mean when it takes 75 percent of America's tactical aircraft and 40 percent of its tanks in order to defeat a country with the national product of Portugal? As it was observed in the *Economist* in the aftermath of the Gulf War: "This is some unipolar gunboat."[3] What does the threat of interstate "anarchy" mean in a world characterized by the diffusion of political and military power, the spillover of a host of transnational problems from one region to the other and the globalization of the economic space. In the words of Stanley Hoffman: "the enemy today is not the violence that results from the clash of mighty powers ..., but the violence that results from the chaos from below ... What is now at stake is the very nature of the state."[4]

In relation to this last statement, one might well remember, with a touch of nostalgia, Kenneth Waltz' remark concerning the longevity of states, "few states die — did he say in 1979 — Who is going to be around 100 years from now? The Soviet Union or Ford and IBM?"[5] This point seems to have been premature. In a nutshell, with the increasing contestability of its key operational concepts, the notion of an established basis of knowledge in security studies has become an oxymoron.[6]

The current period can thus be conceived as a phase of intellectual uncertainty characterized by numerous "morbid symptoms."[7] These include the proliferation of simplistic world views,[8] the tired repetition of old debates and arguments, and widespread "*ad-hocery*" (faddishness) in lieu of strategic analysis. Indeed, one might argue that if the security studies' community does not adapt fast to the new strategic environment, it may very well know the fate of old soldiers and slowly fade away into oblivion. As John Chipman puts it, "In the absence of the conceptual clarity provided by the Cold War, the primary obligation of the strategist is to identify the principal feature of the evolving international system and the consequences for policymakers."[9]

But should our approaches necessarily change because our environment is evolving? If new concepts and theories are needed, this is not because realism is dead and a new paradigm already waits in the wings. We still very much live in a realist's world where states are the main players and military power does count, but there are now many other parameters to be considered. No single concept or theory describes adequately the confusing reality that surrounds us. To reflect a fragmented and complex world, we need a "clash of perspectives *about* world politics."[10] This will afford us the opportunity not to bury one approach or the other, but to enrich our analysis through cross fertilization.

In fact, there cannot be a more opportune moment to open up basic conceptual and theoretical questions and to design a new research agenda.[11] It is the purpose of this volume to contribute in a small way to a new security studies research agenda going beyond ritual pronouncements about what is real and what is not.

Those who remain sceptical about the policy relevance of these theoretical debates should keep in mind that the golden age of strategic studies in the 1950s opened up precisely because the nuclear age was raising new, complex, and frightening questions that military analysts could not answer by themselves. Then, as now, new concepts and theories were needed to make sense of the situation. Although many of the theories put forward by the likes of Kahn, Schelling, and Wohlstetter seemed utterly abstruse, they gave birth to the practice of deterrence and arms control, two major contributions of strategic studies to the real world of policymaking. As Lawrence Freedman has said, "When discussion is forced, despite all the instincts of officers, bureaucrats and politicians, to the conceptual level, then is the time when academics can play their most useful role."[12]

Multilateralism: The Significance of the Concept

This volume focuses on the concept of multilateralism. The reason why multilateralism should be placed at the top of a new security studies research agenda is clear. To belabour a point already made earlier, traditional security threats of direct military attack are no longer the dominant problem to be considered in strategy and defence planning. Traditional security issues have been replaced by numerous nonmilitary preoccupations that favour multilateral responses.

From a global perspective, what was once defined as strategic (military) stability has certainly declined in importance relative to a host of other issues including economic survival, the spread of endemic poverty, population increases, food security, environmental degradation, resource and energy tensions, drug trafficking and large-scale migrations (not to mention ethnic strife and the rebirth of religious and political extremism). Briefly put, there has been a diversification of the notion of security and "a relative decline of the old military/strategic concept."[13]

Moreover, with economic survival perceived as the number one strategic issue for most industrialized nations, their military establishments must now undertake a dramatic reduction in size and restructuring of forces for what Jane Nolan calls the "preventive management of security conditions,"[14] a task significantly different from responding to a large military attack from one specified aggressor.

The end of current geostrategic shifts is still not in sight. The difficulties posed for *national* defence planners by a world with multiple and shifting centres of power are considerable and complicate tremendously the task of defining missions, capabilities, and deployments.[15] No state, however powerful, will be able to deal alone with the all-round military (and nonmilitary) uncertainties we have to face today. In the meantime, the shadow cast by the diffusion of military technology and the persistence of old political quarrels in many parts of the world remains a reality that cannot be ignored.

In short, the evolution of the international system points to the clear conclusion that security issues and more general international issues will have to be addressed in a cooperative multilateral fashion. This — for many experts — is the new strategic imperative:

The Cold War did not end by organized vote or by any strategic design. It was terminated by diffuse, spontaneous historical forces powerful enough to override the prescriptions of established policies, powerful enough also to induce massive social transformation. Those same forces are revising the axioms of international politics. They generate strong incentives to form multilateral cooperative security arrangements to replace the Cold War confrontation whether or not the idea itself is immediately evident.[16]

A principal question for a multilateralist research agenda must be whether and to what extent this analytical appreciation translates itself into political reality.

The Definition of Multilateralism

Before attempting to answer this question, we should have at least some notion of what multilateralism means in theory and practice. When we speak of multilateralism, we usually refer to international institutions like the GATT or the UN; that is to say, to international organizations that promote the coordination of national policies or some form of interstate cooperation and profess to embody certain general principles. Multilateral trade regimes are some examples.[17] In the area of security relations, the concept of multilateralism generates references to collective defence and security arrangements like the North Atlantic Treaty Organization (NATO) and the Organization for Security and Cooperation in Europe (OSCE).

Multilateral institutions comprise (i) organizations with their resources, structures and processes (a much neglected aspect of the study of international institutions), and (ii) a set of persistent and connected rules, formal and informal that prescribe behavioural roles, constrain activities, and shape expectations. Thus, to a large extent, multilateral institutions and *regimes* are closely related concepts.

However, there is more to multilateralism than abstract notions like structures, processes, norms, and rules. Indeed, the key question raised by *regime theory* as well as multilateralism has been central to international relations since the time of Thucydides: namely how is cooperation or rule-regulated behaviour possible between self-centred political entities competing for power and influence in an environment devoid of supranational authority? At the outset, there appear to be two possible answers: the underlying choice they offer is fundamental to the *problématique* of this volume.

From a realist-rational choice perspective, multilateral institutions do (sometimes) count, but they are merely "tools of their member states — instruments of policy — to be used, abused or ignored."[18] They operate within a tight bargaining system in which power and interest play a paramount role. In other words, cooperation will occur in the very limited sense that it suits the short-term interests of major powers. Moreover, nobody really trusts these anony-mous bureaucracies or would be willing to vest any power in them. Beyond this, states usually cheat or "free ride" when it comes to their collective re-sponsibilities. In theoretical terms then, multilateral institutions are marginal phenomena, expressing the distribution of political power rather than becom-ing significant and influential factors in their own right.[19]

From the opposing perspective (call it social-constructivist, liberal-institutionalist, or post-modernist), structures and power are not the only constituent elements of international relations. "Ideas — world views, princi-pled beliefs and knowledge — not only define the meaning of power, but also affect the reasoning process by which state actors define their interest."[20] Power in this sense is not an objective reality, but is what actors make of it. In addi-tion, values do determine states' actions; "world politics is heavily regulated by norms that prescribe appropriate behaviour and are embedded in formal and informal institutions. These institutions form the social structure of inter-national relations."[21] In other words, international relations not only form a *system* where states "interact" (violently or peacefully) but a *community*, an *international society* characterized by common rules and institutions that regu-late the behaviour of individual actors in the best interest of all. Moreover, from this perspective, the boundary between domestic political and social forces and the world of international relations is fluid and permeable. Collective move-ments, values, and beliefs at least partially shape state foreign policies and may contribute to regionwide consensus on a number of desired common goals like democracy or human rights. This consensus, in turn, forms the base on which multilateral *regimes* (like the defence-of-democracy-*regime* of the Americas) are built. The addition of domestic/societal forces to the framework of multilateralism naturally introduces us to the notion of *global governance*.[22] This concept enlarges the scope of multilateral institutions to include all goal-oriented social groupings — from the group to the international organization — whose actions have transnational repercussions.

These contrasting world views have inspired the approach adopted by the editors of this volume. This volume includes both general conceptual analyses of multilateralism and specific regional applications of the concept.

* * *

Andrew Knight provides an historical and anthropological account of the evolution of the concept of multilateralism, stressing that both state-centric and societal understandings of multilateralism have always been present in relations between communities. He distinguishes between "top-down" ap-proaches to multilateralism that focus on states and "bottom-up" approaches that focus on intersocietal relations. He argues that "top-down" approaches have dominated discourse on multilateralism at least since the Peace of

Westphalia, but that in the context of globalization of economies and societies, and dramatic improvements in transportation and communications, "bottom-up" relations are becoming increasingly significant in the study of multilateralism.

Albrecht Schnabel follows with an assessment of the relevance of realist theory to the evolution of great power approaches to peacekeeping in the post-Cold War era. He examines the question of whether the increasing incidence of peacekeeping and humanitarian intervention should be construed as evidence of a shift from a state-centric, national-interest-based structure of international relations to a more communitarian, globalist one. His approach is to examine the motivations of three leading states in peacekeeping. He concludes that the policies of these states are increasingly informed by calculations of interest, prestige, and status; and display little commitment to global humanitarian norms. As such, they are consistent with a realist interpretation of state behaviour. At least in this sphere, multilateralism has little independent explanatory value.

Brian Job tackles the question of multilateralism in regional contexts. Beginning with a working definition of multilateralism that stresses the importance of differentiating between quantitative and qualitative multilateralism, he then goes on to examine the nature of regional security complexes and the interests in multilateralist action of actors operating in such complexes. He argues that the interests of states with regard to multilateralism vary with these states' level of power. This leads to an analysis of the responsiveness and effectiveness of regional multilateral organizations in the management of regional conflict. His conclusions are quite pessimistic. In the short and medium term, there is little prospect for regional support of multilateralism, and little prospect for effective multilateralist management or resolution of regional conflict. In the longer term, however, the existence of a number of nascent security communities at the regional level might be conducive to a more optimistic conclusion with regard to the conflict management roles of such organizations.

This is followed by a number of regional case studies of multilateralism. David Mares analyzes the role of multilateralism in Latin America. After examining the nature of the traditional balance of power system in the region, he analyzes the reasons for the collapse of the structure of security in the region in the 1970s and 1980s. He then discusses the regional experience with multilateralism and the potential for multilateral mechanisms to address the uncertainties of the current security situation in the region. He argues that economic liberalization and political democratization do not necessarily lead to the elimination of regional insecurity and suggests a multitiered (diadic,

subregional, regional, and global) approach to multilateral security cooperation might be a prudent alternative.

As noted above, one of the more compelling reasons for a reexamination
of multilateralism is the growing significance of global and transnational activity lying outside the control of states. One of the more prominent examples of
this is the drug trade. With these considerations in mind, Hal Klepak examines
multilateralism in efforts to control trafficking in narcotics in the Americas. He
argues that there is little evidence of genuine multilateralism in this area. In
general, cooperation is inhibited by the fact that the United States defines the
problem largely in terms of the management of supply, while those states that
are principal sources of drugs tend to see it as a problem of demand. Cooperation is also limited by the historical legacy of American hegemony in the
region. In this context, Klepak sees little new in American behaviour in the
post-Cold War era. What cooperation there is in the field of narcotics is largely
coerced and reflects the deep vulnerability of other states to a United States
that remains hegemonic in a region without counterweights. He concludes
that the record of cooperation in this field is unimpressive and that cooperative behaviour can be explained largely in terms of the realities of power rather
than the emergence of a normative structure.

Gordon Mace, Guy Gosselin and Louis Belanger and company provide a
second functional analysis of multilateralism in Latin America in their paper on
democratic institutions and cooperative security. Noting the necessity of broadening the concept of security to include political development, they analyze
the relationship between threats to democracy and regional stability, noting in
particular the problems of weak civil control over military establishments, the
incomplete character of political and judicial reforms, and the persistence of
poverty and inequitable income distribution in much of the region. They then
turn to an examination of the emergence of a regional strategy of cooperative
security, focusing on democratic institution-building and the record of regional
institutions in practice. On the basis of the accumulation over time of normative instruments, and the OAS reactions to the 1991 coup in Haiti, the *autogolpe*
in Peru in April 1992, and President Serrano's attempt at a civil *coup d'état* in
Guatemala in May 1993, the authors conclude that there is emerging a regional normative consensus on democracy, and that the region is gradually
accepting the right to multilateral intervention in domestic jurisdictions on issues relating to the defence of democracy.

That said, considerable obstacles remain towards the development of this
regime in practice, and notably the discomfort of major regional actors (e.g.,
Mexico and Brazil) with the erosion of sovereignty implicit in the evolution of
this regime. Although there is considerable success in the area of democratic
support, sanctions — let alone armed intervention to restore democratic gov-

ernments — are problematic. Underlying this once again is the problem of political will and the insufficiency of resources made available to the OAS by member states. The authors conclude that in instances where more extreme variants of multilateral action in defence of democracy are contemplated (e.g., armed intervention), UN, rather than OAS action, is preferable. This reflects the fragility of the evolving regional base for cooperative action in this realm of intrusion into domestic jurisdictions.

The second set of cases focuses on Europe. Legault addresses the multilateral structure of Euro-Atlantic security through the lens of regime theory. After a discussion of the substance of the theory and its relation to the realist and institutionalist traditions, it examines metaregulation, rules, and procedure within the Euro-Atlantic security regime. The author then argues that the failure of the regime to cope with the crisis in the former Yugoslavia should not be taken as evidence of the weakness or irrelevance of the regime, since the principal parties to the conflict were external to the regime. Answers to the dilemmas posed by the Yugoslav conflict lie not in the realm of theories of regional cooperation, but in that of theories of conflict and conflict resolution. David Long then continues with an analysis of the current security discourse of the EU, and presents a functionalist critique of this discourse based on the work of David Mitrany. He discusses EU relations with Central and Eastern Europe in terms of these competing approaches to security, and argues that the prevailing discourse on security in the EU is state-centric and heavily focused on military-territorial dimensions of security; and is based on a lack of analysis of potential or actual threats. The confrontational quality of this approach to security limits the openness of the Union to outsiders, thereby potentially creating the threats to European security that it is ostensibly designed to forestall. It distracts attention, moreover, from the EU's strong suit in security — the persuasive dimension of economic power in preconflict and mediation phases of disputes. On this basis, he argues for a functional approach that emphasizes the integrative, community-oriented, and socio-economic aspects of security. Long views current EU policy on Central and Eastern Europe as exclusionary and self-defeating, since it does little to enhance the prospects for recovery that might enhance stability in the region and security for Europe. He presents a number of areas of suggested functional cooperation with the states of Central and Eastern Europe that might enhance security in the region.

Allen Sens follows with an analysis of multilateralism as a means of integrating the smaller states of Central and Eastern Europe into the security architecture of Europe. Picking up on Job's point concerning the need to differentiate among states' interests in multilateralism, Sens first examines the security dilemmas of small states in a neorealist context, with a view not only to understand these states' behaviour, but also to fill a gap in a body of theory that ignores smaller actors. He notes that small states are necessarily dependent on cooperative relationships in the effort to sustain and enhance their national security in an anarchic environment where power is unevenly distributed. In other words, and consistently with the neorealist framework, cooperative behaviour of small states may be explained in terms of national interest. In this context, multilateral structures of cooperation are generally preferable to bilateral ones, and to the option of neutrality. However, certain kinds of multilateralism are more responsive to the needs of small states than others. In particular, inclusiveness and equality are major concerns of small states. Turning to Central Europe, Sens argues that the desire of Central European small states for multilateral cooperation may be explained in terms of a neorealist desire to enhance their security in an uncertain post-Cold War environment. This also explains their preference in the multilateral context for membership in Western European cooperative structures. Sens then examines the question of NATO enlargement from the perspective of these small states, arguing that the expansion of the alliance stands the best chance of addressing their security concerns in a stabilizing fashion.

Zoltan Barany picks up the issue of multilateralism in Central Europe with an extensive historical analysis of the evolution of the Visegrad Group from its origins in the late Gorbachev era through the demise of the Czechoslovak Republic to the present. Focusing also on the question of choice between subregional and Western European forms of multilateralism, he provides substantial empirical backing for Sens' proposition that these states' approaches to cooperation are based largely on perceived interest. The prospects for substantial development of cooperation *within* Central Europe are limited, since such forms do not adequately address state interests. The real issue for the Central Europeans has been whether to seek integration into Western European institutions as a group or individually. The development of relations among the Visegrad states suggests that a collective approach to integration is unlikely to be achieved.

Neil MacFarlane's chapter examines the Commonwealth of Independent States (CIS) as a regional multilateral organization. Departing from a general discussion of the weaknesses of regional organization as purveyors of regional security, the analysis demonstrates that the organization shares most of them. It is non-inclusive, reflects a highly asymmetrical regional structure of power, and is manipulated by Russia as an instrument of a policy of regional hegemony. This is particularly evident in the CIS approach to regional peacekeeping.

Notes

1. Ken Booth, *Contemporary International Relations: A Guide to Theory* (London: Pinter, 1994), p. 111.

2. Ibid., pp. 113-14.

3. *The Economist*, (9 March 1991), p. 15, quoted in Bradley S. Klein, *Strategic Studies and World Order* (Cambridge: Cambridge University Press, 1994), p. 135.

4. Stanley Hoffmann, "The Crisis of Liberal Internationalism," *Foreign Policy,* 98 (Spring 1995):167.

5. Robert Keohane (ed.), *Neorealism and its Critics* (New York: Columbia University Press, 1986), p. 90.

6. Booth, *Contemporary International Relations*, p. 114.

7. Ibid., p. 109.

8. See, for example, Francis Fukuyama, "The End of History," *The National Interest,* 16 (Summer 1989); John Mueller, *Retreat from Doomsday: The Obsolescence of Major Wars* (New York: Basic Books, 1989); James Barber, "Jihad vs. McWorld," *Atlantic Monthly*, (March 1992), pp. 53-63; Mathew Connelly and Paul Kennedy, "Must it be the Rest Against the West?" *Atlantic Monthly* 274, 6 December 1994, pp. 61-91; Samuel Huntington, "The Clash of Civilizations," *Foreign Affairs*, 72 (Summer 1993): 22-29; Ken Jowitt, "After Leninism: The New World Disorder," *The Journal of Democracy,* 2:4 (Winter 1991); Robert Kaplan, "The Coming Anarchy," *Atlantic Monthly*, February 1994, pp.44-76; John Mearsheimer, "Why We Will Soon Miss the Cold War," *The Atlantic Monthly* (August 1990), pp. 35-59; J. Mearsheimer, "Back to the Future: Instability in Europe After the Cold War," *International Security,* 15:1 (Summer 1990): 5-56.

9. John Chipman, "The Future of Strategic Studies," *Survival,* 34:1(Spring 1992):111.

10. Klein, *Strategic Studies and World Order*, p. 134.

11. Ibid., p. 137.

12. Lawrence Freedman, "Outsiders' Influence on Defence Policy: The American Experience," *Royal United Service Institute for Defence Studies Journal*, (1981).

13. Heraldo Muñoz, "A New OAS for the New Times," in *Latin America in a New World*, ed. Abraham Lowenthal and Gregory Treverton (Boulder: Westview Press, 1994), p. 192.

14. Jane Nolan (ed.), *Global Engagement, Cooperation and Security in the 21st Century* (Washington, DC: The Brookings Institution, 1994), p. 3.

15. Ibid., p. 3.

16. Jane E. Nolan, John D. Steinbruner, Kenneth Flamm, Steven Miller, William Perry and Ashton Carter, "The Imperatives of Cooperation," in *Global Engagement, Cooperation and Security in the 21st Century*, p. 19.

17. Robert Cox, "Multilateralism and World Order," *Review of International Studies,* 18 (1992):161-62.

18. Margaret P. Karns and Karen A. Mingst, "Multilateral Institutions and International Security," in *World Security, Trends and Challenges at Century's End,* ed. Michael Klare and D.C. Thomas (New York: St Martin's Press, 1991), p. 267.

19. See, in this regard, the lively debate triggered by John Mearsheimer in his article "The False Promises of International Institutions," *International Security,* 19:3 (Winter 1994/95):4-49.

20. Thomas Risse-Kappen, "Between a New World Order and None: Explaining the Re-Emergence of the United Nations in World Politics," Occasional Paper no. 29 (Toronto: Centre for International and Strategic Studies, York University, 1995), p. 9. See also Judith Godstein and Robert Keohane (ed.), *Ideas and Foreign Policy: Beliefs, Institutions and Political Change* (Ithaca: Cornell University Press, 1993).

21. Ibid.

22. See James Rosenau, "Governance in the Twenty-First Century," *Global Governance,* 1:1 (Winter 1995):13-44.

PART I
The Debate

W. Andy Knight

"Top-Down" and "Bottom-Up" Multilateralism: Two Approaches in the Quest for Global Governance

Introduction

The basic premise of this chapter is that the predominantly state-centric conceptualization of multilateralism held by traditional international relations (IR) scholars is too narrow and ahistorical and, as a result, fails to capture many of the nuances of multilateral evolution.[1] Furthermore, while traditional realist and liberal institutionalist perspectives provide partial descriptions of aspects of multilateralism, they are less than fully adequate in accounting for the current changes in the practice and orientation of multilateralism or in predicting its future trajectory. What is required at this juncture is an historically sensitive perspective that provides a more complete conceptualization of multilateralism and accounts better for its development and changing character.

The argument, simply put, is that multilateralism can be viewed as having two distinct characteristics: (a) a "top-down" trait reflecting a certain state-centric bias that serves to suppress civil societies, and (b) a "bottom-up" attribute which has been present from the early beginnings of intersocietal interaction and is becoming increasingly important today due to the reconstitution of civil societies. Although both versions have coexisted from the beginning of intersocietal interaction, the second has been marginalized in the dominant discourse of IR scholarship whilst the first became entrenched.

In order to develop a more comprehensive and reflective[2] picture of multilateralism this chapter is divided into three sections. Part One critically examines traditional theoretical perspectives on multilateralism. Each perspective highlights particular aspects of the phenomenon, but none provides a complete picture. An alternative approach to understanding and explaining the development of multilateralism is to search the historical and anthropological terrain for evidence of precursors, concepts, and practices that have served to define what has come to be known as "multilateral." The second part of this chapter accomplishes that by (a) describing the three major conceptual models of multilateral organization (pyramidal, diffused, and cosmopolitan); (b) investigating secondary source historical and anthropological literatures for evidence of the germ of multilateral practices; (c) piecing together the evolution of early intersocietal/multilateral governance structures using examples from Sumer society; (d) analyzing the multilateral development within the Hellenistic, Latin Christian, and Modern European societies; and (e) examining the impact of Westphalia on multilateral evolution, the various forms of multilateralism that existed in non-European areas, and multilateral practices and institutions of the expanded international system leading to the creation of the UN system. The third part is a brief look at the impact of recent systemic changes on multilateralism and suggests that a number of forces and new social movements are pushing alternate forms of multilateral activity (of the "bottom-up" variety) to the fore. Finally, the conclusion develops what can be considered as a new way of viewing multilateralism.

The following analysis shows why the uneasy intersection of the two forms of multilateralism at this transitional juncture cannot be fully explained by traditional IR theory. What is required is a new perspective which is sensitive to the historical context surrounding the evolution of multilateral practices; provides a challenge to the ahistorical, state-centric interpretations of multilateralism found in traditional IR literature; and contributes a more comprehensive and plausible explanation of the nature and trajectory of contemporary multilateralism. This chapter attempts to develop such a perspective.

Theoretical Perspectives on Multilateralism

Particularly since 1989, IR observers have recognized how important multilateral norms and institutions are to the management of regional and global changes in the world system. Yet, the dominant IR discourse pertaining to multilateralism has remained largely focused on interstate multilateral activity. This is true of both liberal institutionalism and traditional realism.[3]

Multilateralism is conceived by traditional realists as more or less transitory arrangements designed to achieve collective aims of a group of sovereign states that have discovered a momentary common interest. According to this perspective, multilateral norms, principles, and institutions have a superstructural character and a facilitative function in terms of helping groups of states achieve common ends. Multilateral institutions are not independent of the states that bring them into being. They depend on states for their resources and remain instruments through which state governments can enact collectively-derived policies. In other words, the institutions become (a) a cloak under which the real ulterior motives of major powers are hidden and; (b) a forum in which the acquiescence of the less powerful can be attained.

In contrast to the realist position are a number of paradigms that can be placed under the general category of liberal institutionalism. Each one envisages the emergence of multilateral "institutions that would transform world order by progressively bringing the state system within some form of authoritative regulation."[4]

David Mitrany, for instance, focused on the "low politics" activity of functional and technical agencies as the primary locus of multilateralism.[5] Neofunctionalists developed the concept of "spillover" to demonstrate how the scope and authority of multilateral institutions could be expanded. Carried to its logical conclusion, the spillover of multilateral activity could ultimately result in an irreversible process of sectoral, regional and even global integration.[6] The above argument was carried even further in the empirical studies of Karl Deutsch, except that Deutsch, adopting a transactions approach to multilateralism, conceived of two distinct end-products of the integration process: one leading to the amalgamation of formerly separate states and the other toward a "pluralistic security community."[7] The first path would lead to a community with "one supreme decision-making centre," whereas the second would lead to a community lacking a single centre of authority.[8]

Neofunctionalists and transactions theorists made one other significant contribution to the discourse on multilateralism. They recognized that states were not the only players of significance in the multilateral process. Indeed, the range of relevant multilateral actors was expanded to include elements of civil society (e.g., interest or advocacy groups, trade unions, industrial associations, and political parties),[9] although these actors' actions were generally viewed in the context of legitimating or delegitimating decisions made in state-centric multilateral institutions. This insight aside, traditional theoretical perspectives on multilateralism have tended to obscure "bottom-up" aspects of the phenomenon because these positions are by and large state-centred and ahistorical. What follows next is an attempt to provide a more historically sensitive interpretation of the evolution of the concept and practice of multilateralism.

Developments in the Conceptualization and Practice of Modern Multilateral Organizations

Archibugi notes that contemporary multilateral organizations "were sketched out, if only in embryonic form" in conceptual perpetual peace projects.[10] These projects have continuing relevance to the debate about the beginnings and transformation of multilateralism and derive from a specific juridical strand of pacifist thought.[11] Three basic models of multilateral organization emerge from these perpetual peace projects: pyramidal, diffused, and cosmopolitan.

The *pyramidal model* of multilateral organization[12] represents a "top-down" form of multilateralism. The overall characteristics of this model include provision for:

- creating an international union of sovereign states;

- limiting its membership to sovereigns, thereby excluding the subjects (civil society);

- introducing the principle of sovereign equality by applying a "one state, one vote" electoral criterion;

- giving sovereigns authority to determine constitutional relations within their jurisdiction;

- forming a joint military force under the umbrella of the union to suppress possible rebellion by defector member states;

- settling disputes between sovereigns via the international union arbitration machinery;

- adhering to a nonintervention principle so as to enhance the sovereignty of member states;

- giving the union powers to aid state governments in combating domestic insurrection; and

- implementing a balance of power mechanism in order to maintain equilibrium between the great nations.[13]

While there are several problems with this model, this chapter is concerned only with those that are inherent to "top-down" multilateral structures. By limiting union membership to sovereigns, the pyramidal model excludes large sections of the globe. Since sovereigns are given complete jurisdiction over their domestic area, such a model cannot guarantee that civilians will be protected from human rights abuses meted out by despotic leaders. It provides, at least implicitly, an excuse for sovereign authorities to keep civil society under subjugation. On this issue, Rousseau once raised a very valid question. Why is it necessary to use the union to protect sovereigns against rebellion, when a similar kind of insurance against the tyranny of leaders could not be given to civil society?[14] As Archibugi correctly points out, the pyramidal model sacrifices democracy in order to achieve peace between sovereigns.[15]

The *diffused model*, on the other hand, is an idealized example of a "bottom-up" version of multilateralism. It conceives of an international federation made up of individuals from various states, as opposed to a union consisting only of sovereigns. This arrangement is based on the assumption that individuals within states are likely to appreciate the benefits of multilateral bodies.[16] The main characteristics of this model are as follows:

- a Universal Diet composed of representatives of civil society;

- a dispute settlement mechanism that takes into account the will of citizens of all states;

- an electoral criterion within the federation of "one citizen, one vote";

- a constitution patterned after that of the state with the most advanced constitution;[17]

- an arrangement that would allow sovereigns to appoint members to the Universal Diet, but would also ensure that delegations are proportional to the size of their countries and the value of their territory;

- a provision that would ensure that delegates are not bound by the will of the sovereigns who appoint them but would be able to make decisions based on their own judgment; and

- a voting arrangement using the Venetian method of the secret ballot.[18]

While more democratic than the previous model, the diffused model suffers from a number of flaws. It is based on the dubious assumptions that somehow, sovereigns will hand over some of their foreign policy decisionmaking power to appointed delegations from civil society; the will of the majority of citizens in countries around the world would be consistently just and fair; there can be consensus for this kind of arrangement even in a diverse world; and the voting formula would bring about a measure of fairness to the decisionmaking operations of the Universal Diet. Experience has taught us that sovereigns jealously guard their foreign policymaking power. History has taught us to be wary of the "tyranny of the majority." Empirically, it is possible to show that distributing delegates in the manner advocated by proponents of this model would place rich, populous and geographically large states in an advantageous position over poor, less populated, and smaller states. It is also difficult to imagine that delegates appointed by sovereigns will feel no obligation to support the interest of the persons who appoint them.

The *cosmopolitan model* is usually associated with Immanuel Kant. It represents an intersection of "top-down" and "bottom-up" multilateralism and therefore includes elements of both.[19] However, Kant went beyond previous models in suggesting three definitive articles for his proposed peace plan: (i) that the civic constitution of every state shall be republican; (ii) that the law of nations shall be based on a federation of free states; and (iii) that cosmopolitan law shall be limited to conditions of universal hospitality.[20] These definitive articles attempted to correct what were considered to be basic flaws in previous peace plans. The primary difference between the cosmopolitan model and the diffused model lies in Kant's support for "the existence of both autonomous states and a voluntary confederation of states."[21] Thus, his cosmopolitan model would consist of:

- an assembly of "free" states (based on the criterion of "one state, one vote");

- an international community consisting of both individuals of civil society and state sovereigns;

- a cosmopolitan assembly comprised of citizens of individual states;

- dispute settlement mechanisms within the citizens' assembly to address conflict between states; and

- an international public opinion gauge represented in the form of the cosmopolitan assembly.

Because it combines characteristics of both pyramidal and diffused models, the cosmopolitan model appears strongest of the three. However, it is not free from the following criticisms:

1. The cosmopolitan model addresses the weakness of the pyramidal model by incorporating the "democratic" features of the diffused model. At the same time, it attempts to scale back the ambitious design of the diffused model for a global suprastate organization, realizing that such a goal will be difficult to obtain and may even prove undesirable. However, in trying

to resolve the contradiction found in its predecessors, it creates contradictions of its own.

2. The development of democratic features and structures is not an easy task, especially in those states that do not have a history of democracy. Getting those states to adopt republicanism may require much more than subtle persuasion and the gentle urging of world public opinion. The cosmopolitan model does not address the issue of what is to be done if several units within the international system refuse to adopt republicanism and democracy.

3. The attempt to combine representation from both civil society and sovereigns in a universal organization reveals a major contradiction. Since the interests of these two parties may not coincide on many issues of international affairs, it is difficult to see how the resulting tension can be resolved, especially over essential problems such as protection of state sovereignty, responsibility for human rights issues and decisions concerning war.

4. The respect for the full sovereignty of states may not allow for the blossoming of civil society, and support for the claims of civil society may run counter to the aims of classical sovereignty.

Elements of the above three models can be found in the actual experimentation that led to the creation of modern multilateral organizations. But it is the pyramidal model that has most often been reflected in the practices of mainstream state-centric international organizations. It is important to point out that at the time they were conceptualized, several of the perpetual peace plans were found to be too utopian for practical statesmen to consider. This did not mean, however, that multilateral practices were entirely absent.

Tracing the Germ of Multilateral Practices

Several anthropologists have traced the evolution of societies in primordial relations from family, joint families, clans, tribes, villages, ethnicities, protective alliances, to nation-states.[22] While this is not the purpose of this chapter, what is of interest here is the notion that all societies, even at the most primordial stages, develop "certain complexes of interest" which become a driving logic for the maintenance of a level of cooperation among them. This "consciousness of kind," as one author puts it, is evidence that human beings have not only a perceived need for each other (*unus homo, nullus homo*), but also, "an inner perception of the fact that others strive for similar aims by similar means."[23] Herein lies the germ of what can be called "generic multilateralism."

There is considerable historical evidence to show that formerly disconnected societies developed regulatory mechanisms (norms, institutions, and social customs) as a means of avoiding, or lessening the possibilities of, outright conflict between them and, at times, improving their material lot. This is the essence of multilateral governance.

In the evolution of social formation from family to joint family to clans and tribes, certain myths, customs and institutions were developed to facilitate interaction between these social groups.[24] Such myths help form the ideological base from which shared values, fears, and common world-views emerge. Customs, such as marriage, were also central to early societal interaction and expansion. Out of such customs developed specific norms governing the interaction of early societies. The Tungus clan of Asia, for example, prohibited intraclan marriage, thereby forcing its members to marry outside and in so doing expanded its societal links and network.

The expansion of intersocietal linkages led to the creation of institutional bodies and cooperative arrangements among early tribal groups in such areas as agriculture and defence. Anthropologists and historians have recorded how tribal units in simpler societies cultivated peaceable relations by organizing ceremonial and functional intertribal gatherings in which quarrels between different tribes were openly settled, public entertainment was shared, and cooperative hunting (or fishing) was arranged. Another major conduit for social extension was "multilateral" trade. Through trade and other exchange vehicles, intertribal/societal relations eventually evolved into multilateral relations. Laws and customs were created to regulate such interaction, out of that common or shared values developed which further strengthened social relations.

One early example of the evidence of "multilateral" activity can be found around 2300 BC in Sumer society.[25] Through the exchange medium of trade, a confederal societal network of dynamic, closely connected city-states developed in this region. This network was concerned with: settling disputes between members over water rights, land, and the boundaries of rich agricultural fields; regulating commerce and economic competition between city-states while preserving for them a degree of autonomy; and maintaining a relatively high living standard. Its underlying ideology was based on a belief that Sumer societies were the creation of gods who dominated the world. Although kings ruled, they were merely representatives of the gods who delegated divine authority downwards. Formal and informal institutions were created to regulate and manage increasing volumes of contacts (as a result of trade, commerce, and migration, for example), and hierarchical structures were consciously created and sustained to satisfy the Sumerians' need for order.

Watson describes this top-down structure as consisting of a benevolent hegemon at the apex — a position assumed by one of the kings — who became final arbiter and moderator in dispute cases among the city-states and, at times, enforced certain verdicts. Neither the hegemonic king, nor any other king for that matter, had the right to interfere in the internal affairs of other city-states. Lack of sound judgment could cost the hegemon his prestige and ultimately his position at the top of the hierarchy. If this occurred, the hegemonical city would be replaced by another and the king of the victorious power would issue a claim that the god of the new hegemon had risen to prominence of power in heaven; thus augmenting the history (or laws) of the gods and strengthening the underlying ideology supporting the societal order. Since laws were considered handed down by the gods (i.e., "top-down"), they were strictly applied. Deviants from these laws were harshly punished. Rules and custom, created by the custodians of divine authority, while occupying a lower status, were nonetheless considered important as regulating devices.

A normative element accompanied the institutionalization of intersocietal relations with the objectives being dispute settlement, regulation of economic competition and commerce, and improvements in welfare conditions. Other elements of what we call "multilateralism" can be found in Sumer city-state organization. These include the establishment and development of enforcement, prosecution, adjudication, conciliation, arbitration and consent mechanisms, diplomatic customs, a convention of immunity for heralds or messengers, formalized and codified institutional practices, and procedures, rules and institutions for regulating strategic, economic and cultural relations with outside communities.

Multilateral Evolution from Hellenistic to International Society

Ancient Greek societal practices (during the period around 500 to 100 BC), combined with those of the Persian, greatly influenced the organizational form adopted by the European states system. Since contemporary international society embraced European societal practices, one can make the argument that current multilateral methods derive from Persian-Greco experimentation with such practices.[26]

If one examines carefully the societal and institutional development of the political communities that, in essence, are precursors to the present international society (i.e., Hellenistic society, the Byzantine Oikoumene, the Ottoman empire, and Latin Christendom) one can actually trace the beginnings of what can be called "modern multilateral activity."

The Greeks were colonizers. Overcrowded Hellenic cities induced Greek citizens around 300 BC to explore and conquer other areas in search of economic opportunities. Many of the conquered colonies remained relatively independent of formal Greek governance but adhered to certain traditions, norms, and rules established by hegemonic Greece. Philip II (King from 359 to 336 BC) continued the Greek expansion, enveloping areas that had formerly been conquered by the Persians, using "a shrewd mixture of force and diplomacy to form most of the Greek states, former allies and enemies alike, into what was nominally a league of cities under his military leadership."[27] The league was controlled by a highly hegemonical but relatively benign Macedonian structure. Philip legitimized his control by allowing the various polis and alliances to maintain their individual forms of administration and politics. After Philip's assassination, the weakened Persian empire was brought under the Macedon imperial structure by his son Alexander who proved to be even more expansionist. He used the institution of marriage to blend Persian and Macedonian races and to further his grip on the two empires. The resulting merger of Greek and Persian ideas, norms, techniques of administration, management, and government is referred to as *Hellenistic*.

The Hellenistic concept of authority was "top-down" and based on a legitimacy that was supposedly conferred upon the King by the gods. Religious Amphictyonies, perhaps the first model of a universal general-purpose multilateral organization, heavily influenced intercity-state relations and were staffed by a permanent secretariat charged with the task of maintaining and safeguarding holy shrines and treasures, regulating pilgrimages, and performing important diplomatic functions.[28] Each of the Amphictyonic League members was allowed to send two delegates to the league conference and was granted two votes of equal weight. Each member-tribe, upon entering the league, took an oath never to annihilate any of the other tribes during warfare, and deviant tribes were usually confronted by the collective force of the others.[29] Other Greek "multilateral" institutions of note included the Oracles (which provided widely respected judgments) and the Olympic games (which brought both goodwill and truces amongst participating city-states).

The "multilateral" cooperation exhibited in Greece at the time can also be attributed to the presence of leagues, similar to the ones found in the Chinese multistate system, held together by a common religious ideology which often contradicted geographical logic. These leagues attempted to modify the city-states' behaviour by creating mechanisms for discussing common problems, planning joint action, and formulating rudimentary collective decisionmaking arrangements.

Around 305 BC, after Alexander's death, an antihegemonical compact led by Seleucus and Ptolemy ended the Greco-Persian empire. The Seleucids and Ptolemies dominated the Macedonian system but not in the manner of shared hegemony. They, in fact, became bitter rivals and created what might be called a binary or bipolar system with many of the smaller powers attracted to one pole or the other. There were other counter-hegemonic alliances in Greece such as the Delian League. This league, dominated by Athens, was assembled to provide ships for joint defence of the Athenian empire — similar to contemporary multilateral collective defence organizations like NATO. Like most multilateral organizations of today, league members were obliged to pay assessed contributions to the institution and were expected to follow the dictates of the league's dominant power.

Hellenistic expansion was in many respects similar to the European expansion that occurred in the nineteenth century. When the Romans took over the Macedonian system, the cultural homogeneity of Hellenistic civilization was very much intact and still very attractive to the societies of that day. Even after the collapse of the Roman empire, the Hellenistic culture survived in Christianized form for another thousand years under the Byzantine banner and inevitably clashed with the Islamic counter-hegemony.

Latin Christendom was held together by the firm hegemonic control of the Catholic Church, certain embedded norms of Catholicism, and the socio-political organization of feudalism. By the fourteenth century, however, the fabric of universal Catholicism and stratified feudalism began to fray as conflicts surfaced between the emperor's temporal power and the "divine" power of the Pope in the Holy Roman Empire (the eastern portion of Latin Christendom). The separation of church from temporal authority was the beginning of an unfolding of new secular attitudes and world views that permeated European society during the Renaissance (1350-1650). It was during this period of cultural and intellectual rebirth that the educated elite looked back to classical Hellenic and Roman cultures and norms as models. The new liberal spirit of enquiry together with the growth in desire among people to reach their maximum potential in science, politics, and the arts, resulted in a process of ideological disembedding — the replacement of "old" societal norms, rules, and practices by "new" ones.

As religious political authority declined, the authority of kings expanded. Monarchs subdued local feudal and ecclesiastical power centres and incorporated them into their kingdoms. Formerly homogeneous areas were split up into distinct units.[30] New techniques of acquiring secular power were developed; the *stato* being the most significant. In France, England, and Italy territorial monarchs and commercial city-states took advantage of the papal-imperial rivalry to assert their independence and authority. This paved the way for the creation of the modern nation-state, after the upheaval of the Thirty Years' War — a war that weakened the framework of feudal society and contributed to the emergence of new forces, norms, and institutions.[31] But as the new norms and institutions emerged, after the signing of the Westphalia Treaty, their effect was to loosen further the "top-down" hold of the Church on the majority of European people.[32]

The Impact of Westphalia on Multilateral Evolution

The significance of Westphalia is that it signalled the beginning of a new order that would have implications both within and outside Europe.[33] The treaty recognized a religious stalemate on the continent and confirmed a principle, already ensconced in the Augsburg Treaty (1555), that acknowledged the right of individual principalities to determine the religious affiliation of their subjects. After Westphalia, decentralized political arrangements that characterized the feudal era gave way to more centralized institutional forms.

Gone also was the dominant idea that God controlled the fate of all people. In came the notion of social engineering — empowering individuals to shape their own society and destiny — and the belief that new forms of earthly (as opposed to transcendent) institutions could be created to alleviate human suffering, improve human conditions, and create political communities.[34] Out of this new thinking came the notion of legally equal, sovereign, political, and territorial communities (states) to be headed, not by God's representatives on earth, but by temporal rulers who, with their central administrations, could monopolize the use of force in a demarcated territory and gain external recognition for areas under their jurisdiction. Thus was born the Westphalian state system based on the principle of sovereignty; a principle that would later be recognized as a central plank of international law and would become incorporated into the foundational ideology of multilateral organizations. It is this principle, more than anything else, that has arrested the development of "bottom-up" multilateral practices.

The principle of sovereignty secularized those laws and rules governing individual states and provided the basis for states' defence policies. If a territory was sovereign, then its people would be expected to protect it from outsiders and external influences.[35] For this principle to work, all sovereigns had to recognize the rights each sovereign had over his domestic sphere. This reciprocal recognition (nonintervention), and its corollary principle of sovereign equality, became major elements in international law and survived as persistent features of contemporary multilateral relations. Since the primary concern of Westphalian sovereign states was the survival of state entities, foreign policy necessarily took precedence over domestic policy. The "supreme law of the state" thus obligated its citizens "to organize its internal resources for the purpose of self-preservation."[36]

Using the concept of *raison d'état* — the idea that a state's citizens can collectively have interests that are greater than the sum of their individual interests (or the national interest), foreign policy decisionmaking became an exercise concentrated in the hands of elite groups or individual "heroic" figures who were expected to represent and fulfil the goals and needs of civil society. Thus when sovereign European states decided to engage in reciprocal multilateral activity, the result was necessarily "top-down."

The embryonic European state system eventually expanded beyond the European theatre into an international state system.[37] However, it took some time before a truly international society of states could emerge linking together formerly disparate regional societies through a system of intersubjective understandings of common interests, a common structure of principles and rules that established the rights and obligations of all members, and an agreed upon set of common "international" institutions.[38]

The colonization process became the vehicle for European expansion and resulted in a "top-down" imposition of European standards, principles, customs, norms, and laws upon subjugated peoples. Most Europeans had evidently convinced themselves of their superiority. As a consequence, their relationships with outsiders reflected that of an imperial authority dealing with its vassals. Implicit in this differential practice was the acceptance of the ideology of white racialism, biological superiority, and domination over non-white populations. While it has been argued that racialism, or the notion of a biological difference between the "advanced" Europeans and "backward" non-Europeans, "was never the official doctrine or justification of any European empire," it is hard to deny the reality of its pattern and practice. Euphemisms like "manifest destiny," "civilizing mission," "modernization," and "march of progress," were used to mask this ideology which provided justification for Europeans to enslave masses of people in the "new world." But there were other less malign reasons for European expansion.

One benign ideological reason for European expansion was the idea of *jus gentium* — inherited from Greek and Roman Stoics and given a prominent place in the political theory of Latin Christendom — and *le droit des gens* (the law of nations) propounded by Vattel. As noted earlier, the Peace of Westphalia advanced three basic legal principles upon which the new secular order of the sovereign state would be based, that is, principles of territoriality, sovereign equality, and nonintervention.[39] If such principles were going to be upheld by, and accommodated in the state system, certain devices would have to be created to facilitate their acceptance. One of these was international law which emerged out of the Grotian "natural law" doctrine. Although it was subject to misuse by some, natural law was used positively to support the rights of Amerindians conquered by the Spanish, of African slaves captured and placed into forced labour in the West Indies by the British and French, and of aboriginal peoples who were dispossessed and demoralized by various European settlers.[40] Jeremy Bentham pointed out the emancipatory effects of natural law by showing how it could be used to liberate colonies, disarm nations, and attain a more orderly world.[41]

Whether benign or malign, the European expansionist thrust succeeded, perhaps to the detriment of many non-Europeans. By the nineteenth century, the embryonic European state system became a limited international system. It eventually blossomed into a full-blown universal system as the decolonization process unfolded in the twentieth century. As this international society of states evolved, so did new multilateral institutions that reflected a widening common interest in developing a structure for peaceful coexistence and improved general welfare.

Multilateral Practices Leading to the Creation of the UN System

Based on his analysis of the advent of multilateral institutions, Inis Claude convincingly argues that international organization "was brought into being not so much by prophets who saw it as the legitimate successor to sovereign states, as by statesmen who sought new arrangements and devices whereby the sovereign units of the old system could pursue their interests and manage their affairs in the altered circumstances of the age of communication and industrialism."[42] This position is supported by analysis of the precursors to the United Nations system (i.e., the congress and conference system, the great power concert system, the Hague system, functional public international unions and agencies, private international bodies, and the League of Nations).

Multilateral Activity of Conferences, Congresses and Concerts

The peace conference at Utrecht (1713) and the Congresses of Cambrai (1724) and Sissons (1727) set the stage for the large-scale international meetings that became a prevalent feature of the "Age of Sovereignty." The Quadruple Alliance, formed in 1718, indicated the importance of great powers in the creation of a new international order.[43] The Congress of Vienna (1814-15) established a multilateral framework (an ad hoc conference system) within which European states could build peaceful interactions and develop fruitful reciprocal relationships.[44] Not only did it "lay the diplomatic foundation for a new European order upon the ruins which had been created by the disastrous Napoleonic Wars," it standardized and codified the diplomatic rules that governed the post-Napoleonic era.[45]

The Treaty of Chaumont (1814) established the Concert of Europe after parties to that agreement undertook to act in *"un parfait concert"*. The concert met at least 30 times during the course of the nineteenth century. Through the Holy Alliance, concluded by the Paris Peace Treaty (September 1815), the monarchs of the great powers further committed themselves to govern their subjects "as fathers of families," in accordance with Christian principles, and to practice solidarity in foreign affairs, holding consultations and regular meetings of the congress system in order to safeguard the settlement of Vienna. This "top-down" paternalism was packaged in the form of concert activity (executive collective security).[46] The activities of this self-appointed guardian of the European community of states involved the development of a number of joint security measures to guarantee adherence to norms and rules. In addition, the concert pledged to bring about conditions that would lead to economic prosperity and sustained peace in Europe. But, as an exclusive club of the European great powers, it did little to strengthen the multilateral approach to solving international conflict and much to preserve the status quo on the continent.

The concert system failed essentially because it was exclusive, informal in structure, and unable to guarantee a routinized means of dealing with potential conflicts among states. Despite this, "diplomacy by conference" became an established fact of life in the nineteenth century.[47] The European conference system dealt with several pressing issues of the period; the major one being the establishment of new states of Belgium and Greece, etc. Future conferences were more inclusive and expanded the concern with maintaining multilateral peace beyond the European setting. In 1898, the first "international" disarmament conference was called by Czar Nicholas and 27 states attended, the majority of which were from Europe (with the exception of China, Japan, Mexico, Siam, and the United States). A follow-up Hague meeting in 1907 attracted 44 nations with 18 coming from Latin America. This became the first universal general assembly in the sense that it was the first time that all constituted states in the international system at the time were convened "to discuss interests which they had in common and which contemplated the good of all mankind."[48]

Before the Hague system was interrupted by the outbreak of the First World War, it had established a number of precedents that pointed toward the development of modern multilateral organizations. The expansion of membership at the two conferences also set a precedent for future attempts at universalizing multilateral organization.

The Separation of Public and Private Multilateral Bodies

Up to this point, multilateralism appears as a "top-down" activity addressing problems of security, defined in the traditional state-centric sense as the elimination of military-strategic threats to the territorial and jurisdictional elements of the state ("high politics"). The concept and practice of multilateralism had to be reexamined once it was realized that military threats account for only one type of menace to the survival of humanity and that economic, social, technical, and cultural interactions between people ("low politics") were becoming increasingly complex. New material conditions of increased and fairly complex interconnectedness called for a different type of multilateralism if governments were to be successful in tackling "the difficulties posed and the opportunities offered by the unprecedented international flow of commerce in goods, services, people, ideas, germs, and social evils."[49] Revolutions in industrial technology, international communications, and travel along with the internationalization of labour, production, trade, and finance provided the grist for the development of functional and specialized institutions.[50] However, the emergence of issue-specific functional bodies also revealed another important development, that is, the dialectical tendency in human history "to establish territorial organizations" while at the same time attempting "to transcend boundaries to the furthest extent permitted by technologies."[51]

Not only did the scope of items requiring global administrative attention grow as a result of the above, but the possibility of expanding the range of interstate conflicts also increased as the areas of interaction broadened (posts, navigation, telegraphs, meteorology, measurements, and weight, etc.). The response to this, toward the last half of the nineteenth century, was the creation of several public international bodies and hundreds of private international associations that covered a wide variety of fields and led to unprecedented levels of growth in socio-economic collaboration and cooperation at the international level.[52] As a consequence, the scope of the subject matter of multilateralism expanded to include areas formerly considered "domestic." This development was mirrored at the domestic level as governments in several countries expanded their administrative jurisdiction to cover almost every facet of social and economic life, areas normally considered to be outside the province of government.

Public functional bodies served "as collection points and clearing houses for information, centres for discussion of common problems by governments, instruments for achieving the coordination by agreement of national policies and practices, and agencies for promoting the formulation and acceptance of uniform or minimum standards in the fields of their concern."[53] In other words, these agencies performed service-oriented facilitating and coordinating functions for the benefit of state governments, thereby contributing indirectly to "top-down" multilateralism. Private international organizations, many of which mirrored developments of public international bodies, emerged by contract, as a number of national interest groups (dealing, *inter alia*, with humanitarian, religious, socio-economic, educational, and scientific issues), initiated transnational meetings with counterparts from other civil societies. These private associations were the forerunners of the nongovernmental network we have today and provided clear examples of "bottom-up" approaches to multilateralism.[54] In one sense, they have tried to bridge the gap between sovereigns and civil society — a gap made wider by "top-down" multilateral developments.

The Advent of the League of Nations and the United Nations

The First World War challenged not only multilateral institutions, it also "destroyed the European states system beyond the possibility of repair."[55] It shattered the "balance of power" in Europe and forced the admission that, in spite of attempts to design and build multilateral institutions for the purpose of reducing or eliminating war, "modern European civilization was not immune from destructive forces of military conflict.[56] The devastation and misery of that war, generally thought of at the time as the "war to end all wars," resulted in approximately 15 million deaths. This tragic outcome, while a setback for multilateralism, scorched into the minds of survivors a moral revulsion against the waste of human life and talent and, in turn, became another catalyst for thought focused on means of eliminating war as a social institution. Out of this rebirth of utopian thinking emerged the League of Nations.[57]

As Inis Claude puts it the League "pulled together the separate lines of development into a coherent system. It provided what has been variously referred to as a 'hub' or a 'roof' element, giving the modern world its first taste of institutional centralization."[58] If the nineteenth century experiments with international institutions can be considered as providing the ancestry of modern international organization, "the League of Nations provided the parentage," while building on that ancestry.[59] But the League proved to be another example of "top-down" multilateralism. The League's institutions included a ten-member Council with four major powers given the status of permanent members. This executive body reflected the philosophy behind the Concert of Europe.

The League's main failing was its inability to adapt institutional features to changing international circumstances. Instead of being a locus for facilitating change in the international system, it instead became a body that entrenched the status quo. However flawed in practice, the League Covenant was the first real concrete step in developing a constitution for a global society of states. It laid the groundwork for small states' involvement at the international level by embracing explicitly the concept of universality, by creating a permanent forum where both small, medium and great states' views could be aired, and by establishing a process that provided weak states with an opportunity to help redefine the new legitimacy. In this respect, the League did not die but, rather, evolved into a much more durable second generation international organization — the United Nations.

When the UN system was created in 1945, it became the most universal expression of the historical multilateral process, although it reflected a particular "world order" and the configuration of a set of power relations at a specific conjunctural moment. It also inherited baggage from the past. Seven different kinds of multilateral institutions and/or constitutive practices (from the previous century) converged under the umbrella of the UN system. These are:

- the institution of great power management;

- the codification, through international law, of rules governing the interaction of states;

- the institution of pacific settlement, disarmament, and collective security as instruments for maintaining international peace and security;

- the practice of collective and individual self-defence;

- the principle of state sovereignty/nonintervention;

- the adaptation of the convention of multilateral conference diplomacy to the principles of self-determination and universality; and

- the adoption of the functionalist principle providing for common goods across national boundaries.

These institutions/constitutive practices provided the context for the operations of this "top-down" global governance mechanism and reflected legacies from the past. This baggage is in part responsible for the world body's current inability to adjust its foundational principles and to implement much needed structural reforms that might accommodate better the needs of civil society.[60] The UN is, after all, still a state-centric institution, despite the nominal reference in the preamble of the UN Charter to "we the people" and in spite of the incremental and adaptive reform attempts it has made in the face of systemic change.

Recent Systemic Changes and Their Impact on Multilateralism

A number of recent systemic changes have sparked a call for a rethinking of multilateralism.[61] Most of these changes have struck at the heart of one of the fundamental elements upon which "top-down" multilateralism has been based, that is, the principle of state sovereignty. Since it is not possible to deal with all of these systemic changes in the limited space provided, this section will focus on the impact of two such changes: that is, globalization and powerful technological innovations.

Impact of Globalization and the Technological Revolution

Technological advances in communications and transport have resulted in an increase in the level of complex interdependence.[62] Modern communications (in the form of television, radio, newspapers, telephones, fax machines, electronic mail, etc.), appear to be uniting and fragmenting audiences, exacerbating social cleavages as well as bringing formerly disparate groups together, heightening existing antagonisms as well as providing a means through which such friction can be resolved, eroding national boundaries as well as propelling ultra-nationalist fervour, increasing political cynicism as well as raising the level of civil society's political consciousness. Individual citizens have been empowered as a result of the media's influence. At the same time, because of their adept utilization of communication systems, state leaders have also been empowered *vis-à-vis* civil society. Modern transportation has allowed people of formerly distant societies to interact more frequently. It acts as a conduit for bringing individuals from different countries with similar interests together.

The overall effect of the above has been a shrinkage in social, political, economic, and cultural distances.[63] As a consequence of this phenomenon, formerly dense and opaque frontiers are being dissolved, thus breaking down the Westphalian notion of inside versus outside. National boundaries are no longer able to divide friend from foe. Indeed, the technological revolution seems to be creating in the minds of people around the world a sense of global citizenship which could result eventually in the transfer of individuals' loyalties from "sovereignty-bound" to "sovereignty-free" multilateral bodies. "The changing relationship between the public and private spheres and the virtual collapse of the dividing line separating the domestic from the external environment suggests a fluid but closely integrated global system substantially at odds with the notion of a fragmented system of nationally delineated sovereign states."[64]

Globalization has also contributed to this global shrinkage. The globalization of trade, production and finance has resulted in a marked decline in governments' ability to control these sectors and has challenged the traditional concept of state sovereignty. It has also expanded the number of players that can be involved in multilateral processes. From an international political economy perspective, Robert Cox sees the globalization movement and the seemingly paradoxical adherence to territorialism as two concepts of world order that stand in conflict but are also interrelated. He points out that the globalization of economic processes "requires the backing of territorially-based state power to enforce its rules." But post-Fordism, the new pattern of social organization of production that is congruent with the globalization phenomenon, implicitly contradicts the lingering territorial principle that was identified with Fordism. The results of post-Fordist production have been, *inter alia*, the dismantling of the welfare state and the diminishing of the strength of organized labour. But it also has had the effect of increasingly fragmenting power in the world system, providing fodder for "the possibility of culturally diverse alternatives to global homogenization."[65] If Cox is right, we can see how the dialectic of the globalization process can alter the relationship people have established with the political arena and how it can eventually cause a reaction leading to what Rosenau terms "explosive sub-groupism."[66]

The Rise of New Social Movements: "Top-Down"/"Bottom-Up" Intersection

Since 1989 we have witnessed the multiplication of new social movements. These movements operate at all levels: local, national, transnational, subregional, regional, transregional, and international. Some of them represent a geographically distinct community, while others have a global agenda. Some have interests that are issue-specific, while others have a wide spectrum of cross-cutting concerns. The causes they undertake vary from concerns with animal rights, ethnicity, ecological, the manufacture and proliferation of nuclear weapons, war and peace, feminism, gay liberation, human potential, communalism, religion, indigenous peoples, urban renewal, inner-city crime, taxation, racial justice, youth, "Generation X," disabled groups, to the elderly.[67] As Camilleri and Falk put it: "What makes these actors politically significant is that they are able to translate their alienation and exclusion into concrete social action. They are social movements by virtue of their ability to engender and organize social conflict."[68]

Many of these new social movements reject existing legal and institutional arrangements at all levels, including multilateral arrangements. They also seem, implicitly at least, to be jettisoning traditional IR's dualistic conception of private/public, domestic/foreign, and inside/outside spheres. Civil society seems no longer willing to allow governments to act as exclusive agents on its behalf. Citizens everywhere appear to want more direct representation in the political decisionmaking that affects them. The best possible way of doing this within the present multilateral structure would be for the UN system to undergo major structural reforms that would allow non-governmental organizations (NGOs) and other nonstate actors more than simply the consultative status already allowed for in Article 71 of the UN Charter. But such changes are being resisted by the members of the UN.

The prominence of NGOs, social movements and social forces on the multilateral stage today indicates that "top-down" multilateralism is being challenged by, or at least being forced to intersect with, "bottom-up" multilateralism. Already, in some issue areas some NGOs are effectively positioned at the table with states. They have also been included as major partners in some multilateral agenda setting and at major multilateral conferences (e.g., the sustainable development conference in Rio de Janeiro, the Nairobi and Beijing conferences on women, the Vienna conference on human rights, and the population conference in Cairo). Also, some governments have begun to include backbench members into their delegations at the UN General Assembly sessions, while others have even included NGO representatives in some of their delegations at major multilateral conferences. And, more recently, NGOs have played a major role in helping the UN and other "top-down" multilateral bodies deal with humanitarian crises, such as in Somalia and Rwanda.

What this indicates is that a highly decentralized, almost chaotic multicentric system (comprised of subnational and supranational "sovereignty-free" actors) is being forced to intersect with the relatively coherent and structured state-centric world of "sovereignty-bound" actors. The results have not been all that gratifying for the nonstate actors. "Top-down" multilateralism must either be reconfigured to accommodate these new social movements and forces by expanding its definition of what constitutes a legitimate political community, or it will be bypassed altogether. One author has advocated a possible way out for the UN system. He recommends that Article 22 of the Charter be utilized to create a civil society-centric parliamentary assembly as a subsidiary organ of the General Assembly.[69] However, this particular proposal is highly problematic for a number of reasons: representatives would be elected by national assemblies, rather than the general public within a nation-state; it is difficult to see how the Parliamentary Assembly would be able to pay for the salaries and travel of what could be over 1,000 representatives; this proposal could increase the duplication and waste that already exists within multilateral bodies; very few UN member governments would actually support this proposal.

Other recent calls for "new" multilateralism, however, recognize the emergence and importance of a cosmopolitan global culture and the operations of a global community dealing with matters that refuse to be confined within state boundaries. Most of these calls are pushing for the creation of a body whose members are elected by world citizens rather than nominated by sovereign state governments.[70] Proponents of this measure argue that the creation of a global parliament would enhance the institutional linkages that already exist between states and civil society. The existence of such a body would also allow those that are most affected by decisions made at the international level to have a direct stake in their outcomes. Calls for broadening the political participation, democratizing existing multilateral institutions, and empowering civil societies to take decisions that affect them at the international level are symptomatic of a desire to expand the concept of multilateralism to include the "bottom-up" variety. If mainstream multilateralists continue to ignore such calls, it is possible that "bottom-up" multilateralism will persist outside the confines of "top-down" multilateralism and could even pose a more direct challenge to it.

While one ought to be prudent in recognizing that "top-down" multilateralism will endure as long as the state system exists, one also has to consider that the demands and needs of the new social and political movements may not be fully accommodated within that "top-down" multilateral structure. Something will have to give! New social movements are forcing "top-down" multilateral institutions like the UN system to acknowledge their existence and importance. Perhaps, out of the dialectical clash between "top-down" and "bottom-up" multilateral activity, a window of opportunity might be opened for emancipatory social and political movements to make substantial gains in what was once the preserve of states.

Conclusion: Developing a "New" View of Multilateralism

As noted earlier, the uneasy intersection of "top-down" and "bottom-up" multilateralism cannot be fully explained using traditional IR analysis. For one thing, such analysis tends to be ahistorical, dominated by realist and liberal institutionalist interpretations, and too heavily focused on the interactions of states and state-centric institutions. This chapter offers an alternative approach to understanding developments and changes in multilateralism. We learn from the above analysis a number of important facts about the nature of multilateralism.

First, multilateralism is a deep organizing principle, or architectural form, with a relatively long history. Indeed, the germ of its character can be traced to the interactions of early civilizations. Multilateral practices and institutions reflect, and to a large degree embed, the underlying configuration of power at a particular historical juncture. They embody social practices developed in response to specific problems confronting international society at the time. These social practices originate from broad principles and may over time become routinized, or codified, into specific sets of constitutive rules.

Second, based on anthropological and historical evidence, one can identify at least eight main attributes of multilateralism: (i) a need for reciprocal, cooperative social relations; (ii) an ideological substructure or underpinning; (iii) customs, norms and expectations; (iv) regulative devices and laws; (v) gatherings or *leagues* (ceremonial or functional forums); (vi) exchange vehicles (such as trade) through which concrete multilateral activity is carried out; (vii) a driving normative element (the need for order, conflict avoidance, settling disputes, improving collective welfare, building stronger bonds, protecting the biosphere, and democratization); and (viii) patriarchal, great power/hegemonic leadership (at least when establishing a multilateral regime).

Third, multilateral institutions are sustained within the context of broader structures (world orders) — the products of recurrent patterns of actions and expectations. As has been shown here, such structural configurations are formed through ideas, language, ways of thinking, socio-economic and political conventions, routines, or practices. Because these structures are socially constructed and are part of our intersubjective reality, they can be changed, adapted, reformed, or transformed whenever material circumstances, prevailing meanings and practices, and existing institutions are challenged by emerging powers, meanings, practices, and institutions.[71] Any effort to redefine multilateralism must therefore recognize the links between changing demands of international society, changing societal practices, and material circumstances, and the need to adapt and change multilateral practices and institutions to meet new demands, practices and circumstances.

Fourth, the record of intersocietal interactions confirm that both "top-down" and "bottom-up" multilateral tendencies have co-existed from early times, although the former became dominant with the advent of the European state system. While the evolution in modern multilateralism (roughly from 1648 to the present) has been in the direction of the pyramidal "top-down" model, we have recently noticed a trend toward the revivification of the civil society and, with it, a greater concern with "bottom-up" multilateral processes and practices. It is this trend that has highlighted the need for a reconceptualization of multilateralism.

Fifth, although multilateralism is socially constructed and therefore subject to change as societal demands change, it is important to realize that the trajectories of multilateralism are *facilitated* or *constrained* by historical structures. These structures and historical patterns, while they may exist for long periods of time, are not static nor do they remain forever unchanged. The hegemonic view of world order can be challenged by a counter-hegemonic position, thus creating different patterns of thought and action. Just as the form that multilateralism took over the years has had to adjust, reflecting changed conditions, we should expect that the present form of multilateral arrangements will eventually have to be altered. However, we must be realistic about the pace of change in multilateral organizations. These institutions have to find ways of shedding their historical baggage in order to respond adequately to changing societal demands.

Sixth, we are living in an uncertain and ambivalent period — a time of social disorder, turbulence and transition. Thus, it may not be possible at this stage to outline definitively the kind of multilateral arrangements that will be required in the future. Instead, what seems likely is that existing international institutions will have to engage in an adjustment exercise that would make their structure and processes flexible enough to cope with the waves of change and uncertainty emanating from the dynamic, fluid, and rapidly fluctuating situation.

Notes

1. For a more detailed and comprehensive analysis of this phenomenon see W. Andy Knight, *Multilateral Evolution and Change in the UN System: The Quest for Global Governance?* Unpublished PhD. dissertation, York University, Toronto, 1995.

2. Robert Keohane, "International Institutions: Two Approaches," *International Studies Quarterly*, 32:4 (December 1988): 379-96.

3. Charles Kegley, Jr. and Eugene Wittkoff, *World Politics: Trends and Transformation* (New York: St. Martin's Press, 1989), p. 13.

4. Robert Cox, "Multilateralism and World Order," *Review of International Studies*, 18:2 (April 1992): 169.

5. David Mitrany, *A Working Peace System: An Argument for the Functional Development of International Organization* (Chicago: Quadrangle Books, 1966).

6. Ernst Haas, *Beyond the Nation-State, Functionalism and International Organization* (Stanford: Stanford University Press, 1964) and *The Uniting of Europe: Political, Social and Economic Forces, 1950-1957* (Stanford: Stanford University Press, 1958). But also note that there were discussions and analysis of attempts at integration in regions other than Europe. See, for instance, Gordon Connell Smith, *The Inter-American System* (London: Oxford University Press, 1966); and Hugh Springer, *Reflections on the Failure of the First West Indian Federation* (Cambridge: Harvard University Press, 1962).

7. Karl Deutsch, *Political Community and the North Atlantic Area* (Princeton: Princeton University Press, 1957) and *Nationalism and Social Communication: An Enquiry into the Foundations of Nationality* (New York: Wiley, 1953).

8. See Arend Lijphart, "Karl W. Deutsch and the New Paradigm in International Relations," in *From National Development to Global Community*, ed. Richard L. Merritt and Bruce M. Russett (London: George Allen & Unwin, 1981), p. 236.

9. Cox, "Multilateralism and World Order," p. 170.

10. Daniele Archibugi, "International Organization in Perpetual Peace Projects," *Review of International Studies*, 18:4 (October 1992): 295.

11. See Max Scheler, "The Idea of Peace and Pacifism," *Journal of British Society for Phenomenology*, 7 (1976): 154-66; Francis Hinsley, *Power and the Pursuit of Peace: Theory and Practice in the History of Relations Between States* (Cambridge: Cambridge University Press, 1963).

12. This model was first proposed by Emeric Crucé, *New Cyneas* (1962) and was translated by C. Frederick Farrell, Jr. and Edith Farrell (New York: Garland, 1972). Many theorists have used this model, noteably the Duke of Sully, the priest from Saint-Pierre, William Ladd, and William Jay.

13. This element of the model is taken from the Duke of Sully's memories (1638). See André Puharré, *Les Projets d'organisation européenne d'après le Grand Dessin de Henri IV et de Sully* (Paris, 1954).

14. Jean-Jacques Rousseau, "Jugement sur le projet de paix perpétuelle" (1758).

15. Archibugi, "International Organization in Perpetual Peace Projects," p. 299.

16. Jeremy Bentham, *Plan for a Universal and Perpetual Peace* (1786-89), in *Peace Projects of the Eighteeth Century*, ed. M. Jocob (New York: Garland, 1974).

17. Claude-Henri Saint-Simon, "The Reorganization of the European Community" (1814), with a translation in F. Markam, *Social Organization, the Science of Man and Other Writings of Henri de Saint-Simon* (New York: Evanston, 1964), p. 38.

18. William Penn, *An Essay Towards the Present and Future Peace of Europe* (1693), reprint, (New York: Hildesheim, Georg Olms, 1983, § VII and VIII).

19. Immanuel Kant, "Perpetual Peace: A Philosophical Project" in Hans Reiss, dir., *Kant's Political Writings* (Cambridge: Cambridge University Press, 1970), pp. 93-97.

20. Immanuel Kant, *Perpetual Peace*, translated by Ted Humphrey (Indianapolis: Hackett, 1983), pp. 107-39; Archibugi, "International Organization in Perpetual Peace Projects."

21. Archibugi, "International Organization in Perpetual Peace Projects," p. 312.

22. James Coleman, "Prologue: Constructed Social Organization, in *Social Theory for a Changing Society,* ed. Pierre Bourdieu and James Coleman (Boulder: Westview Press, 1991), p. 1.

23. Ragnar Numelin, *The Beginning of Diplomacy: A Sociological Study of Intertribal and International Relations* (London: Oxford University Press, 1950), p. 18.

24. For example, Albert Hourani, "Conclusion: Tribes and States in Islamic History," in *Tribes and State Formation in the Middle East,* ed. Philip S. Khoury and Joseph Kostiner (Berkeley: University of California Press, 1990), pp. 303-11.

25. This was a cluster of separate communities operating within a common cultural framework "held together by an impressive system of religion and government" in the area around what is now called the Persian Gulf. See Adam Watson, *The Evolution of International Society: A Comparative Historical Analysis* (London: Routledge, 1992), pp. 24-26.

26. This element is presented in a different fashion in Watson, *The Evolution of International Society*, p. 47.

27. Ibid., p.69-70.

28. H. Nicholson, *Diplomacy* (London: Oxford University Press, 1938), pp. 19-20.

29. William Smith, *A History of Greece*, revised by George Greene (New York: Harper & Brothers, 1854).

30. See John Herz, "The Rise and Demise of the Territorial State," *World Politics*, 9 (1959):473-93.

31. Evan Luard, *Types of International Society*, p. 326. A number of "multilateral" institutions and organizational bodies were created during this age of Dynasties which facilitated the interactions of the societies within Latin Christendom. Examples include Church Councils, special congresses called by the Pope, summit meetings between sovereigns, permanent embassies and continuous diplomatic machinery (which became the primary institutions for the resolution of differences). Leagues were established to resolve quarrels among members and general congresses were created to settle outstanding political questions and to facilitate the exchange mutual guarantees. Garrett Mattingly, *Renaissance Diplomacy* (London: J. Cape, 1955), p. 82.

32. Edward Morse, *Modernization and the Transformation of International Relation* (New York: Macmillan Publishers, 1976), p. 25.

33. Leo Gross, "The Peace of Westphalia, 1648-1948," in *The Process of International Organization*, ed. Robert S. Wood (New York: Random House, 1971), p. 42.

34. Michael Walzer, *The Revolution of the Saints: A Study in the Origins of Radical Politics* (Cambridge: Harvard University Press, 1965); Carl Friedirch, *The Age of the Baroque, 1610-1660* (New York: Harper, 1952), pp. 36-38.

35. See Joseph A. Camilleri and Jim Falk, *The End of Sovereignty? The Politics of a Shrinking and Fragmenting World* (Hants: Edward Elgar Publishing, 1992), pp. 13-15.

36. Leopold von Ranke, "A Dialogue on Politics," in *Leopold Ranke: The Formative Years*, ed. T. van Laue (New Jersey: Princeton University Press, 1950), pp. 167-68.

37. Hedley Bull, "The Emergence of a Universal International Society," in *The Expansion of International Society,* ed. Hedley Bull and Adam Watson (Oxford: Clarendon Press, and NY: Oxford University Press, 1984), p. 117.

38. Before the Europeans came, many of these people had already in place a body of rules and a number of institutional practices that governed their interactions. Ragner Numelin, *The Beginning of Diplomacy: A Sociological Study of Intertribal and International Relations*. For instance, in pre-partitioned and pre-colonial Africa there were distinctive patterns of what one could call "multilateral" relations among its many, disparate political communities. For greater elaboration see Grant Hammond and Bryant Shaw, "The Rise of Nations and the Decay of States: The Transformation of the International System?" unpublished paper (1994).

39. A. Bozeman, *Politics and Culture in International History* (New Jersey: Princeton University Press, 1960), p. 514.

40. S. James Anaya, "Indigenous Rights and Norms in Contemporary International Law," *Arizona Journal of International and Comparative Law*, 8: 2 (1992): 1-5.

41. See Bentham, *Plan for Universal and Perpetual Peace.*

42. Inis Claude, *Swords into Plowshares; The Problems and Progress of international Organizations* (New York: Random House, 1971), p. 24.

43. Frederic Kirgis, Jr. et al., *International Organizations in their Legal Settings*, 2d ed. (Minnesota: West Publishing Co., 1993), pp. 2-5.

44. Claude, *Swords into Plowshares*, p. 25.

45. Clive Archer, *International Organization* (London/Boston: Georg Allen & Unwin, 1983), p. 7.

46. F. Hinsley, *Power and the Pursuit of Peace* (Cambridge: Cambridge University Press, 1967), p. 195.

47. Claude, *Swords into Plowshares*, p. 25.

48. J. Scott, (ed.) *The Reports to the Hague Conferences of 1899 and 1907* (Oxford: Humphrey Milford, 1917), p. 201.

49. Claude, *Swords into Plowshares,* p. 34.

50. Industrial developments led to the need for improvements in technology and communications (steamship, railway, telegraph, etc.). Each of these developments had a tremendous impact on the interactions of states. For example, faster travel allowed for the quick convening of meetings between governmental representatives.

51. Chadwick Alger, "Citizens and the UN System in a Changing World," a paper presented at the international conference "Changing World Order and the United Nations System," Yokohama, Japan, 24-27 March 1992, p. 2.

52. See J. M. Keynes, *The Economic Consequences of the Peace* (London: Macmillan, 1919).

53. Claude, *Swords into Plowshares*, pp. 34-36.

54. K. Skjelsbaek, "The Growth of Non-Governmental Organization in the Twentieth Century," *International Organization*, 25:3 (1971): 420-42.

55. Watson, *The Evolution of International Society,* pp. 280-81.

56. Claude, *Swords into Plowshares*, p. 45.

57. W. Andy Knight, "Flawed Vision of World Order," *Compass Magazine*, (March/April 1992).

58. Claude, *Swords into Plowshares*, p. 44.

59. Ibid., p. 41.

60. Hanna Newcombe, "Third Generation World Organizations," in *United Nations Reform: Looking Ahead after Fifty Years,* ed. Eric Fawcett and Hanna Newcombe (Toronto: Science for Peace/Dundurn Press Limited, 1995), pp. 78-93.

61. W. Andy Knight, "Towards a Subsidarity Model for Peacemaking and Preventive Diplomacy: Making Chapter VIII of the UN Charter Operational," *Working Paper Series*, (Halifax: Centre for Foreign Policy Studies, Dalhousie University, 1995).

62. Robert Keohane and Joseph Nye, *Power and Interdependence: World Politics in Transition* (Boston: Little, Brown & Company, 1977), ch 2.

63. James Rosenau, "Distant Proximities: The Dynamics and Dialectics of Globalization," the text was submitted for the annual edition of *l'International Studies Association*, (Washington, 30 March 1994), p. 1.

64. Camilleri and Falk, *The End of Sovereignty?* p. 88.

65. Robert Cox, "Production and Security," in *Building a New Global Order,* ed. David Dewitt et al. (Don Mills: Oxford University Press Canada), pp. 143-55.

66. Rosenau, "Distant Proximities."

67. See Alain Touraine, "An Introduction to the Study of Social Movements," *Social Research*, 52:4 (Winter 1985): 74-78; Jürgen Habermas, "New Social Movements," *Telos*, 49 (Autumn 1981).

68. Camilleri and Falk, *The End of Sovereignty?* p. 207.

69. Dieter Heinrich, "A United Nations Parliamentary Assembly," in *United Nations Reform: Looking Ahead after Fifty Years,* ed. Fawcett and Newcombe, pp. 95-99.

70. Jonas Zoninsein, "Implications of the Evolving Global Structure for the U.N. System: A View from the South," in *Multilateralism and Global Change: Prospects for Reform and Innovation*, ed. Michael Schechter (Tokyo: United Nations University Press), forthcoming.

71. See Cox, "Towards a Post-Hegemonic Conceptualization of World Order: Reflections on the Relevancy of Ibn Khaldun," in *Governance Without Government: Order and Change in World Politics,* ed. James N. Rosenau and Ernst-Otto Czempic (Cambridge: Cambridge University Press, 1992), pp. 137-39.

Albrecht Schnabel

Post-Cold War Peacekeeping and the Feasibility of Collective Security: A Realist Interpretation

Introduction

The international community's response to the many internal military and humanitarian crises at the end of the Cold War suggested to many that an effective peacekeeping regime could finally emerge. This chapter suggests that, on the contrary, the failure of the new collective security regime envisaged in Boutros Boutros-Ghali's, *An Agenda for Peace,* has shown that states are reasserting their position *vis-à-vis* institutionalized and noninstitutionalized international security regimes. Major powers' evolving policies toward the putative peacekeeping regime demonstrate this in international relations. Values have not yet succumbed to interest and power considerations as being the main driving forces of the states that are the members of collective security regimes. It appears that the post-Cold War peacekeeping experience has reaffirmed, not challenged, classical realist interpretations of collective security and international society.

This analysis serves as the basis for several suggestions as to the utility and prospects of multilateral security cooperation in an international system that, at least in the realm of military security, is run by states; and that would have to be changed by states. The post-Cold War peacekeeping experience suggests that states are not willing to make any major changes. As a result, traditional peacekeeping, being more symbolic than effective in containing and solving conflict, is gaining renewed popularity among major powers and UN policymakers.

What may look like a newly emerging international peacekeeping and collective security regime based on communitarian and universal values of human rights and regional and global security, is actually a shallow structure with little substance. What holds it (and the underlying security organizations) together are the national security interests of their member states.

The first section of the chapter addresses the proliferation of UN-sponsored peacekeeping activities since the end of the Cold War and the potential for a new, collective peacekeeping regime. The second section examines three powers' (Russia, Germany, and the United States) foreign policies toward peacekeeping in the post-Cold War period in order to assess their compatibility with the norms and rules that govern the supposed peacekeeping regime. The last section suggests that, unless all contributors to collective security operations see it to be in their short-term national interest to invest resources in peacemaking/keeping/enforcing efforts, they will not commit themselves to such operations beyond inexpensive and risk-free symbolism. Rather than an end in itself, collective action in peace operations proves to be a means toward the maintenance and expansion of peacekeepers' state power and interest.

The Emerging Peacekeeping Regime

Boutros-Ghali's An Agenda for Peace

In 1992, Secretary-General Boutros-Ghali developed a widely cited and discussed report "on ways of strengthening and making more efficient within the framework and provisions of the Charter the capacity of the United Nations for preventive diplomacy, for peacemaking and for peace-keeping."[1] *An Agenda for Peace* was a bold attempt to expand traditional peacekeeping to include various new forms of peacekeeping — from preventive diplomacy to such tasks as election monitoring and peace enforcement. It represented a new and comprehensive way of thinking about global peacekeeping responsibilities. It envisaged peacekeeping as an institutionalized instrument for global security patterns and structures that served two primary functions: (i) to enhance the political and military position of the United Nations System,[2] and (ii) to promote the political and legal status of individuals and subnational groups governed by states that could not or would not fulfil the basic responsibility of providing for their citizens' security.[3]

A Collective Peacekeeping Regime?

Boutros-Ghali's vision takes on life in Legault *et al.*'s account of an emerging collective security regime in the area of peacekeeping where "international organizations have their own role in collective security and are therefore principal actors in collective security regimes: it is through them that countries establish the operating procedures of the system."[4] Their analysis of a collective peacekeeping regime is based on the basic assumption that,

> [a]ccording to our definition of collective security, countries have converging expectations when it comes to controlling the use of force in international relations; countries are interdependent in their security and in their shared objective of maintaining international peace and security; and there are multilateral procedures for taking action and achieving these objectives. The current system is an "evolutionary set of principles and standards, or a code of interstate behaviour, for the purpose of controlling conflict within the framework of interdependence" and thus meets Krasner's definition which maintains that four interrelated features are necessary to create a regime: principles, norms, rules, and decision-making procedures.[5]

Legault *et al.* explain the nature of the peacekeeping regime by utilizing the core components of Krasner's classical definition of a regime:

> The main *actors* are states as well as regional and international organizations. Various "subregimes" can be identified, from peacekeeping to peacemaking to peace-enforcement; international peace operations often do not fall neatly into one of these categories; instead they lie on a continuum between peacekeeping and peace-enforcement.[6]

The principles of this global collective security regime are enshrined in the UN Charter and in Boutros-Ghali's *Agenda for Peace*. The norms for preventive diplomacy, peacekeeping and peace-enforcing are found in regional and international treaties and agreements and in the UN Charter, either explicitly (particularly in Articles 33, 41-47, 52-53, 99) or implicitly (on the margins between Chapter(s) VI and VII) or in general practice and applications stretching Charter stipulations. Rules are created by Security Council or General Assembly resolutions or common practice; in addition to the rules of engagement of traditional peacekeeping, new ones have emerged in the past few years, including those allowing involvement in intrastate conflict, the assistance and protection of civilian populations and refugees, and the "subcontracting" of regional and other "ad hoc multinational coalitions."

Procedures are applied through national (foreign policy), regional and global bodies (formal and informal arrangement within various levels in these organizations); while these are "still in an embryonic state" (UN Charter, p.97), advances have been made through the establishment of a Military Adviser's Office, a 24-hour hotline, proposals for stand-by forces, and cooperation between different regional bodies. Finally, there is increasing activity and cooperation between regional bodies and the UN (although much less so on the part of involved countries) to monitor and control "congruent implementation of rules and procedures" (UN Charter, p.100).

In the context of this chapter, this account of the peacekeeping regime appears not to be a reflection of current peacekeeping practices, but rather a vision of what the peacekeeping regime could or should be like. Legault *et al.* argue that the attempt to describe collective security and peacekeeping in the context of regime theory "extends beyond the old theories of the Cold War — realism and neo-realism — to provide a flexible framework for analysis which takes into account the actors' evolving expectations and behaviours in practice."[7] We have to ask, however, if "evolving expectations and behaviours in practice" do in fact indicate a further strengthening of the proposed new collective peacekeeping regime.

Meanwhile Boutros-Ghali has realized the naiveté of his hopes articulated in the *Agenda for Peace*.[8] The actions of states toward peacekeeping exhibited during the last few years draw into question the regime-like character of collective peacekeeping actions. It is this evolving attitude of states toward peacekeeping to which we will now turn.

Major Power Commitment to the New Regime

To what extent are major powers willing to support this oriented collective peacekeeping regime? As already mentioned above, Legault *et al.* argue that regime theory "extends beyond the old theories of the Cold War — realism and neorealism — to provide a flexible framework for analysis which takes into account the actors' evolving expectations and behaviours in practice."[9] The following section attempts to do exactly that. By examining the evolving post-Cold War peacekeeping policies of a selection of major powers — Russia, Germany and the United States — I attempt to show that, if exposed to the principle attributes of an international regime, the "old theories of the Cold War" are not significantly challenged. Rather, they are reaffirmed by these states' unwillingness to surrender their own national interests and sovereign rights to defend and promote national security interests to regional and global institutions and their universalist *raison d'être*. Legault *et al.* acknowledge that "[f]or the time being, there are still considerable gaps between norms and practice ... However, as the United Nations turns fifty, it is to be hoped that the member-countries will show increased diligence and generosity in their actions."[10] As the following cases demonstrate, there is little evidence that this is occurring.

Peacekeeping and Changing Foreign Policy Imperatives

The evolution of foreign policy imperatives following the end of the Cold War has changed states' attitudes toward peacekeeping.[11] In the case of Russia, peacekeeping responds perfectly to the country's efforts to raise its military and political presence throughout the former Soviet Union, and to reestablish itself as a global actor. In Germany, the end of the Cold War has meant the rebirth of a united nation, and the end of post-Cold War occupation. Peacekeeping allows Germany to pursue its desires and/or responsibilities to assume greater global visibility, but it also reflects the country's efforts to come to terms with its pre-Cold War historical past. In the United States, the end of the Cold War has brought the end of a 40-year preoccupation with upholding and maintaining a Cold War Pax Americana, and a reorientation away from global visibility to domestic security issues. American peacekeeping has been a direct reflection of the ups and downs of American commitments to global politics.

The National Interest and Emerging Peacekeeping "Doctrines"

Russia

The motivations for Russian peacekeeping can be summarized as follows: first, Russia wants to protect Russian minorities in other former Soviet republics. Second, peacekeeping preempts threats to Russia's territorial security and integrity from third countries such as Turkey and Iran in the Caucasus, or Afghanistan in Central Asia; or from spillovers of civil conflicts in other republics, such as in the case of the Ossets and the Abkhazians in Georgia. Third, Russia pursues the long-term goal of regional hegemony, the status of a "great power," which should play the role of "first among equals." Finally, peacekeeping appeases anti-reformist domestic forces, as it helps the government address the issues of ethnic Russians in the near abroad, military spillovers from bordering republics; and it allows Russia to sustain traditional positions of influence and power, while defending traditional allies and restoring Russia's great power status.[12]

Russia's participation in international peacekeeping serves similar reasons: it helps qualify Russia as a civil global actor, willing to support collective security responsibilities along with other Security Council members and world powers. Implicitly, international cooperation on peacekeeping helps avert some of the international criticism of its peacekeeping activities in the near abroad. It includes Russia in the forum of international peacekeepers, and allows it to pursue seriously its plea for receiving official UN acknowledgement and (financial) support of Russian and CIS peacekeeping efforts, a request for international recognition of Russia's regional hegemonic role.[13]

Russian objectives for peacekeeping in the near abroad as well as the far abroad can be boiled down to one single dimension: the advancement of national strategic and economic interests. Commitments to peacekeeping are driven by the protection of Russian minorities throughout the former Soviet Union, the protection of Russia's borders and Russia's interest in a stable, yet militarily and economically highly dependent CIS. There is no indication that Moscow truly desires the cooperation of third parties (be these states or international organizations) to participate in peacekeeping operations within the CIS. Moreover, its willingness to submit itself to the demands of UN postulates in peacemaking operations is severely limited by its partisan approach to situations that require a high degree of neutrality.

In short, Russian "peacekeepers" have much more in common with protection or invasion forces than with the powerless and frail UN "blue-helmet" forces.[14] Nevertheless, Russia's actions are sanctioned, if not explicitly, then implicitly, by the world community. The world community does not wish to get involved in settling conflicts in the CIS, while disorder and instability in this region are in no one's interest. Thus, Russian peacekeeping remains a forceful, partial, and intrusive military operation which may enhance order, but by no means necessarily justice. Moreover, it cements Russia's hegemonic position within the region of the near abroad, and, in the case of Russian involvement in the far abroad, it guarantees the country a seat among the great powers and international decisionmakers. Even the UN Secretary-General seems to take that approach. He praises Russia's role in Bosnia, while he sees " 'no obstacles' to Russian troops carrying out peacekeeping operations on former Soviet territory as long as they did so under the Russian flag."[15]

Germany

Germany's new *Weißbuch*, the annual report by the Ministry of Defence on the security of the Federal Republic and the state and future of the armed forces, defines Germany's approach to peacekeeping as such:

> Even after solving the legal status (of out-of-area missions), the German contribution to securing global peace will be primarily of a political and economic, and not military nature. Every single case will be carefully judged according to German values and interests as well as the consideration of the political goals, risks and possible consequences, and it will then be responsibly assessed and decided upon in awareness of Germany's obligation to history.[16]

This statement can be considered as Germany's peacekeeping doctrine; it relates the country's potential participation in peacekeeping operations primarily to the recognition of Germany's particularistic domestic political concerns. As is the case with the public and political blue-helmet debates, no mention is made of the recognition and defence of universal moral values, or Germany's mandate under Chapter VII of the UN Charter. Moreover, Germany's peacekeeping policy is defined in relation to its status in Europe and the world, in relation to the significance of peacekeeping for responsible membership in NATO and the UN, as a prerequisite for the government's quest for post-Cold War "normalization," and in relation to its chances for a permanent seat on the Security Council.

Other relevant issues are the development of a new purpose for the armed forces at the end of the Cold War;[17] the enhancement of Germany's reputation as not only an economic but increasingly a political force in world politics; and its worthiness as a partner in collective security arrangements. This ties in very well with Defence Minister Rühe's *Verteidigungspolitische Richtlinien*, the defence-political guidelines, published in December 1992. Here, Germany's vital security interests include the protection of the country and its citizens from external threats and political blackmail; the prevention, containment and resolution of crises and conflicts that have an impact on security and stability; the association with nuclear and naval powers in NATO — because of Germany's (weak) position as a nonnuclear middle power with, nevertheless, worldwide interests; the "partnership among equals" between Europe and North America; the maintenance and spread of democracy and free market economic principles throughout Europe and the world; arms control in Europe; and the "influence on international institutions and processes congruent with our interests, and based on our economic power, our military contributions, and our credibility as a stable and capable democracy."[18]

On 24 July 1994, Klaus Kinkel, the Minister of Foreign Affairs, addressed the German *Bundestag* about the consequences that will arise from the Constitutional Court's decision on the use of German forces. He noted that, "[e]ven after the verdict we will stick to our proven culture of restraint. There will not be an automatic participation of German peacekeepers. As we are not in the position to either alone or with others address all of this world's misery, we will have to say 'no' more often than 'yes.'"[19] He envisaged German participation in peacekeeping only when such a mission is justified by international law, when there is a clear mandate, when the military mission is realizable, and when there is a clear link between peacekeeping and political settlement.[20] This is reminiscent of US President Clinton's Presidential Decision Directive 25.

For the most part, Germans will continue their traditional nonmilitary peacekeeping contributions. They will seek political and nonviolent solutions to conflicts. This will allow them to pursue their goal as a global political actor while at the same time will not alienate a public which, after all, has been socialized in "political restraint" during Germany's Cold War years. If Germany's interests are at stake, as in the conflict in the former Yugoslavia, it will likely support more aggressive interpositions through its membership in NATO, WEU, and OSCE.

Germany still is the most "collectivist" of the three states in this sample. However, as it regains its self-confidence as a global actor, and as regional and international organizations face increasing difficulties in effectively responding to conflicts, Germany may take a more unilateralist and noncollectivist approach in its foreign security policy.

United States

As the United States responds to the end of the Cold War by redefining its global role, and as domestic issues gain in salience over foreign affairs, American political leaders are reexamining the nation's increasingly complex national interest.[21] The bipolar superpower competition during the Cold War made it fairly easy to justify all types of foreign involvement, from development activities to military invasions, under the general umbrella of national security interests. Now it is increasingly difficult to define how solutions to a particular crisis may be in America's *vital* interest. As one observer notes, however,

> it is unreasonable . . . to expect Americans and their government to simply ignore 50 years of global leadership as if it never happened and retreat into some mythical era of splendid isolationism. Nor is there any indication of a willingness to do so. Inconsistency and even confusion are not synonymous with a withdrawal from global affairs. Quite on the contrary, they are the result of an effort to remain internationally engaged.[22]

Yet, it has become more difficult to justify global engagement. A number of accounts of America's definition of its vital national interest make this clear. In early 1994, a congressional report of the Working Group on Peacekeeping and the National Interest identified a number of threats which could motivate the US to undertake peacekeeping activities. These include the disruption of economic activities, the proliferation of nuclear and chemical weapons, the spread of conflict into neighbouring countries, mass movements of refugees, and interference with economic development.[23] US National Security Advisor Anthony Lake insisted that a particular mission would have to be evaluated "in terms of our interests, against its presumed costs." He lists seven national interests which "taken in some combination or even alone ... can merit the use of our military, especially in areas of greatest strategic significance": the defence against direct attacks on the United States, its citizens at home and abroad, and its allies; the countering of aggression; the defence of crucial economic interests; the preservation, promotion, and defence of democracy; the prevention of the proliferation of nuclear and other weapons, terrorism, and drugs; the maintenance of America's reputation as a reliable partner; and the combatting of humanitarian disasters.[24]

The Clinton administration's White Paper, the *National Security Strategy of Engagement and Enlargement* listed issues of "broad, overriding importance to the survival, security, and vitality of our national entity" as primary reasons for American troop deployment while secondary issues are those where there is "a sizable economic stake or commitment to allies, and areas where there is a potential to generate substantial refugee flows into our nation or our allies."[25]

The United States' new attitude toward collective security, and peacekeeping in particular, in effect means that the US has retreated from its post-Cold War approach of "assertive multilateralism" — "[m]ultilateral action is still in order, but only if it is conducted in a pragmatic manner and only if U.S. interests are given foremost consideration."[26] The UN "will remain an important source of legitimacy and international support for American foreign policy actions which address issues of *secondary importance* to its national interests (italics by the author)."[27] America's "national interest" is at the heart of the new peacekeeping approach.

If this approach becomes a genuine component of future US peacekeeping policy — and the Republicans' attitude toward American peacekeeping responsibilities suggests that it will — and if it is, in turn, emulated by other major peacekeepers, truly multilateral and principled "humanitarian intervention" would in effect become a utopian concept, symbolizing traditional power politics instead of universal humanitarianism. Such reasoning also suggests the reluctance of peacekeepers to subordinate their own preferences to those of a collective. Without this, multilateral security efforts, if at all possible, depend on day-to-day compromises and — more accidental than planned — confluence of complex structures of perceived and actual national interest. This makes the peacekeeping regime extremely weak, if not impossible to sustain.

National Interest and the Peacekeeper

There are several generalizations one can draw from evolving Russian, German, and American approaches to peacekeeping. First, in all three cases one can only expect limited commitment to peacekeeping solely in response to humanitarian concerns. What drives peacekeeping policies are individual countries' "case-by-case evaluations" of their particular concerns over national security, geostrategic interests, and regional and/or global status. Less particularistic issues such as the defence of universal humanitarian values or global security, peace, and justice have little impact on the actual decisionmaking processes for blue-helmet and peacemaking activities.

Second, gains and losses in peacekeeping missions are defined in terms of political repercussions on elections, on domestic political debates, and on power struggles. They are defined in terms of long-standing historical relationships, one's position within the region or the greater international community, loss or gain in prestige, potential impacts on refugee movements, or other direct threats to one's national security. However, they are almost never defined within the terms of the universal goals of peace and justice as put forward by the UN Charter, nor are they defined in terms of those who are suffering as victims of ethnic and other domestic conflicts.

And finally, all three countries reserve the right to opt out of ongoing missions and to deny cooperation requested by the Security Council. Increasingly pragmatic peacekeeping doctrines assure the states' right to reserve for themselves the final decision to become involved in a particular conflict, or not. As well, structures of command and control are not automatically being transferred to the UN. Nobody appears willing to seriously entertain the idea of a standing UN army, and the proposed standby rapid reaction forces still depends on national legislative authorization to be deployed under UN command.

National Interest and Collective Action

Despite the inhibitions of states to commit to collective peacekeeping ventures, they frequently do so if and for as long as they perceive their interests to be at stake in the development outcome of regional conflicts. Why are self-interested, power-driven peacekeeping nations interested in participating in collective approaches to conflict resolution? As the German and Russian cases show, a major component of a state's willingness to participate in peacekeeping missions might be the opportunity just to be part of a collective security effort. Not only can this enhance a country's reputation as a global military and political actor, but it may also, implicitly, assist in securing membership in other global organizations (i.e., economic ones).

Furthermore, collective approaches do lower the costs of alternative unilateral actions. Here, Russia is a case in point. Although deeply opposed to outside involvement in security affairs within its areas of vital interests, i.e., the "near abroad," Russia is increasingly willing to allow some involvement of such organizations as the OSCE or the UN. This shifts some of the financial burden of peacekeeping to other actors, while it still increases the legitimacy of Russian actions. The United States takes a similar approach. The 1994 National Security Strategy argues that,

> as much as possible, we will seek the help of our allies or of relevant multilateral institutions. If our most important national interests are at stake, we are prepared to act alone. But especially on those matters touching directly the interests of our allies, there should be a proportional commitment from them.[28]

Collective actions add to the complexity of operations, and they are inconvenient because they increase the level of transparency of "invasions in the name of peace." However, they may be a preferred option if they spread the cost of involvement among more actors, if they target conflicts that are of only secondary significance to one's vital national security, and if they provide legitimacy to otherwise dubious actions.

Now, how collective should such operations be? How far should one subject one's national interests and preferences to collective compromises and international rules and practices? One could argue that the current peacekeeping regime does not represent a genuinely collective commitment, as states' commitment to collective action is dependent on individual benefit-cost assessments, rather than the other way around. Furthermore, in the absence of mutual agreements on aims, goals and scope of peacekeeping missions, there is very little or no collective thinking or commitment. At the end of the day, national interest, not collective interest, gives direction to peacekeepers' policies and actions. Multilateral security cooperation for peacekeeping/enforcing purposes takes place only if there is sufficient agreement among all peacekeepers that particular short-term security interests are served — and that the mission will be inexpensive, brief, and successful. Moreover — as the Russian and American cases show — if national security is at stake and, thus, if the national interest is sufficiently served, unilateral action is the preferred option.

An Outlook on the Emerging Peacekeeping Regime

We can summarize the major components of the revised collective peacekeeping regime as follows:

1. The main *actors* of this regime are states that are not particularly interested in prominent roles performed by regional and/or international organizations; the latter are totally dependent on the goodwill of potential peacekeepers, and the presence of security incentives significant enough to persuade them to support international peacekeeping efforts.

2. Various *subregimes* are clearly defined. Defining the tasks and scope of peace operations will be critical for the survival of any international collaboration on peacekeeping in cases where states will have to be persuaded to get involved (i.e., in the absence of unilateral "peacekeeping" intentions). This will be the task of international and regional organizations. The regime itself may survive in the form of traditional peacekeeping — authorized by international institutions, carried out by a representative sample of the international community. In the case of operations that involve substantial human and economic, political and military sacrifice and commitment, that is when peace has to be enforced before it can be kept, there will not be a subregime. Here, case-by-case multilateral or unilateral invasion forces will perform — likely with much more success — the task of current third-generation UN peacemakers;

3. The *principles* of the new, limited, pragmatic and nonprincipled global collective security regime will still be enshrined in the UN Charter, but they will be subjected to case-by-case interpretations. If intervention is preferred by some actors, references to the maintenance of peace, security and stability (Chapters VI or VII) will be made. If intervention is not preferred, reference to the nonintervention commitment in the Charter (Article 2 [4 and 7]) will be made. Instead of Boutros-Ghali's *Agenda for Peace*, day-to-day national interest and foreign policy perceptions will serve as guidelines for collaboration in peacekeeping missions.

4. The *norms* which underlie such operations may still be based on regional and international treaties and agreements, the UN Charter, or on general practice and application in stretching Charter stipulations. But these serve only as secondary sources of justifications and operational frameworks. They are subject to changing interests of peacekeepers involved in conflicts.

5. *Rules* will be established in increasingly pragmatic ways. They will be established and modified by those *who do* the peacekeeping, and they will serve their particular interests and stakes in the conclusion of a particular crisis. The UN and other regional organizations will continue their attempts to be in charge of such operations, or to guarantee peacekeepers' adherence to the principles, norms, and rules set out by the Charter and other international agreements, but their leverage will continue to shrink. How-

ever, they will continue the important, perhaps mostly symbolic, activity of passing resolutions and monitoring crises and outside responses.

6. As an extension of the previous component, *procedures* will develop in response to levels of commitment by potential peacekeepers, that is in response to their approaches to peacekeeping in general. This may range from traditional interposition between warring parties to warfighting against aggressors in local and interstate conflicts. The role of regional and international organizations in establishing rules and procedures of engagement will be minimal.

The true face of the post-UNPROFOR peacekeeping regime will be characterized by the willingness of peacekeepers to cooperate with other actors if, when, and for as long as there is a reasonable perception that the solution or containment of a particular conflict, or simply the participation in efforts to achieve that, will ultimately improve their own security or international (and/or regional) standing.

Conclusions: Realism and Collective Action in Post-Cold War Peacekeeping Operations

Regime theory successfully links traditional state-centric realist thought — as well its more enlightened neorealist companion — with the increasingly interdependent nature of interstate relations.[29] The rational state actor[30] cannot maximize its self-interest in isolation, or without considering domestic factors and international political, cultural and economic relations of other countries. Just as states have to give increasing consideration to domestic forces, they also have to incorporate international or global forces in their decisionmaking process — *if doing so benefits their position at home and/or abroad*. Noninstitutionalized, nongovernmental regimes feed off this need to facilitate cooperation and collective action, based on shared interests and principles, when and as long as this is deemed to benefit regime members.

In the area of security politics, however, the extent to which interdependence affects perceptions of national interest and security depends to a large degree on the perception of the threat to one's society emanating from conflict and instability elsewhere. A potential collective peacekeeping regime requires high levels of threat perception, shared among regime members. In too many cases this simply does not exist, at least when measured in short-term national interest perceptions. Thus, considering the costs of peacekeeping in far-away places with little or no immediate relevance to one's national security calculations, state-centrism and noncompliance with policies of regional and international organizations seem to be the most affordable option. This constitutes a clear impediment to collective security actions which are intended to solve conflicts other than those directly implicating one's nation or that of one's ally.

As long as states participating in collective security arrangements are driven by mutual interests which induce them to coordinate their interests, multilateralism does have a place in regional and international security cooperation. However, if international norms central to UN-sponsored and initiated peacekeeping operations are not part of these mutual interests, the post-Cold War version of a collective global security regime, as envisioned by Boutros-Ghali in 1992, will remain an illusion.

In short, the current so-called peacekeeping regime, at least when used with its humanitarian connotation, holds only as long as its core values, norms, and principles are in congruence with the peacekeepers' national security and status interests. As an extension of this argument, collective security structures and operations can be sustained only if all, or the major contributors, are able to see their interests reflected in the goals of the security collaboration. If they do not, then operations are doomed to fail, as has been illustrated by the failures of recent peacekeeping missions in Somalia and the former Yugoslavia.

If participating nations see that their national security causes have been served, at a reasonable price and with reasonable chance for a missions' success, collaboration may work. This attests to a not-so-new, yet revealing attitude of states in the current context of presumed globalization of international politics: the new peacekeeping regime is based primarily on realist notions of national security and strategic national interest and not on global norms, values, and principles. This applies as well to procedures and structures of the so-called peacekeeping regime. Participating states, and not the regional or international organizations which lend legitimacy to these missions, decide how long and to what degree they will remain committed to a particular operation. The new collective peacekeeping regime is a frail concept with few consequences for traditional — realist — notions of state interest, security, interstate security cooperation, and world order.

Notes

The author is grateful to Pierre Martin and S. Neil MacFarlane for comments and suggestions made on previous drafts.

1. Boutros Boutros-Ghali, *An Agenda for Peace* (New York: United Nations, 1992), para. 1.

2. For further study of Boutros-Ghali's vision for a more forceful and politically aggressive United Nations, see his articles, "Empowering the United Nations," *Foreign Affairs* 71 (Win-

ter 1992/93):89-102; "UN Peace-keeping in a New Era: A New Chance for Peace," *The World Today* 49 (April 1993):66-9; and "An Agenda for Peace: One Year Later," *Orbis* 37 (Summer 1993), pp. 323-32.

3. See Steven E. Goldman, "A Right of Intervention Based upon Impaired Sovereignty," *World Affairs* 156:2 (Fall 1993).

4. Albert Legault *et al.*, "The United Nations at Fifty: Regime Theory and Collective Security," *International Journal* 50 (Winter 1994-95): 80.

5. Legault *et al.*, "The United Nations at Fifty," in *Diplomacy of Hope: Canada and Disarmament 1945-1988,* ed. Albert Legault and Michel Fortmann (Kingston and Montreal: McGill-Queen's University Press, 1992), p. 484. In their attempt to explain what regulates the regulations, the overarching principles of a regime, Legault *et al.* emphasize the existence of metaregulations, covering "both the regime's intended area of action and its norms and principles." Metaregulation "deals with what ought to be or what ought to be done in contrast to what is or what is being done." They rightfully point out that in peacekeeping metaregulations are not clear from the outset of an action. Moreover, "peacekeeping is a fine example" of "instances in which states take action and only afterwards invent principles to support that action" (pp. 82-83). As long as such action reflects, in principle, the regime's overall mission, i.e. to protect human and international peace and security, this is fine. If, however, action reflects other, much less humanitarian and globalist interests, we have to come to the conclusion that these are the prevailing and underlying metaregulations.

6. He defines regimes as "sets of implicit or explicit principles, norms, rules and decision-making procedures around which actors' expectations converge in a given area of international relations. *Principles* are beliefs of fact, causation, and rectitude. *Norms* are standards of behaviour defined in terms of rights and obligations. *Rules* are specific prescriptions or proscriptions for action. *Decision-making procedures* are prevailing practices for making and implementing collective choice" [italics added by the author]. Stephen Krasner, *International Regimes* (Ithaca, NY: Cornell University Press, 1983), p. 2.

7. Legault *et al.*, "The United Nations at Fifty," p. 102.

8. See Boutros Boutros-Ghali, *Supplement to An Agenda for Peace*, UN Document A/50/60, (3 January 1995), in which he takes stock of the developments during the years since the initial publication of *An Agenda for Peace*, and in which he comes to a pessimistic assessment of the feasibility of his originally envisioned collective security regime.

9. Legault *et al.*, "The United Nations at Fifty," pp. 101-2.

10. Ibid., p. 102.

11. The following country comparison has been developed in greater detail in my doctoral dissertation entitled *Ethnic Conflict, Sovereignty, and Humanitarian Intervention: Internationalization of Domestic Conflict and Systems Change in International Relations* and a book chapter with the title " Interventionism Reconsidered: Russian, Germany and America Approaches to Peacekeeping," in *Conflict Management in the CIS: Whither Russia?* ed. Hans-Georg Ehrhart, Anna Kreikemyer and Andrei V. Zagorski (Baden-Baden: Nomos Verlagsgesellschaft, 1995), pp. 78-87.

12. For further elaboration and references on the motivations for Russian peacekeeping, see S. Neil MacFarlane and Albrecht Schnabel, "Russian Approaches to Peacekeeping," in *The 'New Peacekeeping' and European Security: German and Canadian Interests and Issues*,

ed. Hans-Georg Ehrhart and David Haglund (Baden-Baden: Nomos Verlagsgesellschaft, 1995), pp. 78-87.

13. Ibid., p. 85-87.

14. See also, "War or Peace? Human Rights and Russian Military Involvement in the 'Near Abroad'," *Helsinki Watch* 5: 22 (December 1993).

15. Christopher Boian, "Boutros-Ghali Meets Yeltsin on Peacekeeping Role," *AFP*, 4 April 1994. See also James Meek, "UN Rules Out Special Status for Russians," *The Guardian*, 5 April 1994. Meek comments that "Boutros-Ghali went some way towards endorsing Moscow's *de facto* role as regional policeman, supporting Russian involvement in peacekeeping in former Soviet countries whose affairs are already dominated by their relationship with their powerful neighbour."

16. *Weißbuch 1994* (Bonn: Bundesministerium der Verteidigung, 1994), p. 70.

17. On this point, see Rodney Loeppky, "Germany and Peacekeeping: Prospects and Problems," *Forum* 8:4 (Fall 1993): 67.

18. As cited in "Unsere Soldaten tragen Verantwortung für die bedrohte Freiheit anderer Völker," *Welt am Sonntag*, 6 December 1992.

19. Klaus Kinkel, "Erklärung der Bundesregierung," *Bulletin* 70 (26 July 1994), p. 658.

20. Ibid., p. 658.

21. In this context, one should also mention the attack on a federal building in Oklahoma City. Initially, most observers suspected that an international terrorist group (presumably a Middle Eastern, Islamic fundamentalist organization) was responsible for the attack. Soon after, evidence hardened that, in fact, home-grown right-wing terrorists are to be blamed for the attack. As this example shows, America's battles to defend its national security are indeed shifting from abroad (Cold War, immediate post-Cold War period) to its backyard (Haiti, Cuba), and now to its own territory.

22. Joel J. Sokolsky, "Great Ideals and Uneasy Compromises: The US Approach to Peacekeeping," in *The 'New Peacekeeping' and European Security: German and Canadian Interests and Issues,* ed. Hans-Georg Ehrhart and David Haglund (Baden-Baden: Nomos Verlagsgesellschaft, 1995), p. 54.

23. Report of the Working Group on Peacekeeping and the National Interest, *Peacekeeping and the US National Interest*, Henry L. Stimson Center, (February 1994); as cited in Sokolsky, "Great Ideals and Uneasy Compromises," p. 55.

24. Anthony Lake, "American Power and American Diplomacy," Address at Harvard University, 21 October 1994, *U.S. Department of State Dispatch* 5:46, (14 November 1994), p. 766. Although this may have been done unintentionally, one cannot help but notice that humanitarian concerns were listed at the very bottom of this list.

25. It is unquestionable, however, that the threats posed to the United States will weigh heavier than those posed to allies. One could argue that assistance, although forthcoming more reluctantly, is based on concerns over the country's reliability as an ally or partner, over

international standing and the continuation of mutual defence mechanisms, rather than on sincere concerns for the allies' security problems. Office of the Press Secretary, The White House, *A National Security Strategy of Engagement and Enlargement,* July 1994, p. 16.

26. Ibid., p. 16.

27. Presidential Decision Directive 25, unpublished summary and commentary by Stephen Peck, Center for Strategic and International Studies, Washington, DC, p. 6.

28. The White House, *National Security Strategy*, p. 16.

29. See, for example, Robert O. Keohane and Joseph Nye, *Transnational Relations and World Politics* (Cambridge: Harvard University Press, 1972) and *Power and Interdependence: World Politics in Transition* (Boston: Little, Brown, 1977) for compelling analyses of this argument.

30. The degree to which states act rationally is debatable. However, the author believes that actions can be considered as rational if they are based on an informed calculation of *perceived* (or imagined) short- or long-term interests.

Brian L. Job

Prospects for Multilateralism in Resolving Regional Conflicts: "A Little Help from Your Friends"

Introduction

The mandate of this chapter was to provoke thought and discussion. To this end, arguments and conclusions are put forward without tempering nuances and exhaustive examination of the range of empirical evidence that could or should be taken into account. With the end of the Euro-Atlantic Cold War half a decade ago, it is time for some hard thinking about the emerging parameters of the international security order. The realities of the distributions of power and interests within regions and the intractable nature of intrastate conflicts, which are by far the most prevalent and deadly in today's world, have to dispel the overly optimistic rhetoric about a multilateralist "new world order." Attention needs to focus upon promoting realistic expectations for regional multilateralism, and upon strategies for institution building and for enhancement of human security to provide more solid foundations for multilateralism in the next century.

In this context, this chapter addresses certain issues surrounding the prospects for multilateralist action in response to regional conflict in the contemporary international environment. It proceeds from the conceptual to the practical, beginning with considerations of the requirements and forms of multilateralism — as distinct from other forms of collaborative state behaviour, and moving to consideration of the nature of regional relationships and of regional conflict in current international systems. Its conclusions are pessimistic, especially with regard to the short-term future. There is little likelihood in regional contexts for support for multilateralism and equally little for multilateralist institutional action to effectively manage or resolve regional conflicts. For states, regimes, or people caught up in such conflicts, there is, in other words, likely to be "little help from one's [multilateralist] friends." With regard to the longer term, a somewhat more optimistic assessment about the advance of multilateralism in regional contexts may be warranted. There are indications, for instance, of nascent security communities taking shape in selected regional contexts. Somewhat paradoxically, however, the interests of regional states in sustaining such longer term processes, and prospects for regional multilateralism, tend to mitigate against imperatives for joint action on a regional basis to resolve ongoing conflicts. The following section of this chapter takes up definitional and conceptual matters, seeking to distinguish the "quantitative" and "qualitative" forms of multilateralism and to juxtapose various dimensions of multilateralism. From this point on, a regional perspective is adopted. Thus, the third section defines regional security complexes and looks at the interests and motivations toward multilateralism likely to be characteristic of different types of prototypic regional states, for example, regional powers, small states, or "middle powers." Section four confronts the tough question of how and why regional multilateralist institutions are unlikely to be responsive to, or effective in, any interventionary forms of conflict management. While the answers to this question are generally negative, especially in the short term and *vis-à-vis* intrastate conflicts, some hope is held out for longer term progress toward regional security community formation.

Multilateralism: Definitions, Distinctions, and Clarifications

A distinction needs to be made between the quantitative and qualitative senses of multilateral interstate behaviour. In its nominal, quantitative sense "multilateral" refers to any "practice of coordinating national policies in groups of three or more states."[1] Multilateral, therefore, serves as an adjective, a simple descriptor of the number of parties involved in an activity. It does not delineate the nature of this activity, which could range from single events of consultation to the establishment of permanent, collaborative organizations or even the integration of states.

It is the qualitative sense of the term multilateral that provides these important, larger meanings, referring to state behaviours that accord with specific principles. As Ruggie states: multilateralism is a "generic institutional form of modern international life" — one that states demonstrate only when their attitudes and behaviours sustain certain standards or principles. These principles embody three characteristics: *nondiscrimination, indivisibility* and *diffuse reciprocity.*[2] The concept of *nondiscrimination* implies that states must perform their agreed upon behaviour or satisfy their obligations without contingencies or qualifications about which particular states are involved. The most commonly cited example of nondiscrimination is the obligation of states to extend the Most-Favoured Nation (MFN) status to all other states in the GATT/ World Trade Organization (WTO) trading regime. In the context of security relations, states are required to meet their commitments toward all other individual members of the collective (usually requiring action against aggression). Hence, in essence there is an *indivisibility* among the members of the collective, with regard to the commitment/obligation to act and with regard to access to and distribution of outputs. For multilateral security institutions this generally translates into the requirement that peace be regarded as indivisible for and by each member of the collective.

Continuity is an essential third characteristic. Episodic, single-shot instances of interstate coalition behaviour occurring within the context of otherwise individually competitive or hostile relationships among players are not multilateralist. Instead, joint participation has to range over an extended time period and, in doing so, comes to be predicated upon, and become the basis for, anticipations about the longer run functioning of the collective. In other words, states extend their shadow of the future beyond the immediate and short run. In the conduct of their ongoing relations, they are attentive to the need to demonstrate resolve to meet their obligations to the collective. They provide benefits and accept costs on behalf of other members at a given time, feeling assured that these same benefits will be extended to them as necessary in the future. Such an environment exhibits what is described, by Keohane and others, as *diffuse reciprocity*.[3]

Exploring these arguments in any greater depth would take us beyond the scope of this chapter. However, in the following discussions, care will be taken to make clear the appropriate connotation of multilateral which is being invoked. Usual practice will be to use the adjective "multilateralist" when referring to qualitative forms of multilateralism, thus reserving "multilateral" to its nominal, quantitative meaning.

Three points of clarification are important:

First, the presence and operation of formal international organization(s) is neither a necessary nor a sufficient indicator of the existence of multilateralism. In fact, certain institutional mechanisms may be designed to facilitate distinctly non-multilateralist principles of behaviour, including imperialism, hegemonic dominance or bilateralism (as seen, for instance, in the "hub and spokes" architecture of the US-centred, post-Second World War Pacific security order). As Lisa Martin has pointed out, there are circumstances in which the efficient operation of institutions that are multilateral in the nominal sense could inhibit the promotion of conditions and behaviours of multilateralism.[4]

Second, multilateralism needs to be viewed as a continuous rather than discrete phenomenon, that is specific forms of collaborative state behaviour or international institutions will exhibit greater or lesser degrees of multilateralism. Multilateralism encompasses a spectrum of behaviours and attitudes — to focus only upon ideal types or those few empirical examples that are fully developed along all three criteria noted above would be to ignore instances of nascent multilateralism in transitory environments, such as in several current post-Cold War regional contexts. This point will be developed further below.

Third, for analytical purposes, multilateralist arrangements struck by states can be arrayed over two dimensions: the first referring to the nature of the commitment undertaken by and for members, and characterized here as varying from "deep" to "shallow"; the second referring to scope of membership, and described as varying from "narrow" to "broad."

Regarding the first dimension, commitment, the essential feature of multilateralism in a security-oriented context is "some expression or other of collective security or collective self-defence."[5] States "deeply" committed, therefore, promise to assist any one of their membership to address aggression by another state. "Shallower" commitments would involve undertakings of assistance vis-à-vis specifically designated potential aggressors, promises not to assist aggressor states, agreements to make transparent certain information, etc. With regard to the second dimension, membership, a "narrowly" conceived association would involve few states, relative to the overall number of states within the region or system with mutual security interests. One that was "broadly" conceived would be inclusive of its potential regional or systemic membership. Thus, a concert composed of two of five major powers would be viewed as "narrow," as might an alliance of half of the states in a region, while a regionally-inclusive organization such as the Organization of African Unity (OAU) or the United Nations would be seen as "broad."

While not logically necessary, there is in practice a tension between these two dimensions of multilateralism. Although states may strive to expand or enhance their multilateralist relationships along both dimensions, in effect, there will be significant trade-offs involved. Breadth of membership will likely be inversely related to depth of effective multilateralist commitment. Larger multilateralist cohorts, while having the benefit of numbers and geographic scope, will, for a variety of reasons, usually be capable of sustaining only shallow forms of commitments, despite the rhetoric of their charters. Thus, there will be incentives toward association of smaller numbers of "like-minded" states who share common societal characteristics and who fear the same threat(s). But, here the dilemmas will be ones of capability, (Are the members of the group sufficiently capable to meet threats against their numbers?), and of inclusion, (How can the group expand to meet new circumstances and retain the common base of attitudes and understandings which has sustained them to date?). Getting the "balance" right in any particular multilateralist context is a delicate issue for states. As argued below, this has become a special dilemma in today's post-Cold War security environment.

As a final important note, it ought to be mentioned that the form and content of states' actions in response to their security interests is predicated upon the interrelationship of structural, cognitive and (resulting) behavioural factors. Neither the structural features of the environment, i.e., the distribution of power, nor of the perceptions and attitudes of the actors, i.e., the cognitive component, is itself sufficient to determine the configuration of security arrangements that will emerge among a defined group of states. On the structural dimension, the realities of geography, state resources and power projection capacities are critical. As argued by structural realist theorists, the configuration of power amongst the major powers — its distribution, stability and shifts — delimits the parameters and constraints of the security architecture of the system or subsystem in question.

However, it is the cognitive features of the environment — the attitudes of the players toward each other, the rules and norms governing international interaction, the scope and nature of the security dilemmas that the actors perceive and perpetuate among themselves — that effectively determine the particular form of security institutions that might arise. Whether a transitory balance of power holds sway, or a concert among major powers is established, or a polarized system of antagonistic coalitions occurs, depends upon the nature and division of shared attitudes among states, especially the relevant major powers. The same structural distribution of power could give rise to any of these or even other multilateral security orders. Thus, it is the "structure of attitudes" within a system or subsystem that determines, in general terms, the possibilities for multilateralism.

The Regional Context

Specifying a "security region" involves delineation of those states whose security concerns and resultant behaviours intersect to produce what Morgan terms, a "theatre of operation,"[6] or what Buzan has labelled a "security complex."[7] Although membership in a "regional security complex" (again Buzan's term) will be largely oriented in geographic terms, it is defined (i) on the basis of involvement in security relations with other states, for example, the US is therefore a member of several regional security complexes; and (ii) necessarily to include both patterns of enmity and amity, for example, Russia and the

Warsaw Pact were part of the post-Second World War, European security complex.

For analytical purposes, it is useful to think in terms of prototypic regional security complex configurations, involving combinations of actors and structures of capabilities, interests, and attitudes. Four different types of states need to be noted: (i) global powers states that define their interests and may project their power in any or all regions; (ii) major powers states that define their interests and project their power, to a limited extent, beyond their own geographic region; (iii) regional powers states that define their interests and project their power across their own geographic region; and (iv) small states states that cannot project power, that cannot provide for their own security, except *vis-à-vis* each other, and that cannot, in coalition, contest or defend against states (i), (ii) or (iii).[8] A typical regional security complex may involve states of all varieties, that is, a large number of small states, one or two regional powers, several major powers and a global power.

The external security dilemmas faced by the various states within their respective regional contexts will differ substantially. For small states, security guarantees can only be provided by other, more powerful states. Their goal, therefore, will be to ameliorate their security dilemmas through establishment of multilateral arrangements that support principles of nonintervention and/or that promise assistance from one or more other states. Small states may wish to form collective defence pacts or bilateral agreements with major or global powers, usually to deter regional powers; however, the multilateral qualities of such arrangements are suspect in that there is often no meaningfully reciprocated guarantee. Thus, one would look to find small states strongly supporting collective security mechanisms at the regional level, for example, the OAU, and at the systemic level, the UN, for two reasons: first, to promulgate norms of sovereignty and noninterference (in effect to bolster their rights as members of the international system), and second, to acquire assurance that aggression against them will prompt a response by other more powerful states.

Small states, therefore, will have substantial interests in enhancing multilateralist arrangements within their region and the system. They will be drawn to support collective security mechanisms that are broadly based, that is, arrangements that extend multilateral benefits beyond select numbers (such as concerts). On the other hand, they face the dilemma that their individual memberships and the commitments they can make are essentially symbolic. As a result, they are likely to find themselves parties to institutions with shallower, rather than deeper, multilateral commitments. In light of their perceived vulnerability (especially in today's world) as regards more powerful states within their own region, small states will strive toward enhancement of norms of regionalism and regional community and toward mechanisms of preventive diplomacy and confidence building. Certainly, they will be supportive of movement toward regionwide security communities and may regard the establishment of subregional institutions as the kernels from which regionwide multilateralism may develop, for instance, as with the Association of South East Asian Nations (ASEAN).

It is more difficult to characterize the security dilemmas and multilateralist interests of the other regional members. The degree of harmony or consensus of values among the global and major powers in the system becomes the critical variable. If sufficient commonality of attitudes exists among key regional states *and* if they perceive no immediate security threats from each other, the formation of a concert, and/or collective security mechanisms is possible.[9] This is more likely to occur at a systemic rather than regional level. Consensus among all major powers is unlikely to extend to the point where they are in agreement concerning specific regional developments. Thus, for example, one can argue that a concert of major powers has emerged in the United Nations capable of mobilizing against the Iraqi invasion of Kuwait (a singular event which both involved substantial great power interests and violated basic international societal norms) and for humanitarian purposes (on a selective basis). There is little evidence of the emergence of regional concerts capable of conflict management — witness the failure of European powers to act regarding Yugoslavia, or the autonomous behaviour of China in the Asian regional security complex.[10]

In practice, it is more common that the security interests of the major powers are not in harmony. Security dilemmas prevail; states perceive the need to act upon perceptions of immediate and short-term threats. Within regional contexts, this has typically led to the formation of collective defence pacts whose effect is to pit one or more major powers and their regional allies against others. Such arrangements have engendered very effective multilateralism — exclusionary in terms of membership, but often involving substantial depth of commitment, occasionally to the point where a security community is fostered, as in the Western European case. However, as the experience of the Cold War demonstrated, collective defence mechanisms that both represent and are reinforced through the advocacy of incompatible visions of international order are regionally divisive. Movement toward regionally inclusive forms of multilateralism will succeed only to the extent that (a) cognitive transitions occur which break down former barriers and (b) new attitudinal foundations are engendered concerning mutual interests, common security, and expectations of diffuse reciprocity. The last half-decade has witnessed remarkable experiences of the former, but is also demonstrating that progress on the latter is somewhat more difficult.

Probably the most intriguing types of states within regional security complexes today are the so-called regional powers. These states possess complicated security interests, leading them to be somewhat ambivalent or even recalcitrant about regional multilateralism. In the first place, their primary concern will be to avoid the domination or restrictions that could be imposed on them by major powers in whatever mode — intervention, interference in their domestic affairs, constrained membership in collective defence arrangements, or management through major power concerts. Multilateral mechanisms that foster any such results are likely to be eschewed by regional powers. On the other hand, institutions that foster principles of regional identity, that is, to the exclusion of geographic outsiders, will be attractive to them. For instance, Nigeria's support for the OAU or Indonesia's support of ASEAN can be seen in this light. Furthermore, such institutions may provide potential opportunities for regional leadership (as in both of the instances cited above), by providing regional powers with institutional frameworks in which they can block or advance collective initiatives according to their own interests. Insofar, however, as the development of regional or subregional multilateralism is perceived to be likely to constrain the autonomy of regional powers, these states are likely to avoid involvement or tend toward minimalist commitments. (Witness the attitudes of both China and Japan toward incipient multilateralism concerning security developments in the Asia Pacific.)

It is important to note that the discussion above has focused upon states' reactions to their perceived *external* security dilemmas, that is, circumstances arising from the intersection of their interests with those of other states. However, many states also face *internal* security dilemmas, in that the regimes in power find themselves threatened by forces seeking to remove them individually from office, to secede from their jurisdiction, or to alter radically the principles of governance.[11] Such security dilemmas are characteristic of what have been termed "weak states,"[12] a description that can be applied to many in today's international system and to one or more of the parties in most of its ongoing conflicts as well.

What will be the perspective of such states toward systemic or regional multilateralism? The fundamental interest of those in power in these states is regime survival and maintenance of the status quo or restoration of the *status quo ante.* Thus, within their international context, their concern will be to reinforce the principles of noninterference in domestic affairs, preservation of territorial integrity, and entrenchment of sovereignty. International institutions will be attractive to them to the extent that they foster such norms and are capable and willing to mobilize on their behalf. In practice, this has led to support for two forms of multilateralist arrangements: (i) coalitions of states who undertake collective commitments to sustain their current leaders or common form of government; and (ii) inclusive institutions established on the traditional premises of state-centricity noted above and providing multilateral commitments to maintain and restore them.

There are a variety of historical precedents of the former sort, that is, type (i), including the Concert of Europe and ASEAN multilateral arrangements among states within a geographic subregion who feel the need for collective action to stave off commonly-perceived *internal* threats. As for the latter, type (ii) institutions, they emerged as a result of the anti-colonialism and independence waves after the Second World War. The newly created states flocked to the United Nations, a global institution committed to preserving their existence and providing them a voice in the international system, and they moved to create region- wide institutions such as the OAU, whose mission was to promote noninterference in African affairs by outsiders and to preserve the territorial integrity and sovereignty of member states.[13] However, in both regional and global contexts, the participation of weak states was necessarily largely confined to norm enhancement. Being generally also small states, they could provide little weight, even collectively, toward enforcement of multilateral commitments, and, with their precarious internal situations, they have been extremely reluctant to sanction or participate in any actions that might establish precedents for "intervention" in domestic affairs or alter the territorial status quo. Thus, organizations such as the OAU have essentially sustained themselves through their inaction, rather than through multilateral activism.

In sum, four conclusions may be drawn concerning multilateralism in regional security contexts. First, in regional environments in which the ongoing security interests of key players are perceived to be incompatible, the prevalent mode of multilateralism will be found in collective defence arrangements among subsets of state members. Second, in regional environments in which the security dilemma is dampened, that is, there are no immediate threats to the peace among major players, more inclusive forms of multilateralism oriented toward development of common attitudinal bases for security architectures may be found. However, this is by no means assured. Aspiring regional powers, for instance, even if they do not evidence ambitions that threaten other regional actors, may not be eager to find themselves within multilateral frameworks in which their autonomy is limited either directly or indirectly. Thus, the likelihood of the emergence of regional concerts involving these players is problematic. [14] Third, to the extent that clashes of ideology (political, economic, religious, or otherwise) are avoided within regional contexts, there is the opportunity for furthering common regional attitudes and norms of interstate behaviour. It is through the enhancement of regional "strategic cultures" promoting multilateral principles of peaceful change that progress toward commitments of collective security and security community forms will be achieved.[15] Fourth, for a variety of reasons, states, especially small regional players, will be attracted to membership in regionwide institutions that espouse collective security commitments to sustain their territorial integrity and guard their internal sovereignty. The positive impact of these institutions will be seen through their promotion of common identities, furtherance of norms and community-building; but, on the other hand, they are unlikely to be mobilized to engage in proactive activities in conflicts involving their members.

Regional Conflict and Multilateralism

Finally, what are the prospects for the extension of multilateralism in contemporary (post-Cold War) regional security environments in ways that will mitigate or manage regional conflicts? Formulating an answer requires consideration along two lines. These parallel the dual logics of multilateralism, the first concerning the prospects for collective action when regional conflicts occur, (i.e., matters of commitment and action to sustain the peace or punish its offenders); and the second regarding the transition of regional security complexes toward inclusive collective security arrangements and security communities (i.e., matters of identity-building). The dynamics of these two logics, and of developments to further them, are not the same. As explained in abstract terms in the sections above, and as will be illustrated below with reference to recent and ongoing events, the two dynamics may in fact be at odds with each other, making it difficult to draw singular conclusions concerning prospects for multilateralism.

Before proceeding, it is necessary to take note of the key characteristics of regional conflict phenomena in today's world. Empirical evidence supports popularly held views that the end of the Cold War has made a difference to the extent and nature of conflicts in the international system. The most striking features of the records of systematically-compiled data for the post-1989 years are (a) that virtually all conflicts qualify as regional conflicts — only the Persian Gulf War would have counted as a global conflict; (b) that well over 90 percent of conflicts are *intra*state conflicts, with the majority of these being contentions over governance, a minority being secessionist conflicts; and (c) that the regional distribution of conflicts is concentrated in Asia, Africa, and the Middle East, with European conflicts showing a sharp increase.[16] This rise in European conflicts, brought about through the disintegration of the Soviet Union's Eastern European empire, would be one distinguishing feature of the post-Cold War versus the Cold War era. Another would be the decline in regional conflicts arising through "outside" intervention (wars of interest), contrasted with the rise in intrastate violence spawned by ethnic, religious or social ten-

sions, ("wars of conscience"), which occur and spread without regard for traditionally defined state borders.[17]

Collective Action to Resolve Regional Conflicts

Regional conflict will be subject to management attempts by a variety of
actors, including global and regional institutions as well as individual states,
employing a variety of means and approaches. Our interest, however, is centred upon the application of multilateralist principles to address the management
of regional conflicts. To facilitate discussion, consider the two-by-two grid of
four cells emerging from the intersection of conflict type (intra and interstate)
and conflict management mechanism (regional and global).

Starting with the efforts by global institutions to address interstate regional
conflict, note that we are in effect talking about the United Nations and about
a relatively rare type of conflict for the post-Cold War environment, although
there exist a number of key tension points of this sort — India and Pakistan,
North and South Korea, and the territorial disputes in the South China Sea.
Mobilization of the collective capacities of UN members will occur only when
and if the concert of major powers in the Security Council (the Permanent Five
states) wills it, (when they perceive sufficient common interest in facilitating
conflict management). During the Cold War, when almost all interstate regional
conflicts proceeded under the direction of the global powers, collective action
by the UN was allowed to be initiated only when these same powers saw that
the situation threatened to escalate to the pan-regional or global level, for
example, in the Middle East wars. In the current environment, a similar logic
applies to the South Asian or Korean situations, that is, the P5 would be mobilized to act to prevent escalation to nuclear thresholds and to prevent
widespread spillover effects. In these contexts, only a systemic concert of
powers would possess the capacity to act, be it within the United Nations
context or outside it.[18] It is not easy, however, to assess the prospects for
multilateral action in regional interstate conflicts among minor powers. One
has the impression that, absent exceptional factors involving substantial human suffering, delivery on the multilateralist commitments of UN organization
members will continue to prove difficult.

Global institutional responses to intrastate conflicts have not been, and
are not likely to become, either frequently attempted or successful when tried.
The contemplation of such actions runs against what most members regard
as core multilateralist principles of the United Nations, namely noninterference
in domestic affairs and maintenance of territorial integrity and sovereignty.[19]
Only occasionally will it prove feasible, or in the interests of the major powers
in the UN, to mobilize regarding intrastate disputes — in effect for global con-

cert-led collective security activity (Kupchan and Kupchan's terminology) to be initiated. There are, however, many voices calling for more frequent, more preventive, and more forceful action by the United Nations. Often one of the central arguments is of default, that is, global institutions must act given the failure of regional institutions.

There are two lines of argument on this issue. First is how to evaluate the record of the United Nations in resolving regional conflicts that were ongoing as the Cold War wound down, (e.g., Angola, Afghanistan and Cambodia). In these cases, the UN has been given credit for achieving settlements and for attempting to engineer transitions to peaceful, civil societies. Indeed, UN efforts were substantial and serve to demonstrate the capacities for that organization when the major powers combine and/or withdraw their interest in a regional environment. However, what can be achieved through multilateral action by external players to resolve intrastate conflict may ultimately prove to be relatively limited — witness the ongoing troubles of Afghanistan, Angola, and Cambodia, but also in the former Yugoslavia. The second line of argument involves the rise in support for forceful humanitarian intervention to protect civilian populations from the continued ravages of intrastate conflict. With the vast increase in the numbers, the responsibilities and the costs of such peace-keeping missions (Somalia, Yugoslavia, Rwanda, etc.), this has become a major dilemma of multilateralism in the "new world order." While the arguments for mobilizations on behalf of peoples (as opposed to states) are important and, for many, compelling,[20] at the same time, the reluctance of UN member states to undertake such actions (because of their financial costs and potential casualties, however few in number) has grown substantially in the last two years. A cynical attitude must be forgiven the observer who contrasts the rhetoric of multilateralism in the immediate, post-Cold War glow, with the hard realities of seemingly intractable conflicts and the hesitant, half-measures of commitments on the part of the UN and its central members.

As for the prospects for collective action by regional conflict mechanisms: the UN Charter gives precedence to regional institutional responses to threats or outbreaks of conflict. Indeed, for a variety of reasons, regional initiatives could be regarded as more appropriate and more likely to be successful than those of global counterparts.[21] The overall record, however, belies these arguments; the general opinion among analysts is, in fact, just the opposite — that regional institutions have largely proven incapable of effective collective response in either interstate or intrastate regional conflicts. To quote the conclusions of MacFarlane and Weiss:

In reality these organizations are far less capable than the United Nations to deal with regional security.... The institutional capacities of regional organizations are extremely feeble, so much so that they have not been able to carry out mandates in peace and security. Finally, the so-called comparative superiority of organizations in the actual region in conflict — familiarity with issues, insulation from outside powers, need to deal with acute crises — are more than offset by such practical disadvantages as partisanship, local rivalries, and lack of resources.

Whether or not these conclusions should be qualified on the basis of action/inaction in interstate as opposed to intrastate conflicts deserves brief consideration. As noted earlier, most interstate regional conflicts during the previous four decades were substantially structured within Cold War parameters. The superpowers effectively managed both the course of the conflicts themselves and any conflict management strategies that were deemed necessary. Regional institutions were largely cut out of the picture: initiatives by inclusive regional institutions such as the OAS were blocked by their superpower members. Regional collective pacts (such as NATO) were generally themselves party to ongoing conflicts.

However, with the end of ideological confrontation and the decline of the Soviet Union, regional politics have taken on a quite different caste. In particular, aspiring regional powers are often now seen by their fellow regional members as the greatest causes of concern, especially if such states do not appear content with the territorial status quo, for example, China. In response, two types of strategies have been adopted. "Small" regional states, generally individually, have sought security guarantees from major power "outsiders" (e.g., agreements such as those between the US and Singapore and Malaysia), and/or have undertaken broader efforts, combining economic, diplomatic and security-related initiatives designed to draw these states toward acceptance of multilateral attitudes and norms of a regional community (e.g., ASEAN's strategy concerning Vietnam and China). Commitment to this latter approach involves a much longer-range and incremental vision which, in fact, can lead its advocates to want to avoid action on short-term problems with regional powers in order to keep them onside in the larger agenda.

Thus, regional multilateralist institutional responses to intrastate conflicts have proven problematic not only for the reasons stressed by MacFarlane and Weiss, but also because of the overall disposition of regional members to support norms of noninterference. In the instances when action has been taken under the auspices of institutions such as the OAU or OAS, it has generally been engineered by a dominating regional member. Absent such "leadership," regional institutions composed solely of small states have proved largely unable to mobilize action to prevent or manage intrastate conflicts, either through their own collective efforts (which would likely prove inadequate) or through capturing the attention of outsiders, be they major powers or global institutions. The record of ASEAN in the resolution of the Cambodian crisis is instructive in this regard. With a strong interest in achieving stability in Indochina, especially in muting the presence and influence of contending regional powers, ASEAN made extensive efforts of its own over the years to achieve a Cambodian settlement, but with little result. Nor could the Association internationalize attention to the Cambodian case through its collective diplomatic efforts at the United Nations.[22] It was only when the major powers acting on their own initiative, in light of the end of the Cold War, came together in the Paris Peace Agreement of 1991 that the Cambodian conflict was "effectively detached ... from its regional and global dimensions," and only then was the United Nations peacekeeping mission put into place. Thus, while ASEAN states might take "justifiable pride in [working toward] the localization of the Cambodian conflict,"[23] the route to international remedial action in this case demonstrates well the relative capacity of institutions of its sort — collectives of small states — to engineer management of regional conflicts, especially if they are ongoing and involve interests or action of major powers.[24]

Several factors appear important in determining whether or not regional institutions are capable of initiating collective action regarding intrastate conflict. For a select few institutions, this purpose was indeed central to their formation: member states sought to cooperate to fend off threats from internal forces, tangible or intangible, that were perceived to threaten the existence of their regimes. The six founding members of ASEAN, for instance, expressed a common interest in thwarting "communist" insurgency; the members of the Gulf Cooperation Council similarly were concerned to preserve the traditional character of their regimes.[25] The evidence on how effective regional institutions have been in regime preservation is hard to evaluate. While there are indications of bilateral cooperation in the sharing of information, transferring of suspect persons, clamping down on partisan groups, etc., there is little on the record to suggest that regional institutions are willing to mobilize in a formal manner around regime restoration.[26]

It is, however, more likely that intrastate regional conflicts will prove to be divisive within regional institutional contexts and that multilateralist responses toward them, on behalf of any of the parties involved, will be avoided. Witness, for example, the difficulties in mitigating the conflict in the former Yugoslavia, or Ethiopia, Rwanda, Angola, Cambodia, etc. The exception to this rule may be those instances when regional states are in accord that their primary interest is in halting the conflict within a neighbouring state. Such sentiments could arise through desires to stop unwanted spillover effects of fighting, of population movements, of ethno-nationalist appeals to their minority populations and/or desires to put a halt to the outside intervention by a major power. Movement by the Contadora group toward resolution of the Nicaraguan civil war could be cited as an example, also the support of these Central American states for resolution of the Salvadoran troubles. The resources available to small regional states in such situations derive in large part from their familiarity with the participants and their ability to devise specific, locally acceptable compromises (as MacFarlane and Weiss acknowledge), but obviously do not extend to their capacity to impose or even to police settlement within another state.

What has occurred to date in the post-Cold War era, therefore, presents a dilemma for someone looking for multilateralism in approaches to regional conflict management. The rise in the frequency and intensity of intrastate regional conflicts has been accompanied by an increase during the last five years in multilateral efforts to halt and mediate such conflicts, especially through the United Nations. However, these initiatives have been largely at the global level, have been confined to a rather arbitrarily determined subset of cases, and have experienced substantial difficulties in engineering effective collective participation. While the call has gone out for a larger role to be played by regional institutions,[27] there are severe practical as well as attitudinal limitations to the multilateralist responses by regionally-based institutions to address the challenges of regional conflicts.

The Advance of Multilateralism within Regional Contexts

Instead, it is the avenue of the second logic of multilateralism which must be pursued in considering prospects for mitigation of regional conflict and the internal and external security dilemmas upon which they are fostered. This is both because of, and despite, the incrementalism and minimalism that characterize processes of cognitive transition and of community-building around commonly perceived values and norms. Within the current international order several meaningful developments in this regard must be noted.

First, the end of the Cold War was affected fundamentally through a remarkable attitudinal shift, largely on the part of key leaders of the Soviet Union, which undercut the rationale of the established multilateralism of the Cold War's collective defence arrangements and, in turn, their accompanying overlay and penetration of regional security relationships. However, this transformation *per se* did not establish new attitudinal bases for enhanced multilateralist cooperation, particularly at the regional level. In many instances, long-standing social cleavages were brought to the surface, fuelling interstate and intrastate conflicts, which in turn cannot be dealt with effectively by regional or global institutions.

Second, there are, of course, other forms of multilateralism present in the international environment. These range from the relatively "shallow" multilateralism of large collections of states seeking to affirm basic principles of self-recognition and acceptance, to pockets of "deep" multilateralism grounded firmly in the identification by their members with commonly accepted values concerning appropriate forms of economic and security orders and modes of governance. What has been set in motion by the attitudinal shift of the end of the Cold War are processes whereby states within the cores of these (nascent) security communities seek to expand and deepen their multilateral scope. Again in the terms used earlier, committed states are seeking to effectuate cognitive transitions within relevant others in order to draw them toward identification in security communities. Much contemporary discussion, therefore, centres upon the spread of processes of democratization and economic liberalization and their presumed positive impact upon cooperative security relations within and among states.[28] There are indeed signs at both the regional and global levels of the positive, long-term impact of these multilateralist developments.

Third, in the short term and with specific attention to regional conflict, no general positive conclusions regarding multilateralism concerning security relations appear warranted. Ongoing intrastate regional conflicts are not proving susceptible to effective management by either regional or global collective security institutions. Indeed, for reasons discussed above, those states that seek the expansion of their nascent regional security communities are and will remain hesitant to "interfere" in the internal affairs of other members or states which they wish to drawn into their community. The long-term prognosis concerning regional security multilateralism will depend on a delicate balance being achieved between forces promoting common identity among regional players and those forces that capitalize upon identities of distinction, either between states or between groups that intersect currently recognized state boundaries.

Notes

This chapter follows closely to an earlier paper, "Matter of Multilateralism: The Relevance of the Concept to Regional Conflict Management," presented to the 1994 annual meetings of the American Political Science Association and prepared in conjunction with the research project, "Reconceptualizing Regional Relations," directed by David Lake and Patrick Morgan. However, the conclusions drawn in the present chapter are somewhat different than in the noted manuscript. Research for this essay was supported by the Institute of International Relations at the University of British Columbia through its Military and Strategic Studies Program. The author acknowledges the able research assistance of Brian Bow. The opinions expressed in this manuscript are the author's alone, as is responsibility for any errors or omissions.

1.   Robert Keohane as quoted in John Ruggie, "The Anatomy of an Institution," in *Multilateralism Matters: The Theory and Praxis of an Institutional Form*, ed. John Ruggie (New York: Columbia University Press, 1993), p. 7.

2. Ruggie, "The Anatomy of an Institution," p. 11. As an "institutional" form, multilateral in-
    volves "persistent and connected sets of rules, formal and informal, that prescribe behavioural
    roles, constrain activity, and shape expectations." p. 10.

3. See Ruggie, "The Anatomy of an Institution," p. 11. Some scholars go a step further to
    ascribe generative, reproductive, or expansionist qualities to multilateralism. Kahler, for in-
    stance, speaks of "an impulse to universality" in his "Multilateralism Within Small and Large
    Numbers," in *Multilateralism Matters*, pp. 7, 295

4. Lisa Martin, "The Rational State Choice of Multilateralism," in *Multilateralism Matters,* p. 95.

5. Ruggie, "The Anatomy of an Institution," p. 7.

6. Morgan, "The Study of Regional Conflicts: Preliminary Considerations and a Starting Point,"
    unpublished ms., 1994, and in correspondence.

7. Barry Buzan, *People, States, and Fear*, 2d ed. (London: Harvester Wheatsheaf, 1991), p. 169.

8. Under these terms, in the current post-Cold War system, the United States would be a
    global power; Russia, France, the UK, and China are major powers; and India, Brazil, Ni-
    geria, and Indonesia could be regional powers. One could object that not all of the remainder
    are appropriately regarded as small states. However, for the moment, designation of states
    as "middle powers," e.g., Canada, Australia, Italy, introduces unnecessary complications.

9. There has been, of course, substantial debate concerning the ability of a hegemonic power
    to exercise individual leadership and to create and support norms that influence the entire
    system. Certainly, it is the case that the support of any global power would be a necessary
    condition for any concert mechanism. However, it would not by itself be sufficient, (the
    commitment of other, major powers to multilateralism is essential).

10. Management of the North Korean situation might, however, be offered as a counter exam-
    ple. For further development of arguments concerning the prospects for regional or
    systemwide concerts in today's world, see Richard Rosecrance, "A New Concert of Pow-
    ers," *Foreign Affairs*, 71:1 (1992): 64-92 and Richard Rosecrance and Peter Schott, "Concerts
    and Regional Intervention," unpublished ms., 1994.

11. See Brian Job, "The Insecurity Dilemma: National, Regime, and State Securities in the Third
    World," in *The Insecurity Dilemma: National Security of Third World States*, ed. Brian Job
    (Boulder: Lynne Reinner Publishers, 1992), ch. 1.

12. See Buzan, *People, States and Fear*, ch. 2.

13. See Robert Jackson, *Quasi-States, Sovereignty, International Relations and the Third World*
    (Cambridge: Cambridge University Press, 1990).

14. This assessment would be disputed by other analysts of regional security affairs. Prominent
    among them would be Susan Shirk, as seen in her *Asia-Pacific Regional Security: Balance
    of Power or Concert of Powers* (San Diego: Institute on Global Conflict and Cooperation,
    University of California, 1994).

15. See, for example, Desmond Ball, "Strategic Culture in the Asia-Pacific Region," *Security
    Studies,* 3:1 (1993): 44-74.

16. These conclusions are based on the data and interpretation thereof found in Peter Wallensteen and Karin Axell, "Armed Conflict at the End of the Cold War," *Journal of Peace Research,* 30:3 (1993): W331-46. See also annual volumes of the SIPRI yearbook for inventories of ongoing conflicts.

17. "Wars of interest" and "wars of conscience" are terms utilized by *The Economist,* 5 December 1992, pp. 3-5.

18. See, for instance, Paul A. Papayoanou, "Great Powers and Regional Security: Possibilities and Prospects After the Cold War," unpublished ms., 1994.

19. The Secretary-General's *Agenda for Peace* document, while advocating an enhanced role for his organization in promoting peace and peaceful settlement, remains adamant on such points. See also, Lori Fisler Damrosch (ed.), *Enforcing Restraint: Collective Intervention in Internal Conflicts* (New York: Council on Foreign Relations Press, 1994).

20. See, for instance, Robert Jackson, "Armed Humanitarianism," *International Journal,* 43:4 (1993): 579-606.

21. A good review of the arguments is provided by S. Neil MacFarlane and Thomas G. Weiss in their "Regional Organizations and Regional Security," *Security Studies,* 2:1 (1992):6-37.

22. See Pierre Lizee and Sorpong Peou, *Cooperative Security and the Emerging Security Agenda in Southeast Asia: The Challenges and Opportunities of Peace in Cambodia,* YCISS Occasional Paper no. 21 (Toronto: Centre for International and Strategic Studies, York University, 1993).

23. Amitav Acharya, *A New Regional Order in South-East Asia: ASEAN in the Post-Cold War Era,* Adelphi Papers, no. 279 (London: International Institute of Security Studies, Brassey's Inc, 1993), p. 14.

24. Thus, while the Central American states remained very concerned and made various attempts to resolve both the Nicaraguan and the Salvadoran conflicts, movement toward a solution was possible only (a) when the interests of the United States were revised, in light of the end of the Cold War and a change in administrations, and (b) through the actions of the United Nations, that is, a global institution. See S. Neil MacFarlane and Thomas G. Weiss, "The United Nations, Regional Organizations, and Human Security: Building Theory in Central America," *Third World Quarterly,* 15:2 (1994): 277-95.

25. See Amitav Acharya, "Regionalism and Regime Security in Structural and Historical Perspective," in *The Insecurity Dilemma: National Security of Third World States,* ch. 7.

26. The case of Grenada might be brought up as a counter example. Without the "leadership" of the United States, it is unlikely that any action would have been taken by the Caribbean Community (CARICOM) states. See Terry Thorndike, "Grenada," in *Intervention in the 1980's: U.S. Foreign Policy in the Third World,* ed. Peter J. Schraeder (Boulder: Lynne Reinner Publishers, 1989), ch. 17.

27. See especially Boutros Boutros-Ghali in his *Agenda for Peace* (New York: The United Nations, 1992), pp. 36-37.

28. See Etel Solingen, "Democracy, Economic Reform, and the Future of Regional Security," unpublished ms., 1994.

PART II
Latin America

David R. Mares

Looking for Godot?
Can Multilateralism Work in
Latin America this Time?

Introduction

Military force has consistently been utilized in the foreign policies of Latin American countries. The twentieth century has seen more than two hundred instances in which Latin American states either threatened or used military force or were the subject of such threats or force by non-Latin American countries. Democracies have shot at each other (Ecuador and Peru suffered hundreds of casualties in the two border mini-wars of 1981 and 1995), a country with no army was invaded twice by its neighbour (Costa Rica by Nicaragua under Somoza in the 1950s), and six to seven Latin American wars occurred.[1] In the 1970s Peru and Chile engaged in an arms race; in 1978 war between Chile and Argentina was averted at literally the last minute; and democratic Venezuela ordered a full mobilization of its armed forces against democratic Colombia in 1987 and 1993. Clearly, these states do not form a Deutschian security community, in which war among members is not considered. The search for effective and peaceful conflict resolution in Latin America has been a long one. Various versions of multilateralism have historically been attempted. Multilateralism failed in the past as a conflict management system in Latin America for two reasons. First, its proponents ignored the implications of attempting to implement multilateral conflict resolution on a strictly regional basis when one country cannot be constrained by any conceivable combination of the rest. Multilateralism could not function in the face of US unilateralism. In addition, most Latin American countries themselves demonstrated repeatedly that they were not ready to cede any degree of sovereignty over issues that were important enough to develop into crises. Unfortunately, now that many Latin American countries appear willing to reconsider some of these issues, contemporary analysts persist in failing to appreciate the implications of regional power disparities. A new danger has also arisen in the security dialogue:

the belief by market-oriented democrats that military issues are obstacles to effective conflict management. In the face of a failure of the explicit attempts at multilateralizing security management in the region a *de facto* conflict management system developed. The United States was largely unconstrained to define and implement its security agenda in the hemisphere. Within Latin America a Westphalian-type balance of power system served the needs of the Latin American security complex fairly well until the late 1970s. The collapse of that system in the 1980s brings us once again to the discussion of multilateralizing security relations.

This chapter has three sections. Section one presents the Latin American security complex, highlighting the security *problématique* from a Latin American perspective. I argue that security issues in the region incorporate elements from the international, regional, and domestic arenas. The second section analyzes the *de facto* balance of power system which developed in the region. Its successes and failures are highlighted, culminating in its apparent collapse as an effective conflict management system in the 1980s. In the third section I examine three attempts to multilateralize security relations. The reasons for past failures are analyzed and the prospects for future success are evaluated. The fourth and final section proposes that if a multilateral conflict management system is going to be effective, it must incorporate global actors and seriously address traditional balance-of-power concerns.

Latin America's Security Problématique

The Latin American security complex[2] incorporates externalities deriving from three different arenas: international, regional, and domestic. At the international level, the United States is a great power which, irrespective of Latin American wishes, has identified Latin America as belonging to its unique sphere of influence. US power and the region's geographic separation from Europe and Asia combined virtually to eliminate the possibility of Latin American nations balancing the US presence with that of other great powers. The security implication for Latin America has been that US interests and perceptions produce fundamental security externalities for each and every Latin American nation.

Regional security issues are largely remnants of colonial days, namely disputed territorial borders. Many border disputes have been diplomatically or militarily settled. Even today, however, only Mexico, Paraguay, and Uruguay have territorial limits officially accepted by all of their neighbours. The intra-South American militarized disputes of the last two decades all revolved around border issues, although the Venezuela-Colombia tensions also reflect guerrilla activity, the drug trade, and illegal immigration. In Central America, the Guate-mala-Belize and El Salvador-Honduras negotiations are stalled in the legislatures, while Nicaragua and Colombia dispute some islands.[3]

The third security externality develops out of the highly stratified social structure in Latin America and the developing nature of its economies. Be-cause states in the region identify themselves as a community, when the social structure in one country is threatened by political upheaval, elites in the rest of Latin America begin to worry. Even after the Cold War, the domestic social and economic stratification, plus a growing assertiveness of indigenous communi-ties, makes Latin American elites worry about popular reaction to the costs of economic restructuring. These Latin American perceptions of threats to re-gional stability are often reenforced by the US in two ways. The United States may attempt to organize regional opposition, and thus engages in rhetorical excesses, if not the actual fabrication of "evidence" of revolutionary interna-tionalism. In addition, the very willingness of the US to act militarily in these situations raises the spectre of internationalizing domestic conflict (as many feel was done in Central America during the 1980s).

Transborder spillovers of revolutionary upheaval are not merely percep-tual overreactions by Latin America and US elites. Historically, many of those seeking to change the social structure within their country have appealed for support from their Latin brothers and sisters facing the same problems and offered to assist them in return. Sandino's fight against the US intervention in Nicaragua during the 1920s, Cuba's Revolution, Chile's Popular Unity admin-istration, and the Nicaraguan Sandinistas in the 1970-80s all had significant extra-national participation.[4] In addition, neofascist agents from Brazil's Estado Novo travelled South America in the 1930s to build a regional front against "communists," Peron's Argentine labour movement and Peru's progressive APRA party tried to reproduce themselves elsewhere in the continent, Carib-bean democrats set up the notorious Caribbean League to overthrow dictators, and Che Guevara tried to reproduce the Cuban Revolution in the heart of South America.[5]

What then is Latin America's security *problématique*? Given the forced isolation of the region from great power politics, its security *problématique* arises from the region's own internal characteristics. In a region characterized by disputed borders, unequal levels of economic development, and broad dis-parities in the distribution of power, the main security issues for Latin American states revolve around sudden attempts at military resolutions of long-standing border issues and diplomatic stalemates, as well as the spread of rebellion.

Included in this regional security agenda is the manner and timing of US intervention in the hemisphere. US unilateralism and its inconsistent application (meaning that one cannot count on US aid if attacked[6]) produce security benefits and costs for Latin American states which are largely outside their capacity to control. The unpredictability of US behaviour thus becomes a security risk.

Managing Regional Conflict in Latin America:
The Collapse of the Old System of Traditional Conflict Management

The Westphalian system, created in Europe and imposed on the rest of the world through European colonialism, instituted a conflict management scheme with "power," "state," and "sovereignty" as core concepts. There was a sense of "community" because political units were identified as members or not,[7] there were norms concerning behaviour, in particular that of nonintervention in the internal affairs of member states,[8] and occasional great power concerts. Notwithstanding these constraints on international behaviour, the conflict dynamics of the Westphalian system are best understood in balance-of-power terms. It is this conflict management system which gives us the best insight into the Latin American security complex.

Addressing the US Threat. Under a balance-of-power system in which there is no possibility of effectively balancing against one power (i.e., a condition of regional hegemony), weaker states usually have a difficult time in restraining the more powerful state. Multilateral institutions and the development of community norms of nonintervention become the hope of the weak, but in this type of conflict management system they are largely ineffective (see below). The dynamics of a power-restraining conflict management system explains why this particular threat in Latin America's security *problématique* went unanswered.

Dealing with the Intra-Latin American Threat. The danger of intra-Latin American war was minimized by intra-Latin American power balancing and deterrence politics. Balancing and deterring were the result of both military and diplomatic policies.

Arms races by themselves are not evidence of balancing,[9] but evidence abounds that expectations of conflict produced arms build-ups in Latin America. Argentina increased its military budget and arms purchases in the late 1970s when it expected war with Chile. The credibility of a Chilean military response and the ambiguity of potential responses of the British is probably fundamental in understanding why the Argentine military did not engage in war in 1978, but did four years later.

One cannot simply attribute increased arms expenditures to the assumption of power by the military. Not all military governments increase arms expenditures and not all countries that upgrade their military capabilities are run by the military. The left-leaning Peruvian military took power in 1968, but only began a major arms push (including purchases of the only Mirage-2000s in Latin America) in 1973 after rightist coups in neighbouring Bolivia and Chile.[10] Democratic regimes have also not been willing to be caught in a disadvantageous military position, even with respect to each other. Venezuela and Colombia, both democracies since 1958, responded to a disputed border incident in the Gulf of Venezuela by dramatically increasing their military expenditures and reinforcing borders.[11]

Military deterrence can be pursued not only by building up one's own forces, but also by aggregating one's military capacity through alliances. The Rio Treaty, a formal military alliance, is an anomaly in Latin American history. Most alliances have been informal ententes, with some of the most influential in strategic thinking being entirely assumed. Chile has historically been concerned about deterring a possible Peruvian-Bolivian-Argentine axis.[12] A Brazilian-Chilean alliance long haunted Argentine security analysts. Peru assumed that if it became involved in a war with either Ecuador or Chile, the other would take advantage of the situation.[13] In one of the most interesting examples of informal military aid, during the Falklands War, democratic Peru (with a centre-left leaning military) resupplied right wing authoritarian Argentina with 14 Mirages and Exocet missiles.[14]

In an alliance system shifts in coalitions are potentially destabilizing. Argentine behaviour toward the Falklands/Malvinas was affected by the government's perception that it was now in an important alliance with the United States in Central America.[15] Some Chilean security analysts worry that the contemporary Argentine-Brazilian economic integration schemes could have a negative impact on Chilean security,[16] while some Venezuelans worry that developing their portion of the Amazon could make it an attractive asset to seize.[17] Ironically, a better relationship with Chile may have convinced the Peruvians in 1995 that they could now definitively settle the border question with Ecuador.

Balance-of-power-oriented diplomacy in Latin America's security complex appreciated the importance of military factors but also sought to keep the level of armaments low. At the turn of the century the British helped broker a naval arms agreement between Argentina and Chile.[18] More recently, the Treaty of Tlatelolco seeks to keep nuclear arms out of the region.[19] Negotiated force levels in Central America helped diffuse the level of tension there. A ban on bombers was discussed in the 1970s, but Peru's opposition apparently killed it, although Ecuador disposed of its small bomber force. Diplomacy has also been used to develop confidence-building measures among militaries by increasing contact among them. The Andean Group presidents renounced weapons of mass destruction in December 1991 (Declaration of Cartagena). Most ambitiously, some diplomats have advocated disarmament itself.[20] After achieving parity with Chile for the first time in one hundred years, Peru called for regional arms control in 1974 and disarmament in 1985, but nothing concrete was achieved.[21]

Confronting the Domestic Threat. The Latin American security management system addressed the threats of revolutionary contagion in a peculiar fashion. A *de facto* division of labour appeared adequate for a time. Confronted by a revolutionary movement in one country, Latin American diplomats would argue that nonintervention was in everyone's interests. If the revolutionaries failed to moderate their rhetoric, if not behaviour, the United States would isolate and if necessary, covertly overthrow the alleged "communists." But even this constraint on Latin American behaviour was violated in the breach: Latin American countries themselves covertly sought to use money, intelligence, training, and supplies to reproduce preferred political regimes.[22]

Collapse

The regional security management system began to break down in the mid-1960s as the United States returned to the more overt intervention of pre-Good Neighbour days (1890s-1933). The magnitude of the 1965 Dominican invasion (22,500 Marines) and the blatant subservience of the OAS in sanctioning the invasion after the fact,[23] made it impossible for Latin Americans to gloss over US unilateralism. In the 1970s US liberals extended the purview of foreign policy to cover the domestic policies of Latin American countries (human rights and democracy), much to the chagrin of traditional US anti-Communist allies in the region.

This conflict management system effectively collapsed in the 1980s. For the first time since the 1930s, interstate war threatened to engulf Latin America. The Argentines prepared to take on the Chileans and fought the British; Peruvians clashed with Ecuadoreans twice; Central Americans became intimately involved in each others' civil wars; and even the long-standing democracies of Colombia and Venezuela mobilized their troops. The United States invaded Grenada and Panama, threatened Cuba, and stoked the Central American conflicts with military manoeuvres, material, and rhetoric.

Three factors seem to account for the collapse of the conflict management system. Weapons became more destructive, diplomacy became more ideological, and the foreign debt crisis made disputed resources seem more important and produced domestic political pressures which could possibly be mitigated via diversionary external conflicts.

US unilateral arms control via military assistance programmes that refused to provide post-Second World War weapons had helped dampen the severity of the arms competition up through the late 1960s.[24] In the 1970s, as Latin Americans sought to replace their antiquated equipment, the international arms market was tapped to increase dramatically the military capabilities in the region. Soviet T-54 tanks and Sukhoi fighter bombers, French Mirages, Super Etendards, and Exocet missiles of various configurations, Israeli Dagger and Kfir fighters, British Hunter fighters and Canberra bombers, and finally US F-16s and A-4s made their way into Latin American arsenals. In addition, Argentina, Brazil, and Chile began to develop an arms industry that could retrofit existing weapons systems; develop missiles, light aircraft, light armoured vehicles; and even embark on nuclear submarine and bomb programmes.

Mexican and US diplomacy attempted unsuccessfully to modify the arms build-up. The Tlatelolco Treaty against nuclear proliferation was accepted by all Latin American countries except the four most likely to proliferate: Argentina, Brazil, Chile, and Cuba. The impact of US human rights sanctions on the regional arms build-up, was limited by alternative sources of supply. There were also real security needs fuelling the purchases. Chile was vulnerable at the time of the Peruvian (1977) and Argentine (1978) war scares. Cuban, Soviet, and US weapons flows to Central America also produced perceptions of imbalances. Nicaragua's neighbours worried about the massive increase in its army's personnel and equipment, while the Sandinistas focused on Honduras' air superiority and the flow of resources from the United States.

The result of the disjointed efforts at arms control, arms build-ups and reductions, and arms embargoes was to create a situation in which strategic surprise might resolve long-standing disputes. Neither democrats nor authoritarians, economic liberalizers nor statists, pro-Communists nor anti-Communists were immune to the new strategic environment. The Argentine military sought to surprise both the Chileans and the British, Ecuadorean democrats believed they could present Peru with *a fait accompli* in the Amazon, Sandinistas feared a replay of the Dominican intervention, and Venezuelan democrats worried that Colombian actions were a prelude to a definitive settlement of their border dispute.

The diplomatic structure of the hemispheric security system appeared irrelevant to many of the conflicts of the 1980s. This structure teetered in the wake of the US invasion of the Dominican Republic in 1965 and the opening of Latin American ties to Cuba in the 1970s, and broke down dramatically with the Falklands/Malvinas War and the end of the Cold War. Not only was the OAS unable to resolve peacefully the war in the South Atlantic, the United States actively supported an extra-hemispheric power in a military confrontation with an American nation.[25] Finally, the legitimacy of a system set up primarily for hemispheric defence was seriously undermined by the sudden absence of an extra-continental threat.

The Reagan administration fuelled the ideological polarization of Central America, extended it into the Anglo-Caribbean (Grenada) and sought to re-isolate Cuba from Latin America. The impact on Central America interstate behaviour was predictable: interstate tensions increased dramatically. But the impact of the Reaganite "holy war" mentality was not limited to fighting communists in the US "backyard." The Argentine military government, actively aiding the US in Central America, came to believe that the United States would remain neutral if Argentina unilaterally sought to resolve the Malvinas question.[26]

The economic collapse of many Latin American economies in the early 1980s may have also contributed to increased interstate conflict in South America. Oil is exploited on the Colombian-Venezuelan and Ecuadorean-Peruvian borders and explorations were underway in the South Atlantic. But adverse economic factors alone do not explain the heightened level of regional conflict. Both Ecuador and Peru experienced strong economic growth before their 1995 border skirmish.

Ironically, democratization may also be partially responsible for increased tension. Democratic politicians in Colombia, Venezuela, Ecuador, and Peru used external tensions to garner domestic support.[27] Diversionary threats, however, are not limited to democratic polities. The Argentine military may have engaged in a diversionary war.[28]

In short, Latin American leaders do not feel secure with a unilaterally and significantly diminished military presence, even in the absence of immediate security threats. Contemporary Argentina, democratic for ten years and with clear civilian control of a dramatically downsized and politically weakened military, has significantly increased its radar capabilities in the most recent fighter aircraft purchases, even threatening to buy the radar from Israel if the United States continued to respect British desires for a permanently weakened Argentine air force.[29] Not only the leaders feel the need for a deterrent military force. In a 1992 public opinion survey 17 percent of Argentines and 36.5 percent of Chileans believed that military threats from neighbouring countries were either likely or highly likely.[30]

Looking for Godot? Multilateralism Without Weapons

Historically, there have been many attempts to create multilateral structures for conflict management in Latin America. Given the acknowledged failure of the traditional system, discussion of new multilateral management schemes for regional security is widespread within diplomatic, military, and academic circles.[31] The contemporary redemocratization of Latin America and the dramatic liberalization of its national economies suggest to many that, in the wake of the end of the Cold War, the moment is propitious for an entirely new security relationship in the region. This section examines the different paths to regional security proposed, from the most to the least ambitious.

Pluralistic Security Community. The search for a pluralistic security community (one in which community norms against the use of force are subrationally effective), has a long and unsuccessful history in Latin America. After achieving independence, the new states sought to create a peaceful society of nations in the New World. Between 1826 and 1889 at least 50 conventions among Latin American states pledged to resolve disputes amicably.[32] Yet this was the period of the bloodiest Latin American wars.

Pluralistic security communities place great faith in international law as a mechanism for conflict resolution. This diplomatic approach is held in particularly high regard in Latin American international relations. Latins joined with the US in seeing the Americas as a special place, far from the power politics of Europe. This uniqueness was expected to produce a special style of international politics, governed by "American Law," which would protect the sovereignty of all states. Even when it became clear that this perspective did not prevent the United States or even Latin American states from violating the sovereignty of American states, the idealism of an "American system" remained. In a rebuke to European practice, Latin American diplomats and jurists formulated the first attempts to legally limit the ability of nations to use force to protect the interests of their national citizens in foreign countries (Calvo and Drago Doctrines).[33]

At times Latin American countries resolved disputes without recourse to military threats. Binding arbitration was popular among many countries at the turn of the century, although it met with the disapproval of Brazil and Chile,[34] both of whom were busily establishing effective control over border areas in dispute. From 1885-1925, settlement of interstate conflicts by arbitration in Latin America prospered.[35] Still, arbitration seemed to fall out of fashion, and militarized negotiations gave the lie to the idea of a Latin American pluralist security community.

Unfortunately, neither economic liberalization nor democratization seems to have diminished the nationalist zero-sum perspective which undermines the prospects for a pluralist Latin American security complex. El Salvador and Honduras and Chile and Argentina recently arbitrated their border disputes. Nevertheless, the Central American countries continue to dispute the 1992 World Court ruling.[36] The Chilean government, in the midst of creating a free trade zone with Argentina but also confronting domestic protest of the 1994 decision favouring Argentina, accused the commission of "technical errors" and petitioned for reconsideration.[37] The 1992 public opinion polls in Argentina and Chile were most disheartening (see above). Only in the US-Mexican relationship, and only since the 1930s, can we find evidence of an effective pluralistic security community.[38]

Collective Security. Collective security schemes overlap pluralistic security efforts in Latin America. Collective security arises because, although the use of force is acceptable, it is undertaken only with the collective sanction of the community. The normative and material bases of the community which gives the sanction are similar, though not as well developed as those in a pluralistic security community.

Two attempts at creating an inter-American collective security management system stand out: the Pan American Union (PAU) and the Inter-American Treaty of Reciprocal Assistance (Rio Treaty). The first failed to materialize on paper, while the second was moribund from the time it was negotiated. The historical reality is that neither the United States nor some of the major Latin American states have accepted subordinating their freedom of action to the inter-American community.

The years of the Pan American Union (1889-1945) included the heyday of overt US intervention in Latin America, 1890-1933.[39] The United States attempted to keep political matters, including security issues, off the PAU agenda until the 1930s. But some Latin American states consistently pushed two security topics into the discussions. Argentina proposed the Drago Doctrine on debt collection, while others pushed for the obligatory peaceful resolution of conflict among American states. The US was opposed to both measures, and important Latin American nations also refused to constrain their freedom of action. Brazil, a creditor itself, opposed the Drago doctrine.[40]

US hemispheric policy appeared to change with the adoption of the Good Neighbour Policy and the return home of the last US troops in Latin America

and the Caribbean (from Nicaragua and Haiti in 1933). Hemispheric cooperation became the rhetorical order of the day after 1936 as the United States
sought to create a common neutrality position *vis-à-vis* the prospect of another European war. The United States worried that Latin America's European
ties would draw the hemisphere into a coming war.[41] Nevertheless, the US
was rebuffed in its plan for a strict neutrality stance that would isolate the
Americas from Europe and had to settle for a vague agreement to consult in
the event of a threat, "if they so desire."[42] In 1938, after the Munich crisis, the
United States sought an outright mutual defence pact, but Latin American
opposition limited cooperation to consultation.

The outbreak of war in Europe stimulated closer inter-American cooperation. A hemispheric neutrality zone was implemented in September 1939. In
response to the fall of the Low Countries and France to Germany in 1940, the
United States and Latin America declared that an attack against one American state by a non-American state was an act of aggression against all. Mexico
participated in the Pacific war, while Brazil sent troops to Italy. Even in the face
of the global threat by fascism, there were important limits to cooperation. The
US effort to isolate the Americas from Europe before 1941 via a hemispheric
economic cartel failed. In addition, the United States wanted Latin America to
consult before taking any action that could provoke Axis retaliation, yet it did
not consult with Latin America regarding the aid it provided to Britain before
Pearl Harbor. There was also no consultation with Latin America concerning
the United States decision to join the European war. The US also faced difficulties in undertaking bilateral military negotiations, particularly with Argentina,
which only abandoned its neutrality stance in 1944, despite years of United
States' sanctions.[43]

The period 1945-47 marks a watershed in the development of inter-
American relations. The PAU was reorganized into the Organization of American
States (OAS), with explicit recognition of its role in hemispheric political and
security matters. The Inter-American Treaty of Reciprocal Assistance (Rio Treaty,
1947) specifically allowed the use of force if necessary to ensure peace and
territorial integrity.

The OAS and the Rio Treaty give the appearance of a far-sighted collective security community at the regional level. In addition to advocating peaceful
resolution of conflict and military cooperation against aggression, the OAS
Charter called for the defence of democracy and human rights.[44] Under Article
51 of the United Nations Charter regional disputes were to be referred to the
OAS before the UN Security Council would intervene.[45]

The OAS conflict management system, however, had few successes. Some Caribbean and Central American disputes were at least temporarily settled under OAS auspices, but war was not prevented between Honduras and El Salvador in 1969. The OAS did block the Carter administration's attempt to use an inter-American force to save the pro-US regime in Nicaragua in 1978, but it could not stop the Bush administration from invading Panama a decade later. Mediation in South American disputes failed and in 1960 Ecuador even denounced the Protocol of 1942 which had ended the war with Peru.[46]

Most importantly, once the United States became involved in a dispute (as would occur when the US sought to overthrow leftist regimes), the system became marginalized. The US veto in the UN Security Council and denial of World Court jurisdiction effectively meant that there was no appeal of a US decision to act unilaterally.[47]

The United States found numerous opportunities to act unilaterally against both perceived communists (e.g., Guatemala in 1954 and Cuba in 1961) and noncommunists (e.g., embargoes against military regimes in the late 1970s and the invasion of Panama in 1989). In recognition of the reality rather than the rhetoric of the inter-American security arrangement, Canada explicitly refused to join the military components of the inter-American system when it recently became a member of the OAS. Chided by an American diplomat for not wanting to undertake full responsibilities, a Canadian diplomat noted that Canada would join when the United States ceased to act unilaterally in security matters.[48]

The problem with collective security via either a military alliance or adherence to the norm of nonintervention was that it served few interests. Wary of a return to the days of US intervention via its policies of diplomatic recognition, Latin American governments were willing to condemn communism as a threat but unwilling to sanction intervention to overthrow an allegedly communist regime. Castro's government in Cuba was expelled from the inter-American system, but its overthrow by external force was not sanctioned, even as Castro tried to export the Cuban Revolution.[49]

Unable to restrain the giant, Latin Americans refused to bind themselves to a common response even in their struggle against revolutionary movements that threatened to overthrow their stratified social structures. In the 1970s Panama, Costa Rica, Mexico, and Venezuela provided aid and comfort to the Sandinista revolutionaries against the Somoza dictatorship in Nicaragua, while the bureaucratic-authoritarian regimes of the Southern Cone collaborated in tracking down suspected communists. Nevertheless, and despite hemispheric cooperation in military and police training programmes, South American states essentially confronted domestic revolutionaries on their own, as did Central American nations until the 1980s.

Contemporary efforts to revive the notion of collective security are unlikely to get very far as long as the power disparity between the United States and the rest of Latin America is such that no one can sanction the US for behaving unilaterally. This fact explains why it is chiefly the American analysts and policymakers who favour this approach to regional security.

Cooperative Security. Cooperative security differs from collective security primarily via the credibility of the commitment to defend each other. Collective security requires confidence in the response of the community to aggression against any member of the community. Cooperation means mutual adjustment for mutual gain and such concessions are more likely to become the "shadow of the future."[50] Consequently, cooperation implies that there is an element of constant negotiation among the parties. Confidence in the commitment to act is thus necessarily less in a cooperative than a collective security arrangement.

This negotiation does not have to occur among equals and it can include side payments linking security with nonsecurity issues in order to get collective action. What each side brings to the table does not have to be the same; for example, in the inter-American drug wars one side could offer to attack supply while the other focuses on demand. Cooperative security is thus especially applicable to heterogeneous communities.

Cooperative security schemes for the Latin American security complex have been forwarded by both the Canadian and Argentine delegations to the OAS. Lowenthal has suggested the necessary conditions which would have to be met for such a conflict management scheme to function at the hemispheric level.[51] We can think of these conditions in terms of mutual adjustment of behaviour in order to realize the mutual gain of cooperative security. Latin America, Lowenthal argues, needs to change its past behaviour and norms, and commit itself to democracy and the "hemispheric community." The United States, on the other hand, must commit itself to banishing unilateralism.

Advocates of a cooperative security regime in the Americas believe that the political and economic ties implied by having a liberal democratic hemisphere will dramatically reduce conflict and make that which occurs manageable without recourse to force. Hence military considerations are marginalized, while defending democracy becomes the new key to regional security.

Unfortunately, conflict management in these schemes does not depend upon domestic politics. What fundamentally matters is the stance that the "international economic order" (IEO) takes on the question of regional conflict. The argument requires that the IEO sanction those who disturb regional cooperation. Foreign private capital in particular is expected to shun away from governments that undertake policies which do not promote regional cooperation. Economic liberalizers are alleged to be most hurt by possible international sanctions (because they need access to foreign capital and markets) and most helped by international interdependence. Thus they will be the leading force for regional cooperation. The end result is that those domestic groups that favour cooperation will be strengthened in their national coalitional struggles and the government will prefer a foreign policy that strengthens regional cooperation.[52] Using the same logic of the democratic peace proponents,[53] regional peace develops as more dyadic groupings are made up of liberalizing governments.

The fundamental problem with this analysis lies in its conception of the IEO and empirical reality. The liberal IEO is not a unified structure and the logic of sanction is not clear. At different points it appears to be the profit orientation of private sources of capital, the security interests of the governments of the advanced industrial countries, or the financial concerns of the major international economic organizations. Even with the end of the Cold War, the interests of these three groups of actors are not the same, either across groups or within them. Governments compete against each other; multilateral organizations disagree on who should be sanctioned and when; and the private sector not only is divided amongst itself, but also may disagree with governments and multilateral organizations. The end result is a case-by-case evaluation by the various international forces, which significantly undermines the argument that liberal economies and democratic politics inevitably lead to regional peace.

A few examples will illustrate the problems. The United States and Latin American governments condemned President Alberto Fujimori's coup in Peru, but private capital flows into Peru increased dramatically as the guerrillas were corralled and inflation came down. Mexican stocks and the peso rallied in February 1995 on the news that President Ernesto Zedillo had sent the army into Chiapas and ordered the arrest of rebel leaders.[54] Argentina's ratcheting up of the level of Southern Cone air power was initially opposed by the US, but when the Argentines turned to Israel for the radar, the United States capitulated. Even during the Cold War (which Solingen claims imposed a global security imperative which allowed regions to destabilize to avoid sanctions), the United States sanctioned the egregious human rights violators in Latin America in the 1970s. Still, neither US disapproval nor aggressive foreign policies by some of these Latin American governments kept private capital or European and Israeli arms out of South America. Ironically, the easy access to international credit helped bring down the authoritarian economic liberalizers in the debt crises of the 1970s and 1980s.

Not only are the international sanctions not forthcoming, the behaviour of national liberalizers also does not follow expectations. The economic liberalizing coalitions in Chile and Argentina[55] allowed their 1978 conflict over the Beagle Channel to develop right up to the drafting of a declaration of war. Lest one want to claim that because these governments were authoritarian they were isolated from the international community and thus such constraints were weak, one must remember that at this time the Chilean economic experiment was taking off, and shortly thereafter the Argentine followed suit, both fuelled by international speculation.[56] The Argentine junta wanted to remain in the good graces of the Reagan administration and international bankers as they dealt with an economic collapse beginning in 1980, yet went to war with Britain in the Falklands/Malvinas in 1982, most likely intending to extend the war to Chile after the British recognized the *fait accompli*.[57] It is also not sufficient to argue that the military dominated the civilian liberalizers in the authoritarian governments. Democratic liberalizers in Colombia and Venezuela (where the military were not noted for having significant political power) clashed in 1986 leading to increased military budgets[58] and nationalist rhetoric by campaigning politicians. Democratic liberalizers in Peru and Ecuador sustained a week long skirmish with up to 200 dead in 1981, another militarized dispute in 1984, and in February 1995 continue to shoot at one another. Peruvian President Fujimori, a favourite of Wall Street who presided over the world's fastest growing economy in 1994, adamantly rejected Ecuadorean and international calls (including that of the Pope) for a ceasefire, choosing instead to intensify the skirmish with saturation bombing and another 1,000 troops.[59]

The liberal roots of the cooperative security argument works when the international flow which the country needs is under oligopolistic or monopolistic control and domestic politics in the sanctioning country do not oppose the sanctions.[60] Nuclear power plants, supercomputers, and perhaps massive debt bailouts are more effectively controlled by the leading governments of the liberal IEO than are the competitive markets in stocks and bonds, light manufacturing, and services. The irony of what "letting the market work" and "democratic foreign policy" mean for the effectiveness of international sanctions is lost on liberal security analysts.

Multilateralism in a Global Context in which Weapons Matter

Economic growth and democratization in the absence of a stable and credible balance of power are more likely to be recipes for increased conflict, rather than steps toward a pluralist, collective, or cooperative security community. Historically, the Cold War made little difference in the pattern of either US intervention or Latin American interstate conflicts.[61] In the post-Cold War, the United States invaded Panama, continued the embargo against Cuba, and pushed for an invasion of Haiti, demonstrating its willingness to use a big stick. Even in the new regional context, Ecuador and Peru have gone to war, while border tensions push Colombia and Venezuela to the precipice.[62]

This analysis suggests that prudence and cautious optimism, rather than euphoric idealism, promise to deliver more security to Latin America. The challenge in the current formulation of Latin American security arrangements is to push the military threshold farther back, rather than to search for its elimination. The most viable alternative conflict management system for Latin America must also recognize that the United States will continue to define its security needs unilaterally. The system must not be built on either an assumption that the US will behave or that its behaviour is irrelevant.

A multitiered and integrated security structure could meet these demands. It would be multitiered to facilitate working out disagreements locally first, and as necessary, subregionally, regionally, and globally. It would be integrated in that military, diplomatic, economic, political, and social aspects of interstate relations would be utilized to support the nonviolent resolution of conflict. Structured in this fashion, the regional security management system may convince the United States both that its legitimate needs are being addressed and that an early decision on its part to utilize force will meet opprobrium not only at the regional level, but the global as well. Such a conflict management system could also diminish the security dilemma among Latin American countries themselves.

The basic underpinning of the management scheme proposed here is found in the military and diplomatic structures in which Latin American conflict dyads play out. The chief elements of these structures are the balance of power, arms control, and confidence building measures (CBMs). The challenge is to minimize the level of armaments and keep them defence-oriented, not eliminate them.

While defence budgets in general have declined in most countries, the push for a professionalized military[63] (which requires force modernization), should produce smaller but more powerful militaries. Unfortunately, the Ecuador-Peru conflict will probably send ambiguous messages about the best use of that power. Ecuador's anti-air capabilities kept Peru's superiority in fighter bombers and helicopters from making a difference in the war. For some analysts the experience will emphasize the advantages of defensive orientations, but others will seek new jamming capabilities.[64] Increased transparency in the arms acquisition process[65] could stimulate both a more defensive orientation and perhaps even a greater sense of security at lower levels of armament. Bilateral and multilateral meetings among Latin American militaries for confidence-building purposes have been gaining momentum for the last decade,[66] but clearly more is needed.

Building on a stable and minimal balance of power would be military, diplomatic, political, and economic groupings at the subregional (i.e., Latin American subgroups) and regional (the OAS,[67] possibly a hemispheric free trade regime along the lines of President Bush's Initiative for the Americas) levels. Their basic contribution to security in the region would be via developing and training for defensive missions, support of confidence-building measures, economic development which promotes economic interdependence, political development which reinforces democratic government, and mediation of disputes when these other measures fail.

Many of these subregional and regional groupings are currently functioning.[68] It would be important, however, that any regional or subregional organization that had the United States as a member, not have a military capacity. US resources would overwhelm everyone and the group would fall under its influence, repeating the unhappy experience of the Rio Treaty. Hence, collective inter-American security schemes are inappropriate.[69]

The next level up in the security system would incorporate the diplomatic-military structure of the United Nations. Its role would consist of mediation, confidence-building measures, coordination of sanctions when necessary, provision of peacekeeping forces where appropriate, and training of peacekeepers in Latin America. Argentina has participated in numerous UN peacekeeping missions and has offered to turn a military base formerly used to guard its Brazilian border into a peacekeeping school. It is more appropriate that Latin Americans collaborate with UN-provided trainers than with the United States on this mission because US forces are trained to seek military victories rather than help keep a tenuous peace. (Note the disastrous consequences of US military participation in Somalia.)

Finally, and hopefully far down the path to peace and security, comes the traditional US presence. One cannot eliminate this "bull in the regional china shop." But incorporating Latin American bilateral, subregional, regional, and global structures into a multitiered and reinforcing security system offers the best hope for keeping red flags from the bull's sight.

Notes

1. There are six as defined by the standard 1,000 battlefield deaths cutoff: Dominican Republic-Haiti, 1937; Bolivia-Paraguay 1931-35; Peru-Ecuador 1939-41; El Salvador-Honduras, 1969; and Argentina-Great Britain, 1982. The Peru-Colombia clash in 1932 produced 868 deaths.

2. For a discussion of security complexes, see Barry Buzan, *People, States and Fear* (Boulder: Lynne Rienner, 1991).

3. In 1993 Colombia accused Nicaragua of attempting to buy missile boats from North Korea to contest Colombian sovereignty over the San Andres Islands. Nicaragua denied the charges, claiming that it was downsizing its military establishment, and citing the sale of helicopters to Ecuador as an example. *Diario*, (Caracas: Venezuela, August 1993), vol. 32. It would be interesting to see how such a purchase affected Ecuadorean and Peruvian calculations at the time of their 1995 border war. Peruvian President Fujimori claims that he was aware of Ecuadorean preparations for war in 1992 and sought to delay Ecuadorean action until Peru defeated the Shining Path rebellion and revitalized its armed forces. *Hoy*, Quito, Ecuador, 4 April 1995.

4. US government officials and security analysts often point to such participants as evidence of "external" security threats. But they conveniently forget that the US War of Independence itself attracted idealists from outside its territorial boundaries, as well as money and troops from a prerevolutionary France which had not progressed politically to the point of having a British type Magna Carta.

5. Stanley E. Hilton, *Brazil and the Soviet Challenge* (Austin: University of Texas Press, 1991); Lloyd J. Mecham, *A Survey of United States-Latin American Relations* (Boston: Houghton Mifflin, 1965); Jorge I. Dominguez, *To Make the World Safe for Revolution: Cuba's Foreign Policy* (Cambridge: Harvard University Press, 1989); Samuel L. Bailey, *Labour, Nationalism and Politics in Argentina* (New Brunswick, NJ: Rutgers University Press, 1967); and Rober J. Alexander (ed.), *APRISMO* (Kent, OH: Kent State University Press, 1973).

6. Ecuador was abandoned to the Peruvians in the 1939-41 war and Chile felt isolated in 1977-78 as it confronted war scares with first Peru, then Argentina. The landed oligarchy throughout Latin America believed that the US push for land reform after the Cuban Revolution meant that they were being abandoned by the US anti-communist military regimes in the 1970s which perceived US human rights policies in a similar light.

7. Steve Chan, "Mirror, Mirror on the Wall ... Are the Freer Countries More Pacific?" *Journal of Conflict Resolution,* 28:4: 617-48.

8. Richard W. Mansbach and John A. Vasquez, *In Search of Theory* (New York: Columbia University Press, 1981), p. 4.

9. Graham T. Allison, "Questions about the Arms Race: Who's Racing Whom? A Bureaucratic Perspective," in *Contrasting Approaches to Strategic Arms Control*, ed. Robert L. Pfaltzgraff, Jr. (Lexington, MA: Lexington Books, 1974), pp. 31-72.

10. On Peruvian threat perceptions, see Ronald Bruce St. John, *The Foreign Policy of Peru* (Boulder: Lynne Rienner, 1992), pp. 203-5; and Daniel M. Masterson, *Militarism and Politics*

in Latin America (New York: Greenwood Press, 1991), p. 265. The Soviet Union provided Peru with 115 military advisors in the army and air force, and trained 200 commissioned and noncommissioned officers citing Pentagon sources, CLADDE-RIAL, *Limitacion de Armamentios y Confianza Muta en America Latina* (Estudio Estrategico de America Latina, 1988) vol. 2, p. 348.

11. *Defensa*, Madrid, November 1988, XI, p.127, as cited in Serbin: 288. CLADDE-RIAL, *Limitacion de Armamentios y Confianza Muta en America Latina*, pp. 300-1, 371. Venezuela had already been reinforcing border defences after Colombian guerrillas crossed. But the 1987 appearance of a Colombian navy vessel in Venezuelan-claimed waters provoked mutual military mobilizations. Similar incidents in the early 1970s also fuelled arms acquisitions. *Diario*, 20 December 1993, p. 30

12. Robert N. Burr, *By Reason or Force* (Berkeley: University of California Press, 1965).

13. Juan Velit, "El Contexto Politico-Estrategiico del Peru," in *Percepciones de Amenazas y Politicas de Defensa en America Latina,* ed. V.A. Rigoberto, Cruz Johnson and Varas Fernandez (Santiago, Chile: FLACSO, 1993), p. 233.

14. Adrian J. English, *Armed Forces of Latin America* (London: Jane's, 1984), p. 401.

15. Chaim D. Kaufmann, *U.S. Mediation in the Falklands/Malvinas Crisis* (Washington, DC: Georgetown University, Pew Case Studies in International Affairs #431, 1994 [1988]).

16. An interview with Professor and General Augustin Toro (ret.), Insituto de Estudios Internacionales, Universidad de Chile, 1990.

17. *Globo*, Caracas, Venezuela, (28 June 1993), p. 18. Cites Alberto Muller Rojas, a retired General, current Senator, and respected security analyst.

18. Burr, *By Reason or Force*, (1965)

19. John R. Redick, "The Tlatelolco Regime and Nonproliferation in Latin America," *International Organization* 35:1 (1981): 103-34.

20. Since 1987 the Latin American Centre for Defence and Disarmament (CLADDE) and the Joint Study Program of Latin American International Relations (RIAL) have edited an annual study of progress in this area, *Estudio Estrategico de America Latina*, (Santiago, Chile). In January 1992 the OAS charged its working group on Hemispheric Security to prepare three reports on the security of small states, the relationship between the OAS, and the Inter-American Defence Board, and arms proliferation. (OAS April 1992). The United Nations has a regional Centre for Peace, Disarmament and Development in Latin America and the Caribbean in Peru.

21. St. John, *The Foreign Policy of Peru*, p. 210.

22. Nineteenth century liberals in power throughout Central America and Mexico helped each other gain and retain political power. The leaders of the Mexican Revolution initially felt more secure with radicals in power in Central America and supplied Sandino in Nicaragua during the 1920s. In the 1940s and 1970s Argentine military governments supported coups in Bolivia. Right wing authoritarian regimes in Chile and Bolivia exchanged suspicions with the left-wing military government in Peru. Venezuelan democrats overthrown in 1948 informally organized a "Caribbean League" to promote democracy in the subregion via covert

action. Ralph Lee Jr., Woodward, *Central America* (New York: Oxford University Press, 1976); Michael J. Frances, *The Limits of Hegemony* (Notre Dame: University of Notre Dame Press, 1977); St. John, *The Foreign Policy of Peru*; Lloyd J. Macham, *The United States and Inter-American Security, 1889-1960* (Austin: University of Texas Press, 1962). In the late 1940s, and early 1950s Peron's government in Argentina financed the ATLAS labour movement throughout Latin America. Brazilian intelligence services helped track down communists into the late 1930s. Argentina helped train the CONTRA in Central America from 1979-82. Bailey, *Labour, Nationalism and Politics in Argentina*, Hilton, *Brazil and the Soviet Challenge*; and Kaufmann, *U.S. Mediation in the Falklands/Malvinas Crisis*.

23. Abraham F. Lowenthal, *The Dominican Intervention* (Cambridge: Harvard University Press, 1972).

24. Jack Child, *Unequal Alliance: The Inter-American Military System, 1939-78*. (Boulder: Westview, 1980).

25. Discussion with Peruvian General (ret.) and ex-Foreign Minister Merado Jarrin, 1989. Other Latin Americans, while not agreeing with the manner im which Argentina attempted to resolve the long-standing dispute were dismayed by the clear preference of the US for the British. Venezuela cancelled an arms contract which it had with the British. See the critique of the RIO Treaty shortly after the war by the current Chilean ambassador to the OAS: "The mechanisms for the peaceful resolution of conflicts within the inter-American system did not function appropriately to manage the South Atlantic war precisely because they had been discredited and paralyzed along with the overall system." Heraldo Munzo, "Beyond the Malvinas Crisis: Perspectives on Inter-American Relations," *Latin American Research Review*, 30:1: 158-72.

26. Kaufmann, *U.S. Mediation in the Falklands/ Malvinas Crisis*, p. 3.

27. "Border Incidents Add to Tension in Venezuelan-Colombian Relations" *Latin American Regional Reports*, 3 February 1994; *The New York Times*, 9 February 1995, p. A3.

28. Jack S. Levy and Lily I. Vakili, "Diversionary Action by Authoritarian Regimes: Argentina in the Falklands/Malvinas Case," in *The Internationalization of Communal Strife*, ed. Manus I. Midlarsky (London: Routledge, 1992), pp. 118-46; but Virginia Gambo, *The Falklands/Malvinas War* (Boston: Allen&Unwin, 1987), pp. 74-77, 131-33, presents a strong case against it.

29. See the discussions concerning the recent purchase of Skyhawk A-4s with look-down radar from the US. Though old, the Skyhawks had been responsible for destroying some of the British ships during the Malvinas War. English, *Armed Forces of Latin America*, pp. 27-29.

30. Andres Fontana and Augusto Varas, "Percepciones y Opiniones Sobre las Fuerzas Armadas en Argentina y Chile: niellists comparativo de Dos Estudios," *Fuerzass Armadas y Sociedaad*, VII, 2 (April-June): 33.

31. For example, the Organization of American States created a committee to examine the relationship between the social-political-economic components of the organization and their military counterpart. The North-South Center at the University of Miami and the Latin American Program of the Woodrow Wilson Center of the Smithsonian Institution have funded conferences and research on this topic. The National Defence University has had a series of workshops for policymakers, officers, and academics on the new inter-American security environment, highlighting civil-military relations.

32. Mecham, *The United States and Inter-American Security*, p. 46.

33. Gordon Cornell-Smith, *The United States and Latin America* (New York: Wiley, 1974), pp.111-15.

34. Mecham, *The United States and Inter-American Security*, pp. 59-60.

35. Hector Gros Espiell, *Conflictos Territoriales en Iberoameriaca y Solucion Pacifica de Controverias* (Madrid: Ediciones Cultura Hispanica, 1989), p. 16.

36. *The New York Times*, 5 February 1995, p. E4.

37. Chip News, Santiago, Chile, 31 January 1995.

38. This state of affairs is largely due to two factors. After losing a disastrous war with the US (in 1849, Mexico lost one-half of its territory to the US), suffering a war scare in the 1880s, and experiencing two military interventions during the Mexican Revolution (1914 and 1916), it became objectively clear that militarizing relations with the great power US could not benefit Mexico. In addition, Mexican political leaders in a one-party system born of military revolts and surrounded by the militarized polities in the rest of Latin America, have deliberately kept the Mexican military small and backward.

Nevertheless, the United States has been increasingly militarizing its southern border in a largely futile attempt to control the inward flow of drugs and people. The US public and their leaders may not believe war is thinkable with Mexico, but they believe that using military force against Mexico is legitimate. Hence we may in the future have a pluralistic security between the United States and Mexico in name, but not in spirit.

39. While the United States was unwilling to risk military conflict with Chile during its land grab against Bolivia and Peru in the War of the Pacific (1879-81), by 1891 the US was prepared to declare war if the Chilean government did not apologize for the injuries suffered by US sailors in a bar room brawl. In response to European use of military force to collect debts in Venezuela, US Secretary of State Olney protested, declaring that the United States was "practically sovereign" in this area. The Roosevelt Corollary to the Monroe Doctrine (1904) stipulated that the US would use military force to collect European debts.

40. Bradford E. Burns, *The Unwritten Alliance* (New York: Colombia University Press, 1966), pp.120-21.

41. The issue of a common policy had been around in 1917 when the United States entered the First World War along with Brazil, but Mexico and Argentina favoured neutrality. Mecham, *A Survey of United States-Latin American Relations*, pp. 77-86.

42. David G. Haglund, *Latin America and the Transformation of U.S. Strategic Thought, 1936-1940* (Albuquerque: University of New Mexico Press, 1984), pp. 36-41; Mecham, *The United States and Inter-America Security*, pp. 124-35.

43. Frances, *The Limits of Hegemony*; and Mecham, *The United States and Inter American Security*, pp. 186-87.

44. Despite widespread violations of human rights and the prevalence of nondemocratic governments, until the 1990s only two countries were sanctioned for violating these inter-American norms: the Dominican Republic and Cuba, both in 1960. The US overcame

reluctantly Latin American unwillingness to sanction Cuba by acquiescing in the sanction of the Dominican dictatorship. Mecham, *The United States and Inter-American Security*, pp. 282-315.

45. Ibid., pp. 282-315.

46. Ibid., pp. 406-8.

47. Guatemala (1954) and Cuba (1960) unsuccessfully tried appealing to the UN while Nicaragua turned to the World Court in the 1980s. Cornell-Smith, *The United States and Latin America* (New York: Halstead Press for John Wiley and Sons, 1994), pp. 215-19, 228-36. Sung Ho Kim, "The Issues of International Law, Morality and Prudence," in *Reagan and the Sandinistas*, ed. Thomas Walker (Boulder: Westview Press, 1987), p. 265.

48. Comments during the workshop "North American Security in the Time of NAFTA," National Defence University, Washington DC, September 1994.

49. Dominguez, *To Make the World Safe for Revolution*.

50. Robert O. Keohane, *After Hegemony* (Princeton: Princeton University Press, 1984), p. 5.

51. Abraham Lowenthal, "Latin America: Ready for Partnership?" *Foreign Affairs: America and the World,* 72:1 (Winter, 1992/93).

52. Etel Solingen, "Economic Liberalization, Political Coalitions, and Emerging Regional Orders," in *Regional Orders: Building Security in a New World,* ed. David A. Lake and Patrick Morgan, (University Park: Pennsylvania State University Press, forthcoming)

53. Michael Doyle, "Liberalism and World Politics," *American Political Science Review,* 80: 4: 1151-61.

54. *The New York Times*, 11 February 1995, p. A4

55. The liberalizer credentials of the Chilean and Argentine bureaucratic-authoritarian regimes in the 1970s are unassailable. For an analysis of their radical Chicago-style economic programmes, see Alejandro Foxley, *Latin American Experiments in Neoconservative Economics* (Berkeley: University of California Press, 1983); and Joseph, Ramos, *Neoconservative Economics in the Southern Cone of Latin America, 1973-1983* (Baltimore: John Hopkins University Press, 1986). The post-authoritarian government in Chile has made only minor modifications in economic policy, while in Argentina the Menem administration has been significantly more active, especially selling state-owned enterprises. But the liberalizing reforms of Menem appear most different when compared to the economic policies adopted in 1980, when the economy collapsed.

56. Ramos, *Neoconservative Economics*.

57. Martin Middlebrook, *Task Force: The Falklands War, 1982*, rev. ed. (London: Penguin, 1987); Interview Emilio Meneses, Santiago, Chile, 1990, indicative of the security concerns Argentina had *vis-à-vis* Chile, they left their best troops on the border with Chile and out of the war with Britain. Gary W. Wynia, *Argentina* (New York: Holmes and Meier, 1986).

58. The percentage of GDP/GNP devoted to defence expenditure in Venezuela increased from 1.3 percent in 1985 to 4.3 percent in 1991; comparable figures for Colombia are 1.6 to 2.8, *Military Balance* (London: International Institute for Strategic Studies, 1995), pp. 226-27.

59. *The New York Times*, 10 February 1995, p. A5.

60. For a discussion of the political economy of sanctions in general, see Robert Paarlberg, "Lessons of the Grain Embargo," *Foreign Affairs,* 59:1 (Fall): 144-62; also the critique in John J. Mearsheimer "The False Promise of International Institutions," *International Security,* 19:3 (Winter 1994/95): 25.

61. David R. Mares, "La Guerra Fria en los Conflicots Latinoamericanos: Mitos y Realidades" *Fuerzaas Armadas y Sociaedad,* X:2 (April/June 1995): 19-25.

62. *El Nacional,* Caracas, Venezuela, 17 March 1995, p. 1.

63. There is a broad concensus throughout the Americas that military professionalization keeps them out of politics. For the theoretical justification, see Samuel P. Huntington, *The Soldier and the State* (New York: Vintage, 1957).

64. Interview with Major Antonio L. Pala (USAF), Washington, DC, March 1995.

65. Not all countries participate in the United Nations' army registry and the data produced by Washington-based Arms Control and Disarmament Agency (ACDA) and the London-based International Institute for Strategic Studies (IISS) are not identical.

66. CLADDE-RIAL, *Limitacion de Armamentos y confianza Mutua en America Latin* (Estudio Estrategico de America Latina, 1988), vol. 2.

67. Latin American diplomats attached to the OAS have recently been active in attempting to revive the inter-American security system. At the same time, they are also seeking to make it less necessary by having other components of the regional system address political, economic, and social factors which are believed to affect peace and security in the Organization of American States.

68. For example, the Group of Eight; the Group of Three; the Andean Pact; and Mercosur.

69. As soon as the United States began discussing the possibility of using force to overthrow the dictatorship in Haiti, Latin America, as well as Canadian diplomats objected. *New York Times,* 9 May 1994. Even after the United Nations approved the use of force, major Latin American states continued to object and Canada refused to be part of the invasion force. For an elaboration of the general point, see David Mares "Inter-American Security Communities: Concepts and Challenges," in *Security, Democracy and Development in U.S.-Latin American Relations,* ed. Lars Shoultz, William Smith and Augusto Varas (Miami: Transaction Books, 1994), pp. 265-77.

Harold P. Klepak

Multilateralism, Regionalism and Cooperation in Fighting the International Narcotics Trade in the Americas

Introduction

Few problems have been more vexing for the international relations of the Americas in recent years than the question of how to deal with the international illegal drug trade. The inter-American dimensions of this worldwide problem have been vast and complex and have placed heavy strains on many parts of the United States-Latin America relationship which was seemingly improving as the troubles caused by the Cold War declined and then largely disappeared.

The end of the 1980s and the first half of the 1990s have been characterized by what some authors have referred to as "the cocalization" of United States policy toward Latin America. Accusations have been many in Latin America that the United States has found the argument of drugs to justify its unilateral interventions in the region.[1]

This chapter seeks to discover to what extent one can speak of true regional cooperation in the Americas in the fight against the illegal narcotics trade. It takes as its context the discussion between realist and liberal institutionalist schools of thought on the issue of the value of regional approaches in forwarding cooperative action in selected realms of international concern.

The "liberal" contention is roughly that regional cooperation allows for building habits of collaboration which can improve relations in general and can effectively address major international problems shared by more than one state. Realists contend that the old rules of power still prevail, that it is in the power relationships among states that one sees the reality of regional politics, and that such collaboration results from the outcome of the interplay of these relative power positions.

I will look first at the nature of the problem and how it has been seen by the United States and a variety of Latin American countries. I will then turn to discuss briefly the nature of the inter-American "region," or "system" as it is often termed. Only then can one assess the actual handling of the drug trade and the responses to the challenges it poses. In doing so, I will lay out briefly key individual Latin American responses as well as collective ones at the regional and subregional levels.

I shall argue that the anti-drug experience in the inter-American context is more consistent with the arguments set forth by the realist school than with liberal institutionalist thinking on this matter. That is, the degree of inter-American collaboration in this area has been much more a function of the abilities of the regional superpower to compel compliance from its potential partners than it has been one of all sides coming together, sharing values and approaches, and wishing to work for the common good.

The last 20 years have shown a marked dominance of virtually coerced collaboration in the face of wide disagreement on the nature of the problem and the best means to combat it between the main regional consumer (the United States) and the main regional suppliers (Colombia, Peru, and Bolivia). And while other Latin American countries, as well as Canada, may find themselves between the extremes of these poles of perception, they also have found their policies dominated by the need to placate the regional giant.[2]

This is not to say that this issue is in any way black and white. The evolution of the problem in the last decade, leading to the impossibility of labelling countries as either exclusively suppliers or exclusively consumers, has meant that there has been a sort of meeting of the ways, even if only a rather limited one. But, as will be shown, even this progress has been slowed dramatically by the continuation of very different perceptions of the problem and the best means to deal with it.

What is the Nature of the Problem?

The current illegal international drug business is estimated to be worth some $500 billion a year.[3] It is one of the most important business operations in the world, outstripped probably only by the international legal commerce in arms and petroleum. The three main traded finished drugs are marijuana (now legal in quite a number of countries but not in the United States), cocaine, and heroin.

The Latin American dimension of the trade is largely in cocaine, made from the coca leaf, grown overwhelmingly in South America and especially in Peru, Bolivia, and more recently, in large quantities in Colombia as well. But a disturbing current trend is the increasing regional production of the poppy, from which heroin is derived, in Colombia and Guatemala especially. Marijuana is produced in many, perhaps all, countries of the Americas. Indeed, the United States is in fact itself a massive producer of this so-called "light" drug.[4]

These illegal drugs find their main markets in North America and in Europe, although there is also growing demand in parts of Asia and in Latin America itself. But by far the most important source of demand is the United States, responsible alone for the bulk of the market for both the more lethal drugs in question.

For the purposes of this chapter, the process that interests us is that which takes the coca leaf or the *amapola* poppy and converts them (via precursor chemicals) into cocaine or heroin proper, and then usually transports it to the northern markets. There it is distributed by sellers in the dark and massive drug underworld of North American and European cities to both casual users and addicts ("abusers" as they are often termed). The dominant role of Latin America in the production, transformation, transport, and commercialization of the drug ensures that consumer countries focus on this region as at least part of any answer to the problem.

That problem takes the form of huge costs to northern societies, and especially the United States; drug abuse has a bill attached in the form of crime in the streets, law enforcement related to this, medical services, educational and publicity costs connected with fighting the spread of the scourge, absenteeism from work, disruption to family and social life, and myriad other elements. At least 85 percent of North American urban crime is reckoned to be drug-related, as addicts desperately seek extra income in order to pay for their extremely expensive habit.[5] Anti-drug agencies put the actual financial cost of the drug problem to the citizens of the US in the order of several billion dollars a year, but the price in terms of insecurity in the streets and other social costs is, of course, incalculable.

The US View

The United States has tended to see itself as the victim of a foreign plot by unscrupulous non-Americans who poison the nation's youth with drugs and thus attack the very fabric of US society. If there were no drugs coming into the country, this view holds, then there would be no problem. Until the Clinton administration, almost the whole thrust of US policy was aimed at countering supply, that is the arrival of the drugs from abroad in the United States. While President Bush was willing to pay lip service to the idea of *joint* responsibility for the problem when he met Latin American leaders at a series of drug summits, the reality was that the issue in Washington was almost always put in terms of stopping supply rather than dealing with demand.

The budgetary results of this were clear. For most of the now decade-long heightened struggle against drugs some 70 percent of US expenditure on the drug problem has been on repression and interdiction of supply, while only roughly 30 percent has been on educational, publicity, medical, and related efforts to deal with demand.[6] And while President Clinton's new drug "czar," White House Drug Control Policy Director Lee Brown, suggested in October 1993 that the new government was going to draw the two efforts into more equal balance, this promise seems to have remained largely rhetoric.[7]

Latin American Views

The first point to be made here is that there is not one Latin American view on this issue; there are at least 20 — one from each of the Latin American states — and no doubt several more from the over one dozen states of the Commonwealth Caribbean. This reflects not only the diversity inherent in what Marcel Niedergang has aptly called *les vingt Amériques latines* but also the fact, alluded to above, that no state can truly claim to be exclusively a supplier or exclusively a consumer, or even exclusively a transhipment zone.[8]

What is usually referred to as *the* Latin American view on the drugs trade is that most often put forward by the main producer states of Bolivia, Colombia, and Peru. These three Andean republics have responded to the popular US view that the problem is one of supply by arguing that, on the contrary, if there were no demand in northern, especially United States, cities, then there would be no incentive for Latin American farmers to grow the base plants nor for entrepreneurs to undertake such a risky business.[9]

They reinforce this argument by suggesting that it is absurd to think that the Latin American *campesino*, desperately poor, but with a strong tradition of honesty and love of peace, would sacrifice that status because of some nasty streak in his character. However, the argument goes, when there is no other crop that can bring him anything like what he gets for poppy or coca leaf, and when he has a family to support in a crumbling agricultural economy, it is simply illogical to think he will not opt for the only way out of his predicament.

Thus the responsibility for the scourge, in this view, is almost exclusively in the camp of the consuming north. Former Peruvian president, Alan García, has even quipped that drugs are Latin America's only successful multinational enterprise and it would be nonsense to suggest abandoning it.

For those holding this view, the only possible answer to the problem is crop eradication *coupled* with crop substitution. That is, farmers have to be given an alternative crop that can be sold for at least something like the money they make with illegal ones like coca or *amapola*. This, however, is ferociously expensive, as it implies usually not only assistance with the crop but also with its transport and marketing. Since the regions where coca is grown are almost always well into the hinterland, and capital is generally scarce in the extreme, the *narcotraficantes* appear to be likely to hold the upper hand for some time to come.

Be that as it may, this view is altogether at variance with the generalized one of the problem being supply. Thus the two *sides* come at the problem with diametrically opposed ideas about the nature of the blame to be assigned for the existence of the problem. Hence, they are hardly likely to have the same views on to how to deal with it.

These three countries do not, however, represent the only Latin American views on this matter. The Southern Cone countries of Uruguay, Chile, and especially Argentina, with sophisticated, largely white, urban and *bourgeois* populations, have considerable sympathy for their Latin neighbours in their desire to escape the blame for the problem, but also feel threatened by the increasing invasion of their own streets by the phenomenon and its attendant violence. Their reaction thus is rather nuanced compared to either the three Andean states mentioned or the United States.

The countries of the Central American and Caribbean regions also form something of a patchwork, where attitudes toward the problem are concerned. While extensive production of lethal drugs occurs in Guatemala and to a lesser extent Jamaica, almost all the region's countries see their territories, air space and surrounding seas used by drug dealers to move their drugs north to the United States and Canada and northeast to Europe. Most countries here are small and weak, and there is a widespread feeling that the drug barons represent a serious threat to national sovereignty managing as they do sums of money greatly in excess of the national budgets of most of the states of the area.[10]

These countries, particularly the mini-states of the Caribbean, are crying out for greater international efforts to stem the trade, and especially military, coast guard, and police assistance from the United States and Western Europe. The level of such assistance has so far been surprisingly low given the priority supposedly assigned to the problem by the governments of developed states.[11]

The Americas: Region, System or What?

Considering the Americas at all as a region is fraught with problems. Despite the currently popular myth in the United States that the ideals of hemispheric unity date back to Monroe and even Simón Bolívar himself, the historic reality is that Monroe and his Cabinet considered Latin America a sphere of natural dominance for the United States and not a zone for profitable collaboration.[12] Even more dramatically, Bolívar believed his proposal for "American" unity should end at the borders of the United States, a country he felt to be only slightly less menacing for the newly independent Latin American states than Spain and its Holy Alliance partners in Europe.[13]

Most nineteenth century Latin American attempts at unity were responses to pressures and aggression from either Europe or the United States. But at no time did any Latin American state suffer from powerful European nations the territorial losses, unilateral interventions, and humiliations that Mexico, Central America, and the Caribbean states have received at the hands of the United States throughout that century and the first three decades of this one.[14] The combination of support for filibusterers (in Florida and later in Texas, California, and Central America), an officially supported policy of Manifest Destiny involving territorial expansion into Latin America, the Monroe Doctrine itself, and outright aggression, made Latin American societies extremely suspicious of Washington and its objectives in the region.[15]

The idea of Pan Americanism has faced heavy weather for all of its history. Latin American states looked unabashedly to Europe for support against US pretensions although on more than one occasion they equally wished Washington to stand between them and meddlesome and pushy Europeans. The Southern Cone was most successful in this, but even Mexico and the Caribbean sought, often desperately, for counterweights to US power, and such a thing could only be found in the United Kingdom and Europe, especially the former.[16]

Despite conferences in the late 1880s and the first actual underpinnings of a Pan American system as of the last year of that decade, the reality was that *all* Latin American states, to at least some extent, sought the protection and room for manoeuvre afforded by a European counterweight to the US. Even when Pan American rhetoric was at its most high-flown, *raison d'état* cried out for options outside the hemisphere. From the earliest years, the basic feature

of the Americas has been the inherent asymmetry of one great power or superpower dealing with 20 or more essentially minor actors on the world stage.

This does not mean to suggest that there is no meaning at all to Pan Americanism, or if one prefers, the *Western Hemisphere Idea*.[17] There is a feeling in
some circles that the Americas have been fortunate enough to build a region
of relative peace, at least in this century, and that conflicts tend to be controlled better here than in other regions.[18] Within Latin America, there is certainly
a widespread belief that there is a sort of commonwealth of Latin countries
who feel they have a special relationship, but it must be emphasized that this
relationship in no way includes the United States and, in fact, in many ways is
a result of common perceptions of the threat that country has meant for Latin
America over more than a century and a half. Even the Commonwealth Caribbean is not included in this essentially cultural self-perception, and Haiti is
included only *par courtoisie*.[19]

Latin Americans, not surprisingly given their history, consider themselves
Argentineans, Brazilians, Cubans, Hondurans, Mexicans or whatever first, and
only then as members of a cultural reality which it pleases the north to call
Latin America. Historically, given the imperial systems in existence, the links
among these countries were much weaker than between them individually
and their European *métropoles*.

Conflicts of all kinds have occurred among these republics ever since independence, and as one has been reminded this year in South America, these
are not necessarily over.[20] While recognizing a cultural commonwealth, in no
way is that identity in the same league as the sentiment of nationalism, even if
the latter has taken in some cases some bumps in this age of globalization.

The Southern Cone nations in particular have insisted throughout their
independent history on the closest of relations with Europe, taking their models from the old continent and not from the new. Paris, London, and Rome
were the sources of inspiration, not Washington, New York, or even their own
Latin American neighbours. Geography, in any case, continued to reduce effectively the connections among themselves much more than the thousands
of kilometres of oceans did with Europe.

Thus, regional coalescence, when it occurred, was based on direct national self-interest. And while the threat in the last century was more often the
Old World than the New, in the last nine decades it has much more frequently
been, or been seen to be, the United States. A common front against the US
could on occasion bring some results while unilateral action against that country
almost always courted disaster. On the other hand, in most cases, the

asymmetries were such that even multilateral action *vis-à-vis* Washington was doomed to failure, at least when issues at stake were of real significance to the northern colossus.

The Pan American system was therefore slow to develop and real substance in any Latin American unity even slower. The first major conference of the hemisphere, in 1889, certainly began the process but it was not until the first years of this century that it began to take real form. From the beginning, the US role was paramount, as evidenced by meeting agendas, the siting of headquarters, and the chairmanship of agencies.

In this century, the possibilities of counterpoise, so obvious in the European (essentially British) dominance of the international division of labour into which Latin America had been integrated, grew weaker and weaker. By the Hay-Paunceforte Treaty of 1901, the United Kingdom served notice that it was yielding hegemony in the Caribbean and Central America, and the military and naval ground more widely in Latin America, to the United States. The French had largely done so since the disastrous intervention in favour of the Emperor Maximilian in Mexico in the 1860s. Germany became important, but was in no way able to stare down the United States in time of crisis.

While European dominance of trade and investment survived in the south until the Second World War, in the Caribbean, Mexico, and Central America, it was waning decades before. The two world wars, especially the second, had shown Latin America how feeble the ties to Europe could become. The United States was only too willing, especially during the periods of wartime neutrality in 1914-17 and 1939-41, to fill the gaps the Europeans left.

Indeed, it is in the security field that the inter-American system became most developed. Feeling threatened by events in Europe in the late 1930s and early 1940s, most Latin Americans were willing to follow the US lead in sealing the hemisphere from outside interference.[21] President Roosevelt was extremely keen to solidify this connection and the years of neutrality and war brought the region, especially the north, solidly into a United States sphere. The shattering of European power by the two wars merely hastened this result.[22] After the war, for its own reasons the US moved to make permanent the wartime arrangements that included basing rights, Lend Lease programmes, training, massive transfers of equipment and weaponry, the arrival of US military missions, and accords on importation of labour into the US, recruitment of foreigners into the US armed forces, and even guaranteed access to strategic resources.

The result was what many began to call a true inter-American "system," whose three pillars were to be hemispheric arrangements for common defence (Rio Pact of 1947), peaceful settlement of disputes (Pact of Bogota of 1948) and the actual Charter of the Organization of American States (OAS), successor to the Pan American Union set up in 1948. The Latin Americans, anxious to stimulate a US interest that might see the latter offering them a "Marshall Plan of the Americas," agreed to this system, having now accepted that there simply were no longer any potential counterweights to US power.

Reinforced by a series of bilateral Mutual Assistance Pacts in the early 1950s, the system held in the face of a leftist reform movement in Guatemala (crushed in 1954), and proved mobilizable in the face of the perceived threat of Castroism in the 1960s "export of revolution" phase of that regime. It even assisted direct US military intervention in places like the Dominican Republic in 1965.

When issues of less direct interest to the US arose, however, the system proved much less useful. Indeed, the legitimizing role of the OAS for what were essentially unilateral US initiatives eventually sapped whatever strength and vitality the organization was ever likely to have. The OAS proved powerless to stop, and indeed in many ways encouraged, the wave of coups that toppled civilian governments in the 1960s and early 1970s. Worse, it was incapable of doing anything very effective to control the spread of revolution and war in Central America in the late 1970s and 1980s. The same proved true when Ecuador and Peru fought each other in 1981. And most telling was the obvious uselessness of such an organization, from a Latin American point of view, when the Falklands War broke out. In the vital security area, bedrock of the system in many ways, there was obvious failure or, even worse perhaps, irrelevance.[23]

Thus when the Cold War ended, many authors began to ask what was now the utility of the OAS and the inter-American security system. If such questions were difficult ones for other multilateral security arrangements, even NATO, they were much more so for the Rio Pact and other elements of the inter-American system. For the first few years of the Cold War era, among governments of the hemisphere it was felt to be little less than opening up Pandora's Box to suggest having a serious look at making the system relevant. After all, for many members, the actual most likely direct military threat of recent decades had not been from outside the hemisphere, but rather from the "alliance" leader itself.[24]

The US Response

The drug issue has been moving into this context for multilateralism and regionalism over the last two decades and particularly over the last nine years, since President Bush emphasized even more than previous governments the security threat drugs represented for his country. The United States has tried, first with Mexico and then more widely, to orchestrate a multilateral response from the whole region to the scourge of the drug trade.

As mentioned above, this response in the US was largely one of repression and interception. The United States reinforced and multiplied its agencies dealing with drugs and by the late 1980s, had even given a major role (principally intelligence and indirect support to the police) to the armed forces in the fight.[25]

A plethora of agencies (some put the figure as high as 35) within the United States are involved with federal, state, and municipal lines crossed regularly. When the inevitable "turf wars" produced inefficiencies in what was already an almost impossible struggle, the reaction in Washington was to appoint a director of a national strategy against drugs but this merely underscored how divided the agencies really were.

Massive deployments of resources and manpower did little more than make a dent in the problem and indeed, by sending prices up, reinforced the link between drug abuse and crime. The problem was clearly an international one, as it had been in the earlier opium crazes of the previous century.[26]

Thus, carrying on a tradition of considering the trade a legitimate target of US diplomacy, Washington stepped up its attacks on it. But in the new context of middle class conversion to drugs in the 1960s and 1970s, the new target was not opium from Asia, but marijuana and later cocaine from Latin America.

Again, the idea of drugs as an international issue was not new, even in the 1980s. President Nixon had tried hard to cajole Mexico into a cooperative effort against marijuana in the early 1970s. Mexico had indeed tried to collaborate closely, involving the army in stepped-up operations to eradicate the crop and interdict the marketing system. But little was accomplished and the marijuana epidemic soon seemed minor as cocaine gained ground as the *chic* drug in the late 1970s and 1980s.

Cocaine, however, came from farther south, arrived in the United States through a wider range of entry points, was vastly more profitable to the *narcos*, was more difficult to intercept because it came in smaller (more valuable) packets, was more disruptive to users and society, and was grown in more difficult to influence countries than Mexico. It also had legitimate uses of long standing in the countries of the Andes and could not simply be declared illegal.[27]

As a national drug strategy became more formal in the mid- to late-1980s, the international dimension of the problem came further to the fore. When politicians proved incapable of delivering the goods in US cities by action at home, they turned to foreign targets. Action against drug use at home was in any case unpopular with the middle classes who not only often partook of some drugs but also obviously, if inconveniently, voted.

Thus, international action, where the blame could somehow be placed on the suppliers, proved more popular and more comfortable for US public and government alike. That action has been loud if not very impressive.

Washington has led the moves in the United Nations, in the OAS, and in many other venues, to smash the trade. Making policy on drugs something of a litmus test of loyalty to the new power in a unipolar world, the United States has expected anyone who wished to be considered its friend to play the game in fighting drugs.

Latin American Responses

The ways Latin American countries dealt with this *test* have been divergent and have reflected geopolitical, fiscal, and security realities of great variety. The Andean countries have attempted to convince the United States, sometimes by taking diplomatic initiatives of their own, that they are serious about dealing with the drug trade, and that they share a great deal of the US perception of the problem. Thus the Andean so-called *producing* states called for a summit at Cartagena to discuss the problem. And although this summit, like others, would bring to light the extent of the divergence in views between producing and consuming states, it did serve the purpose of showing some degree of seriousness on the part of key Latin capitals and thus reducing calls for more dramatic and unilateral action in and by the US.

Lima, La Paz, and Bogotá have, however, insisted that no real progress can be made unless the basic problem of crop substitution is addressed. That is, *campesinos* in the Andes must have another crop to which they can look for real profits if they are to abandon this lucrative virtual gold mine. And while this at first received lip service from the United States (and from the UN and other international agencies), when the bill for such a programme became clear, the developed countries, led by the US, scampered off quickly.

Given domestic pressures not to be seen as kowtowing to Washington, these governments have had to walk a tightrope between US demands for action and domestic pressures to go slow on the drug issue. For Colombia and Peru, this issue has been further complicated by the army's resolve to put beating insurgency first and fighting drugs second. Cooperation with the US has proven terribly difficult in this sense, as US efforts at home have appeared to many to prove that the country is only serious about *others* fighting (and often dying) in the drug war. The idea that the United States "will fight till the last Latin American" is widespread and, it must be admitted, the casualty figures do seem to bear this out to a considerable extent.[28]

In places where production is nonexistent or at least not so widespread, cooperation at any level with the United States has been even more long in coming. Argentina, Brazil, Chile, Paraguay, Uruguay, Venezuela, with this area today, as in other areas in the past, have used their relative distance and independence *vis-à-vis* Washington to resist calls for what they see as excessive energy deployed to this area. Such efforts as they have made more recently have tended to some degree to reflect their own domestic drug problems and agenda, but have in most cases also been clearly the results of wishing to please the United States.

Argentina is the most obvious case in point. While this country is no doubt suffering from quite a serious drug problem in its big cities, there is little doubt that most of its new-found keenness under President Menem to appear active in the struggle against the drugs trade has been part of what is called *el nuevo realismo* (the new realism). This is the series of policies of recent years whereby Argentina has jettisoned its tradition of distancing itself from the United States, and has instead done everything to gain legitimacy with that country. The despatch of forces to US-inspired operations in Iraq and Haiti, and to UN peacekeeping operations elsewhere is part of this realism. So are major efforts to adopt structural adjustment policies approved by Washington and efforts to strengthen the inter-American security system.[29]

Other countries are rather far behind, but none have actually dared to oppose the United States in this sphere now that successive presidents have considered the problem a matter of national security. Indeed, history has taught Latin American governments that if the US considers a problem to be a security issue, then they had better do so as well.

Closer to US borders and waters, no such freedom of action has been considered or indeed countenanced. The century-old relationship of dominance still in play has not allowed this. Even Cuba has had to go out of its way to show Washington that it is doing its best to deal with the problem of the island's airspace and territorial seas being used for transhipment in the direction of the US.[30] This is not to say the Cubans would not wish to help in any case, but merely to suggest that international factors have been at least as important as domestic ones in bringing about Cuba's active anti-drugs programme and its cooperative efforts with the Bahamas, Jamaica, and other regional states in this area. Needless to say, the US does not formally cooperate with Cuba on this matter, even though informally there is some degree of connection.[31]

Other Caribbean and Central American states have been even closer in their willingness to cooperate although these countries tend to have less of a problem of consumption in their own countries than do some of the South American republics. Many have accepted incorporation into various military and related schemes for interception of aircraft and boats bringing drugs north. US radars have been deployed in several countries ringing the Caribbean, producing a network of intelligence allowing improved interception. Military, police, and coast guard cooperation, shepherded by the United States, but including virtually all these states and the European territories still belonging to the United Kingdom, France, and the Netherlands in the region, is generally close, although not necessarily effective.[32]

Only among the Caribbean islands themselves can one say that there is a truly close similarity of government views with that of the United States on this issue. As mentioned, their small size, position on routes of importance to the *narcos*, their lack of significant military or even police forces, and their poverty make these islands obvious targets. The *narcos'* success in avoiding interception, joined to the suborning of officials, has made many of them virtual safe havens for these traffickers. The vast sums of money available to the trade's bosses ensure an ability to more than match the financial resources and even weaponry and equipment of these mini-states.[33]

The United States' cooperation is thus generally welcome among the governments of these countries. Such is their dependence on Washington, in any case, that they would no doubt wish to assist. But the only too real threats to sovereignty represented by the trade make the matter a pressing one for them as well.

Mexico has attempted to cooperate closely with the United States. For historical reasons, this is not easy and nowhere more difficult than in the area of military collaboration. Even so, some coast guard links have been established with the Mexican Navy, police, customs and excise cooperation is constant, and cross-border linkages abound between all manner of services connected with the anti-drug effort. The involvement of the armed forces in crop eradication and interception of the product has been exceptional with tens of thousands of troops made available for special operations and at least three thousand constantly on the job.[34]

Thus, a patchwork of reactions is joined to a patchwork of responses on the part of Latin American and Caribbean states. In general, cooperation has been poor and inefficient. Increases in "hauls" of intercepted drugs have done little more than prove that the trade is flourishing. While optimists at United States Southern Command in Panama have recently argued that the rate of interception may have reached as high as 20 percent at present, most observers tend to stick to the figure of a maximum success of 10 percent. Thus, in the real terms of dealing with the problem, there is clearly little success here.

The "Regional Response"

The inter-American system, and various subregions of it, have also reacted to the requirement for joint action in the anti-narcotic trade. At subregional levels, the Andean countries have attempted to adopt common procedures in the wake of their own summit on the problem leading to the Declaration of Quito of 1985, where they promised to join together in dealing with the issue. In Central America, the Esquipulas peace process always had an anti-drug element to it and formal arrangements of all kinds among the subregion's armed forces, police, and judiciaries have been established. Mercosur, the quadripartite effort at a common market under way among Argentina, Brazil, Paraguay, and Uruguay has adopted a largely common approach. And the Caribbean countries have gone a long way in doing the same.

For most activity in this area, the formal inter-American machinery has been left aside. The security system was ill-placed to respond to a nontraditional problem such as drugs and the difference in perspectives on the problem made this impossible in any case. Even the OAS itself was often considered too inefficient to be brought into the fray in any effective way. Nonetheless, in 1986, as part of a wide-ranging US effort to internationalize the responses to the threat, an OAS agency was created with the objective of coordinating an inter-American effort against the drug trade.

CICAD, the Inter-American Drug Abuse Control Commission after its Spanish acronym, was welcomed by the United States as the only hemispheric organization in the anti-drug business, but Washington has reservations about the tendency of the agency to see the control of demand as central to success. CICAD also feels that no effort which does not provide crop substitution possibilities has any chance of success.[35]

Much to the pleasure of the United States, however, CICAD has made some, if limited, real progress in standardizing judicial approaches to the problem, and in getting things going in the vital fields of money laundering and control of precursor chemicals.[36] Canada in particular places real hope in this multilateral instrument of the inter-American system as a whole.

If one excepts CICAD, however, it must be emphasized that there is little being done on an institutional inter-American level to date. It is, however, true that new and informal approaches are being tried. The most obvious of these is the hemispheric summit idea. In December 1994, the Miami Summit of the Americas (except Cuba) was held. At this occasion, Latin American, Caribbean, and North American leaders joined in (yet another) ringing denunciation of the drug trade and promised to do something serious about it in the future.

While this had happened at annual meetings of the OAS, and of course at a subregional level at the San Antonio, Cartagena, and other "summits," this was the first time it had taken place at the level of hemispheric heads of state and government. While it is too early to tell, the planned subsequent series of meetings among the hemisphere's defence, justice, finance, and other key ministers will probably address the drug question more closely. Whether anything of note will come of it, however, is a matter of conjecture at this time. It is troubling to think that once again the OAS mechanism is being shunted aside in favour of highly visible but not necessarily more effective, *ad hoc* arrangements.

Final Considerations

As in so many other spheres, so in drugs the main feature of inter-American cooperation appears to be the continuation of a tradition of ringing calls for joint action followed by desultory results. Despite President Clinton's promises of new approaches, Latin American states often feel that only they are expected to actually *do* something. As the new Congress in Washington is making clear, a shift to more US unilateral action, including direct action, is more than just a possibility.

The humiliating process of *certifying* Latin American states as having cooperated properly with the United States still goes on and is likely to be more acerbic in the future. The weight of the United States, as "the only game in town" for Latin America, is real. Access to international lending agencies passes through Washington. Access to US markets and investment passes through Washington. In many ways, even access to European and Asian sources of interest can *pass* through Washington.

As Augusto Varas, one of Latin America's foremost strategic thinkers, has put it, the region has passed from a relationship based on hegemony to one based on "coercive control."[37] Latin Americans are keenly aware that the world is breaking up into blocs, and to varying degrees they greatly fear this trend, especially if it leads to antagonistic groupings. They realize that, here again, despite some recent successes with their own subregional free trade arrangements, the US relationship may well be the only game in town. Under such circumstances, the relative power position of the US has been raised in a truly extraordinary fashion.

Cooperation on drugs has therefore not been an option for them. But, given nationalist and economic issues in their own domestic situations, they have had to walk the tightrope between the pressures coming from Washington to do something serious, and the necessity to avoid annoying their electorates closer to home. As new and largely fragile democracies, this circus act has proven all the more difficult.

Since Latin American public opinion is divided on the issue, and since cooperation with the United States is in several countries not well seen, such collaboration as there has been has not proven very impressive. In any case, the challenge is so great that only the most exceptional level of joint effort could be expected to yield any significant results.

Conclusions

The members of the inter-American community meet, discuss, and issue long and strident communiqués on the issue of drugs and how they intend to fight the illegal trafficking. This level of action is now over a decade old and shows no signs of levelling off. Indeed, with the summit *process* now an ongoing one, it will just increase.

Real action will, however, remain limited and ineffective unless a serious attempt is made to bridge the gap between two (and more) essentially different ways of perceiving the problem. The view of jointly targeting supply and demand, repeatedly stated in recent years, has not been translated into action. Latin American nations and the United States are all responsible for this. Key countries in the south do not really wish to do anything very serious about the trade because it is, frankly, very profitable in a region where little else is.

The US seems only to wish to do something if it does not seriously disturb voters at home.

Under such circumstances, one will probably continue to see the same pattern. That is, the US will use its considerable arsenal of financial, political and, on occasion, military resources to compel Latin American states to at least appear to be doing something noteworthy in this field. Some Latin American countries will do so voluntarily, at least to some extent, facing the problem themselves in their own streets. Others will bend their knees, but will do so to the minimum possible degree in order to retain US goodwill. Unfortunately, this smacks of power politics more than the cooperative measures jointly arrived at for the common good. One might well ask, in the inter-American context, "so what else is new"?

Notes

1. The most strident statement of this sort of thinking, much more widespread than many think, is found in Gretchen Small and Dennis Small (eds.), *El Complot*, (Mexico: Centro de Investigaciones Económicas, 1993); and more seriously, Edgardo Mercado Jarrín, *Un Sistema de seguridad y defensa sudamericano* (Lima, CONCYTEC, 1990).

2. For an analysis of Canadian policy, see Harold P. Klepak "The Impact of the International Narcotics Trade on Canada's Foreign and Security Policy," *International Journal*, 1 (Winter 1993/94): 66-92.

3. Alison Jamieson, "Global Drug Trafficking," *Conflict Studies*, 234 (1990): 4.

4. Ibán de Rementería, "Production: panorama mondial de cultures de drogue," in *La Géopolitique de la drogue*, ed. Guy Delbrel (Paris: La Découverte, 1991), pp. 40-49.

5. See the figures for Canada and the United States given in Victor Malarek, *Merchants of Misery: Inside Canada's Illegal Drug Scene* (Toronto: McClelland & Stewart, 1990), esp. pp. 18-28.

6. Andean Commission on Jurists, "New? Anti-Drug Policy," in *Drug Trafficking Update*, March 1994, pp. 4-5; and Stephen Fidler, "US Tries to Break the Vicious Circle," *Financial Times*, 5 November 1993, p. 7.

7. Michael Isikoff, "Administration seeks $200 million cut in Caribbean drug interdiction," *Washington Post*, 29 October 1993.

8. Marcel Niedergang, *Les Vingt Amériques latines* (Paris, 1969).

9. See the series of arguments brought forward in Diego García-Sayán (ed.), *Coca, cocaína y narcotráfico: laberinto en los Andes* (Lima: Comisión andina de juristas, 1989).

10. For the Caribbean, see the several excellent works by Ivelaw Lloyd Griffith, the most extensive of which is his *The Quest for Security in the Caribbean* (Armonk, NY: Sharpe, 1993), esp. pp. 243-75. For Central America, see Peter Smith, *Drug Policy in the Americas* (Boul-

der: Westview, 1992); and the more controversial, Peter Dale Scott and Jonathan Marshall, *Cocaine Politics: Drugs, Armies and the CIA in Central America* (Berkeley: University of California Press, 1991).

11. These issues are all addressed in Griffith, *The Quest for Security,* pp. 206-12.

12. Pierre Queuille, *L'Amérique latine, la Doctrine Monroe et le panaméricanisme* (Paris: Payot, 1969); and Hugo Luis Cargnelutti, *Seguridad interamericana: ¿un subsistema del sistema interamericanco?* (Buenos Aires: Círculo Militar, 1993), pp. 10-24.

13. María Eloísa Alvarez del Real (ed.), *Pensamientos de Bolívar* (Panamá: Editorial América, 1988); Margarita González, *Bolívar y la independencia de Cuba* (Bogotá: El Ancora, 1985); and Leopoldo Zea (ed.), *Bolívar y el mundo de los libertadores* (Mexico: UNAM, 1993).

14. For the Mexican experience in this regard, see Josefina Zoraida Vázquez and Lorenzo Meyer, *México frente a Estados Unidos: un ensayo histórico 1776-1988;* for Central America, Walter Lafeber, *Inevitable Revolutions* (New York: Norton, 1983); and Jan Knippers Black, *Sentinels of Empire* (New York: Greenwood, 1986).

15. See the interesting analysis on both the California case and wider issues of this kind in Angela Moyano Pahissa, *La Resistencia de las Californias a la invasión norteamericana 1846-1848* (Mexico: Consejo Nacional para la Cultura y las artes, 1992), esp. pp. 15-27.

16. In the Mexican case, see Lorenzo Meyer, *Su Majestad británica contra la revolución mexicana 1900-1950* (Mexico: Colegio de México, 1991), pp. 56-60.

17. This useful term of analysis, and its history and prospects, is developed in Arthur Whitaker, *The Western Hemisphere Idea* (Ithaca: Cornell University Press, 1954).

18. Germán Arciniegas, *O.E.A.: la suerte de una organización regional,* (Bogotá: Planeta, 1985).

19. See, for example, Francine Jácome (ed.), *Diversidad cultural y tensión regional: América latina y el Caribe* (Caracas: Nueva Sociedad, 1993).

20. Robert N. Burr, *By Reason or Force* (Berkeley: University of California Press, 1974).

21. David G. Haglund, *Latin America and the Transformation of US Strategic Thought* (Albuquerque: University of New Mexico Press, 1984).

22. See Harold P. Klepak, "The Inter-American Security System 1889-1989: Sometimes an Alliance, Sometimes Not," in *Canada and Latin American Security,* ed. Harold P. Klepak (Montreal: Méridien, 1993), pp. 63-85.

23. Héctor Faúndez-Ledezma, "The Inter-American System: Its Framework for Conflict Resolution," in *Latin America: Peace, Democratization and Economic Crisis*, ed. José Silva-Michelena (Tokyo: United Nations University, 1988), pp.168-86.

24. Heraldo Muñoz, "La agenda de seguridad en las políticas exteriores sudamericanas," in *Seguridad democrática regional: una concepción alternativa,* ed. Juan Somavía and José Miguel Insulza (Caracas: Nueva Sociedad, 1990), pp.161-88.

25. For two views of this process, see Bruce Michael Bagley, "Myths of Militarization: The Role of the Military in the War on Drugs in the Americas" (Miami: North-South Center, 1991); and Washington Office on Latin America, *Clear and Present Dangers* (Washington: WOLA, 1991).

26. Olivier Brouet, *Drogues et relations internationales* (Paris: Complexe, 1991), pp. 93-117.

27. Alejandro Camino, "Coca: del uso tradicional al narcotráfico," in *Coca, cocaina y narcotrafico: laberinto en los Andes*, ed. García-Sayán, pp. 91-108.

28. See the figures for Colombian and Mexican dead among the security forces in respectively, Colombia, Office of the President, "The Fight against the Drug Traffic in Colombia," March 1990; and Sergio Aguayo Quezada and Bruce M. Bagley (eds.), *En Busca de la seguridad perdida* (Mexico: Siglo Veintiuno, 1990).

29. Roberto Russell, "Argentina: ¿una nueva política exterior?" in *El Desafio de los '90: anuario de política exteriores latinoamericanas 1989-90*, ed. Hugo Muñoz (Caracas: Nueva Sociedad, 1990), pp. 15-29; and Jorge Lavopa et al., *El Rol de las Fuerzas armadas en el Mercosur* (Buenos Aires: Fraterna, 1992).

30. See the series of Cuban government publications on this issue, Jose Marti, "Cuba against International Drug Trafficking 1987," *Havana*, Editorial, 1987.

31. See Harold P. Klepak, "Medidas de confianza mutua y reacercamiento entre Cuba y los Estados Unidos," *Estudios internacionales*, 107:8 (October-December 1994): 605-17.

32. For the military side of this, see Harold P. Klepak "The Use of the Military against the Illegal Drug Trade," *Jane's Intelligence Review,* 4 (November 1992): 525-528.

33. Griffith, *The Quest for Security*, pp. 243-75.

34. See Maria Celia Toro, "México y Estados Unidos: el narcotráfico como amenaza a la seguridad nacional," in *En Busca de la seguridad perdida*, ed. Aguayo and Bagley, pp. 367-87.

35. James Rochlin, *Discovering the Americas: The Evolution of Canadian Foreign Policy towards Latin America* (Vancouver: University of British Columbia Press, 1994), pp. 223-4.

36. Andean Commission of Jurists, *Drug Trafficking Update*, July 1993.

37. Augusto Varas, "La Post-guerra fría, la seguridad hemisférica y la defensa nacional," in *Percepciones de amenaza y políticas de defensa en América latina*, ed. Rigoberto Cruz Johnson and Augusto Varas (Santiago: FLACSO, 1993), pp. 3-69, esp. 35-40.

Gordon Mace
Guy Gosselin
Louis Bélanger

Regional Cooperative Security in the Americas: The Case of Democratic Institutions

Introduction

The objective of this chapter is to evaluate the pertinence of regional co-operation in resolving problems linked to the development of national democratic institutions which constitute a threat to security and stability in the Americas. An examination of this question should improve, however modestly, our understanding of the nature of the relationship between two phenomena that have contributed to shaping the new post-Cold War international reality: the regionalization of the international system, and the broadening of the notion of security.[1] On one hand, the end of the bipolarity associated with the Cold War appears to favour the return of regionalism as one of the organizing principles of international relations. On the other hand, the notion of cooperative security has emerged. In its collective dimension, security has traditionally taken the form of military alliances destined to counter exterior threats. Cooperative security, for its part, refers to an interstate enterprise intended to reduce threats in every guise through multidimensional cooperation between participating countries. It targets threats that are not uniquely military in nature, and which may well originate inside participating states just as often, if not more frequently, than outside their borders.[2]

The increased political significance acquired by American regionalism since the mid-1980s has come, in part, from its association with the democratization movement which has swept the continent. Examples of this can be seen in the Protocol of Carthagena (1985), which linked peace and democracy, through the diplomatic mobilizations provoked by disruptions in the democratic process in Haiti (1991) and Peru (1992), and right up to the Plan of Action defined by the Summit of the Americas (1994), with its provisions for the reinforcement of democracy. Studies bearing on this new regional activism in the development of democratic institutions and human rights have focused primarily on OAS action, underlining its potential and, especially, its limitations.[3] For our part, we will attempt to evaluate the appropriateness of regional cooperative security action in this area from a synthetic perspective on American regionalism that goes beyond a strictly institutional analysis. The analysis has a double focus. The first refers to the socio-political situation of states, and calls for a description of the nature and extent of the threat to regional security posed by obstacles to democratization and respect for human rights in the Americas. The second refers to regional action, and leads to an analysis of the form that regional cooperation has taken to meet the aforementioned threat within the framework of the inter-American dynamic.

The Shape of the Threat to Democracy and Regional Stability in the Americas

Democratic regimes are not necessarily less belligerent. Nonetheless, as Raymond Aron suggests, they are better diplomatic partners: "Only those regimes whose leaders are virtually free in the short term from the influence of public opinion can, from one minute to the next, burn what they had once adored and adore what they had once burned without the people being profoundly disturbed, some no longer believing in propaganda, others believing in the truth of the moment, still others ready to place their confidence in the excessive cunning of their masters."[4]

Despite the establishment of democratic regimes throughout the region major problems that restrict the extent of political democratization remain. Above and beyond the simple organization of free and fair elections, these include limited civil control over the military, incomplete political reforms, and low respect for human rights and the struggle against poverty. These elements allow us to trace a portrait of the threat to regional stability and provide a general idea of the collective task confronting the states of the region.

Limited Civil Control Over the Military

The insufficient control exercised by civil authorities over the military threatens peace and security in the region.[5] This problem is most significant in countries where guerrilla and terrorist activities are ongoing or have only recently come to an end, situations justifying, or at least favouring, the maintenance of considerable military influence over civil authorities. This is most notable in Nicaragua, El Salvador, Colombia, Peru, and, potentially Mexico. In this last case, the Zapatista National Liberation Army (ZNLA) rebellion is recent (January 1994), and military influence seems less of an issue than the PRI monopoly over the state. Nonetheless, Mexico is a major regional power[6] that appeared sufficiently stable to participate in a free trade agreement with the United States and Canada. The impact of the Mexican situation on regional stability could thus be important. The same can be said for Colombia and Peru, medium powers where guerrilla activity is linked to drug trafficking. The drug trade primarily concerns Colombia and US policy toward drug-producing countries, whereas the Peruvian situation is complicated by the 1992 civil coup (*autogolpe*) and subsequent fears of repercussions for other political regimes and, ultimately, for regional security.

Despite the absence of centres of active violence, the reemergence of democratic regimes that began in the 1980s has proven to be relatively slow and problem-ridden in several other countries. In effect, old putschist traditions in countries such as Paraguay, Bolivia, and Argentina are often paralleled by constitutional provisions which give military authorities a say in politics, as is the case in Brazil, Chile, or Ecuador.[7] It is in Brazil, Latin America's foremost power, that the situation is the most worrisome for regional stability. There, the military has conserved tutelary power,[8] even though the attitude of the military authorities during the period when allegations of corruption forced the resignation and replacement of President Collor by Vice-President Franco suggests that their power is waning. Likewise, the subordination of military to civil authorities appears as yet incomplete in two other important regional powers, Argentina and Chile. Venezuela, too, a major oil producer with no recent tradition of military government, has provoked concerns over regional stability in the wake of two attempted military coups, one in 1989 and one in 1992.

In short, subordination of the military to civil authority is not yet complete throughout the region. Military power still escapes political control even in some of the democratic regimes most important for regional equilibrium, such as Brazil, Peru, and Colombia.

Incomplete Political Reforms and Lack of Respect for Human Rights

A second category of problems also appears to threaten regional stability because it affects values and practices contributing to the implantation of democracy. A solid democratic regime finds expression in strong public institutions, the integration of all political forces into political life, the struggle against corruption, respect for human rights, and punishment of human rights violations when committed. Presently, however, new democratic regimes remain fragile because the reforms that launched the democratization process are incomplete and often difficult to pursue. This fragility can be a source of instability.

Political reforms, albeit still incomplete, are progressing quite normally in two important countries, Argentina and Chile, as well as in others like Nicaragua and El Salvador. In contrast, the situation in the two principal regional powers appears to be essentially blocked. In Brazil, reforms have been left hanging, and have produced chronic failure at the government level. As for Mexico, change appears imperceptible, particularly with regards to the question of free and fair elections and the alternation of power, as the ZNLA rebellion so clearly indicated. Although both Brazil in 1992, and Venezuela in 1993, were able to replace presidents accused of corruption without placing their democratic regimes in jeopardy, both regimes were shaken by the bids for consolidation of power (autogolpe) undertaken by Presidents Fujimori in Peru and Serrano in Guatemala during the same period (1992-93). Serious problems thus remain within countries of pivotal importance for regional equilibrium.

An examination of the issue of human rights completes this general overview of the evolution of political reforms. A democratic regime does not necessarily guarantee complete respect of human rights, but the human rights situation is a good indicator of democratic health. On one hand, several countries in the region were obliged to assume the legacy of massive human rights violations attributed to former military regimes in pursuing the transition to democracy. In most instances, to use Garreton's terms,[9] a policy of amnesty and impunity prevailed, accompanied by occasional efforts to establish guilt and administer justice for appearance's sake. This was the case, for example, in Argentina, Brazil, Chile, Guatemala, Nicaragua, and El Salvador.

On the other hand, Table 1 indicates that, whereas the overall human rights situation in Latin America has improved over the longer term (1975-90), the assessment is much less conclusive in the specific area of civil rights.[10] In 1990, the last year of the period, respect for civil rights effectively deteriorated in several important countries, particularly those, like Colombia and Peru, that face ongoing guerrilla and terrorist activities. As for Mexico, where guerrilla activity is recent, it is the lack of progress that stands out. In addition, the civil rights situation also deteriorated or stagnated in several other nations, most notably in Brazil, Venezuela, and Argentina.

In sum, the consolidation of democratic regimes appears to be an arduous task. Although the situation varies from one country to another, certain states still face grave problems, including Brazil and Mexico, the two most important. Rights violations are of major significance in Mexico and notable in Brazil. Corruption is widespread and institutional reforms unsatisfactory in both countries. The situation prevailing in these two nations exercises an important influence on regional stability.

TABLE ONE: CIVIL AND POLITICAL RIGHTS IN THE AMERICAS

	1975 PR[2]	1975 CR[3]	1980 PR	1980 CR	1985 PR	1985 CR	1990 PR	1990 CR
Argentina	2	4	6	5	2	2	1	3
Bolivia	6	5	7	5	2	3	2	3
Brazil	4	5	4	3	3	2	2	3
Canada	1	1	1	1	1	1	1	1
Chile	7	5	6	5	6	5	2	2
Colombia	2	3	2	3	2	3	3	4
Costa Rica	1	1	1	1	1	1	1	1
Cuba	7	7	6	6	6	6	7	7
Dom. Rep.	4	2	2	3	1	3	2	3
Ecuador	7	4	2	2	2	3	2	2
El Salvador	2	3	6	4	2	4	3	4
Guatemala	4	3	5	6	4	4	3	4
Haiti	6	6	6	6	7	6	4	4
Honduras	6	3	4	3	2	3	2	3
Mexico	4	3	3	4	4	4	4	4
Nicaragua	5	4	5	5	5	5	3	3
Panama	7	6	4	4	6	3	4	2
Paraguay	5	5	5	5	5	5	4	3
Peru	6	4	2	3	2	3	3	4
U.S.A.	1	1	1	1	1	1	1	1
Uruguay	5	5	5	5	2	2	1	2
Venezuela	2	2	1	2	1	2	1	3

Notes:

[1] On a scale of 1 to 7, 1 corresponds to a situation where rights are most respected, and 7 to a situation where they are least respected.

[2] The score for *political rights* is determined by the degree to which a given country satisfies the following requirements: (a) leaders are chosen in decisions made on the basis of an open voting process, (b) significant opposition is allowed to compete in this process, (c) there are multiple political parties and candidates not selected by the government, (d) polling and counting of votes is conducted without coercion or fraud, (e) that a significant share of political power is exercised by elected representatives, (f) all regions, even the most remote, are included in the political process, and (g) the country is free of foreign or military control or influence. Countries assigned a rank of 1 most closely satisfy these requirements and those assigned a rank of 7 most seriously violate them.

[3] The score for *civil rights* is determined by the degree of liberty a given country grants its news media and individual citizens, primarily as it applies to political expression. The survey looks at censorship applied to the press or radio. It also assesses the rights granted any individual to openly express ideas, to belong to an organization free of government supervision, and the individual's right to a free trial, i.e., the degree to which the judiciary is independent of administrative control. Also important is the number of political prisoners held in a country, the use of torture or brutality, and the degree to which the state security forces respect individual rights. Countries assigned the rank of 1 grant the greatest degree of civil liberties and those assigned the rank of 7 most seriously violate them.

Source: *Statistical Abstract of Latin America* (1993), p. 275; Freedom House, *Freedom at Issue* 22:1 (January/February 1991).

The Struggle Against Poverty

In the eyes of numerous observers,

> the new Latin American democratic regimes are being built atop social powder kegs, and often as ramparts against them. The difference between socioeconomic exclusion experienced under dictatorship and exclusion dressed up in democratic virtues is not always very clear to its victims.[11]

The depth and extent of poverty undermine the foundations of democratic regimes and are an important source of fragility, as the expression "social powder keg" aptly suggests.

It is possible, first of all, to identify the contours of poverty in several important countries by combining the UNDP human development index (HDI) with fragmentary UNDP data on the distribution of wealth.[12] According to this index, the two largest Latin American nations, Brazil and Mexico, occupy a median position. Their relative weakness in this regard is also apparent in partial data on the portion of wealth possessed by the 40 percent of poorest households. While this portion varies between 7 percent and 15 percent for Latin American countries as a whole, the figure is 7 percent in Brazil, and 10 percent in Mexico. These percentages are inferior to those recorded for countries like Argentina, Bolivia, Colombia, Costa Rica, El Salvador, and Guatemala.[13] In addition, prevailing liberal economic policies tend to accentuate inequalities and challenge social policy.[14]

Secondly, it is important to try to draw out perspectives on the evolution of this situation of incomplete and unequal development. Given that wealth must increase if it is to be redistributed, the weight of national debt is a good indicator of prospects for growth of wealth in the medium term. Table 2 indicates the extent and evolution of the debt in Latin American countries between 1980 and 1992. Political conditions favourable to economic reform must also be taken into account. On this point, Williamson and Haggard have concluded that determined leadership and solid political support within parliament are determining factors in the success of any socio-economic reform programme.[15]

Consequently, it can be argued that perspectives for growth and economic reform appear good in Argentina, Chile, and Peru, where the burden of debt is either low, rapidly declining or moderate, and where political leadership seems strong, and parliamentary support solid. The outlook is less encouraging in Brazil or Venezuela, and probably in Mexico as well. Burdened with a slowly decreasing but still sizeable debt, Brazil is saddled with a political leadership lacking in assurance, and political institutions that tend to hinder more than

TABLE 2: DEBT LEVELS (MILLIONS $US) AND PROPORTION OF GDP FOR THE PRINCIPAL COUNTRIES IN THE AMERICAS, 1980-1992

	1980	%	1985	%	1990	%	1991	%	1992	%
Argentina	27157	35.6	50946	61.1	62233	46.0	65397	35.6	67569	30.1
Bolivia	2702	93.4	4805	176.6	4278	100.5	4077	85.3	4243	83.6
Brazil	71012	31.3	106121	50.3	116417	24.9	117350	29.7	121110	31.3
Chile	12081	45.5	20384	141.7	19227	67.9	17947	55.9	19360	49.28
Colombia	6941	20.9	14245	42.6	17232	45.1	17338	43.4	17204	36.7
Costa Rica	2744	59.7	4401	120.8	3772	69.1	4053	74.0	3965	63.2
Dom. Rep.	2002	31.2	3502	84.0	4387	65.2	4494	66.0	4649	61.9
Ecuador	5997	53.8	8703	77.4	12109	122.7	12468	113.8	12280	102.1
El Salvador	911	26.2	1845	47.0	2137	40.3	2174	37.4	2131	33.4
Guatemala	1166	14.9	2656	27.9	2838	38.0	2823	30.6	2749	26.8
Haiti	302.4	20.9	717.4	36.0	883.8	36.6	747.1	28.8	772.8	..
Honduras	1472	60.6	2729	78.5	3698	135.0	3360	119.0	3573	114.2
Mexico	57378	30.5	96867	55.2	105958	44.8	115291	41.2	113378	35.2
Nicaragua	2192	103.1	5821	220.3	10692	793.8	106629	825.2	11126	822.3
Panama	2975	87.5	4759	105.1	6679	147.9	6733	129.0	6485	111.8
Paraguay	954	20.7	1817	57.98	2128	40.77	2177	34.94	1747	27.8
Peru	9386	47.6	12884	86.2	20268	88.7	20720	98.2	20297	95.4
Uruguay	1660	17.0	3919	89.7	4335	54.0	4649	48.6	5253	46.8
Venezuela	29344	42.1	35334	59.1	33170	70.3	34046	65.0	37193	62.5

Source: World Bank, *World Debt Tables 1993-1994* (Washington, DC: World Bank, 1993).

support change. Venezuela, for its part, must deal with a debt which, although moderate, remains largely undiminished, along with a leadership that appears rather weak in the face of a political situation nearing the crisis point. As for Mexico, the debt load is undoubtedly light, but the Mexican leadership and its political support appear more fragile than previously as the country confronts a major financial crisis. The "social powder keg" thus appears to be more of a threat in these three countries, as well as in Colombia where the situation is highly specific.

The Shape of the Threat to Democracy

The three types of problem examined above limit the extent of democratization in several Latin American countries and maintain political regimes in a state of fragility. This situation constitutes a threat to stability and security in the region because democratic government authority remains limited in the face of internal problems requiring firm decisions on urgent solutions. The crises of political regimes and internal political upheaval provoked by pressure from national political forces have repercussions on other countries and on relations between countries, as international reactions to the recent *coups de force* in Peru, Guatemala, and Haiti demonstrated.

The threat to regional stability is proportional to the position which countries experiencing difficulties in democratic development occupy in the hierarchy of power (see Table 3). It is for this reason that internal developments in Brazil and Mexico give rise to the most concern. The two major regional powers are experiencing difficulties in their pursuit of political reforms and, with weak HDIs, seem less able than other important countries to significantly reduce poverty. Furthermore, civil control over the military is still incomplete in Brazil, whereas respect for human rights remains at a low level in Mexico. The mid-range regional powers of Peru and Colombia are also cause for concern due to the importance of drug traffickers, limited respect for human rights and the influence of the military in the face of guerrilla activity. The Peruvian *autogolpe* again produced a rather authoritarian civil regime in a country with a low HDI. Finally, Venezuela, Latin America's third power, has drawn attention with its two attempted *coup d'états*, justified by military rebels on grounds of corruption and growing social inequality.

The Development of Cooperative Security in the Americas

After having traced the shape of the threat to regional security, we will now examine the manifestations of cooperative security initiated in the Americas in response to that threat. To do so, we will first look at the system of norms, principles, and rules established for the protection of democracy and human rights,[16] and then study manifestations of support for democracy undertaken on the basis of this system. We will conclude by evaluating the role of cooperative security initiatives, particularly those piloted by the Organization of American States (OAS), in supporting and protecting democratic institutions in the Americas.

To begin, however, it should be recalled that what Bloomfield[17] has termed the "OAS regime for the defence of democracy" was virtually nonexistent until the mid-1980s. The commitment to the respect and promotion of democracy

TABLE 3: THE SHAPE OF THE THREAT: DEMOCRACY, HUMAN RIGHTS AND POWER

Country		Power	Threat		
		Aggregated Index		Civil and Pol	
Name	Rank	1986-1989[1]	Characteristics 1988-1994	Rights[2] 1990[3]	HDI
United States	1	1000.00		1.0	0.976
Canada	2	348.35		1.0	0.982
Brazil	3	233.71		2.5	0.730
Mexico	4	170.99	Guerrilla warfare (active since 1994)	4.0	0.805
Venezuela	5	132.67	Attempted coup d'état. (1989 + 1992) Drug traffickers	2.0	0.824
Argentina	6	129.55			
Colombia	7	94.02	Drug traffickers and active guerrilla warfare	2.0	0.832
Peru	8	85.90	Disruption of the democratic process (April 1992). Drug traffickers. Active guerrilla warfare	3.5	0.592
Chile	9	79.76	Authoritarian regime until December 1989	2.0	0.864
Uruguay	10	71.08		1.5	0.881
Ecuador	11	70.84		2.0	0.646
Panama	12	61.15	Authoritarian regime until December 1989. Drug traffickers	3.0	0.738
Nicaragua	13	57.64	Authoritarian regime until February 1990. Guerrillawarfare ending in 1990	3.0	0.500
Costa Rica	14	57.27		1.0	0.852
Guatemala	15	56.99	Attempted coup d'état (May 1993). Active guerrilla warfare	3.5	0.489
Bolivia	16	51.36	Drug traffickers	2.5	0.398
Paraguay	17	45.08	Authoritarian regime until February 1989, Drug traffickers	3.5	0.641
El Salvador	18	44.27	Guerrilla warfare: Military activities ceased in January 1993	3.5	0.503
Dominican Rep.	19	43.02		2.5	0.586
Honduras	20	39.70		2.5	0.472
Haiti	21	31.09	Coup d'état (June 1988, January 1991, September 1991). Authoritarian regime until Oct. 1994	4.0	0.275

Notes:
[1]See Gordon Mace, Louis Bélanger, Jean-Philippe Thérien, "Regionalism in the Americas and the Hierarchy of Power," *Journal of Interamerican Studies and World Affairs,* 35:2 (Summer 1993):115-57.

[2]Average of civil and political rights results combined. Freedom House, *Freedom at Issue,* 22:1 (January/February 1991).

[3]UNDP, *Rapport mondial sur le développement humain* (Paris: Economica, 1990 and 1993).

was essentially established in the OAS Charter[18] and in the 1969 American Convention on Human Rights.[19] However, the impact of the relevant articles was weakened by the importance accorded in equal measure to the respect of the principles of sovereignty and nonintervention on which all OAS action was also based.

Early difficulties in undertaking regional action in favour of democracy and human rights in the Americas can thus be explained by the institutional weakness of the OAS, as well as by the context of a period dominated by the Cold War, the bipolarity of the international system, the asymmetrical distribution of power between the United States and other countries of the region and the unilateralism characterizing Washington's policy on Latin America. In these conditions, it is not surprising that most Latin American governments considered the OAS to be a simple instrument of the United States, depriving it, by the same token, of much of its legitimacy as a vehicle for cooperative security.[20]

In the same way that the context of the 1945-80 period influenced inter-American cooperation at the time, the international environment of the 1980s played an important role in the evolution of values and mentalities which allowed for the emergence of a regional initiative for the promotion of representative democracy and human rights. The strategic element central to this change was undoubtedly the disappearance of the communist world, the implosion of the Soviet bloc and the subsequent elimination of an alternative to American domination that certain governments of the region had turned to in the past.

However, the most fundamental impact may have come from the external debt crisis and the world economic crisis of the early 1980s. The external debt crisis meant that the majority of Latin American governments no longer had sufficient financial resources for extensive state intervention, and were forced to envisage a new model of economic development. The global financial crisis revealed, for its part, that the industrialized countries themselves no longer had the same financial room for manoeuvre as it previously had. In consequence, support for Latin American economic development would no longer come from international public financial institutions, but rather from the private sector, much more sensitive to political stability, and perhaps to some form of "normality" in democratic practices.[21]

In the context of emerging economic blocs, the fear of exclusion, of a certain "Africanization" of Latin America, played a non-negligible role in spurring the appearance of new values and ways of doing things in the region. These changes in culture and practice created the conditions necessary to the emergence of new forms of inter-American cooperation concerning democratic institutions.

The Doctrine

The regional strategy for the defence of democracy in the Americas was thus truly put in place beginning in 1985. It was in that year that OAS member states adopted the Protocol of Carthagena, which was essentially an amendment to the charter of the organization establishing the promotion and consolidation of democracy as fundamental principles of OAS operations.

Five years later, and at Canada's initiative, the OAS Secretary-General created the Unit for the Promotion of Democracy. The mandate established for the unit by the OAS Permanent Council set out three priorities: technical assistance for the organization of elections; support for the legislative process; and support for education in democratic practices.[22] Although very active since its creation, and particularly well-known for its election supervision missions, the Unit for the Promotion of Democracy has nonetheless suffered from organizational difficulties and a lack of resources.[23] The support obtained at the Summit of the Americas in December 1994 should, however, translate into additional resources that will allow the unit to expand and extend its action on behalf of local democracy through increased links with community organizations and improved coordination with other OAS agencies.[24]

At the third plenary session of the XXIst regular meeting of the OAS held in Santiago, Chile in June 1991, the participating governments adopted the Declaration of Santiago reaffirming their firm commitment to the support and promotion of representative democracy and human rights. Although the mention of "respect for the principles of self-determination and non-intervention" still represents a constraint on collective action, the adoption of Resolution 1080 nonetheless constitutes the first significant challenge to the traditional conception of sovereignty in the regional juridical order. For this reason, its adoption was difficult, with several of the more conservative countries like Mexico rallying only reluctantly to the majority position.[25] Under the terms of the resolution, the Secretary-General is now obliged to call a meeting of the OAS Permanent Council to determine the measures to be taken in the case of a disruption in the normal democratic process within a member state. Although insignificant in appearance, Resolution 1080 is nonetheless important given that it requires foreign ministers to meet. Once together, it is difficult for them to avoid taking action.[26]

Another important step in implementing a regional strategy for the defence of democracy was the adoption of the Protocol of Washington in December 1992. Under the terms of the Protocol, an OAS member state whose democratic government has been overthrown by force can be suspended after a vote by two-thirds of member countries.[27] Combined with Resolution 1080, the adoption of the Protocol of Washington marks an important moment in the evolution of the OAS: for the first time in the history of the organization, collective action was envisaged in response to an event of an internal nature, the interruption of a democratic government.[28] Unfortunately, however, the Protocol has only been ratified by three countries to date: Argentina, Canada, and El Salvador.[29]

The laying of the doctrinal foundations of regional support for democracy and human rights was recently completed by the Declaration of Managua and by the Summit of the Americas held in Miami in December 1994. Adopted at the June 1993 OAS General Assembly in Managua, the former committed member states to consolidating democratic structures in all countries of the region, as well as to encouraging the development of a "democratic culture" throughout the Americas. The declaration also recognized the fundamental link between the development of democracy and the eradication of extreme poverty, a connection rarely referred to in the past by members of the OAS. The importance of economic development in consolidating democracy has been given concrete recognition with the decision to create an Inter-American Council for Integral Development (CIDI) destined to replace the Inter-American Economic and Social Council (CIES), and the Inter-American Council for Education, Science and Culture (CIECC).[30]

The Summit of the Americas, for its part, confirmed commitments made since 1985. The Declaration of Principles effectively reaffirms the clear resolve of OAS member states to "preserve and strengthen our democratic systems for the benefit of all people of the Hemisphere." It also reiterates the inseparability of democracy and development.[31]

Thus, even if constraints on member states are not yet complete, it is difficult to deny the establishment from 1985 onward of an environment favourable to representative democratic institutions in the Americas. In effect, the Protocol of Washington and Resolution 1080 constitute serious breaches of the once immutable principles of sovereignty, territorial inviolability, and nonintervention. Let us now examine what this has meant in terms of concrete action.

Practice

It was Resolution 1080 which formed the juridical foundation for OAS intervention in three cases where democracy was disrupted: in Guatemala, Peru, and Haiti. In Guatemala, Jorge Serrano Elias was elected president in January 1991 in elections held under the scrutiny of OAS observers. Having campaigned as the candidate of national reconciliation, Serrano immediately took steps toward meeting his campaign commitments by presenting a Plan for Total Peace. An agreement was reached in April in Mexico City with the Guatemalan National Revolutionary Union.[32] However, the process later ran into problems over respect for human rights and increasing military reticence with regard to demilitarization.

At the beginning of May 1993, the peace process appeared completely deadlocked. President Serrano, invoking corruption within the state apparatus, then attempted a civil *coup d'état* by suspending the Constitution and dissolving Parliament and the Supreme Court. One week later, international pressure forced the army to depose the president, who subsequently left for Panama.

Certain observers consider OAS action in Guatemala a success, given that it allowed a rapid and orderly resolution of the crisis.[33] It is true that the condemnation of the civil coup and the immediate dispatch of an OAS delegation to Guatemala City clearly demonstrated the existence of a real regional will to support democracy. But the OAS intervention alone would perhaps not have brought the crisis to such rapid resolution had it not also been for the unilateral suspension of American and German aid, and the birth of an important coalition of social forces within Guatemala itself.

Peru was also the theatre of a civil *coup d'état* on 13 April, 1992. Confronted with serious economic difficulties and the struggle against guerrilla forces and drug producers, President Fujimori dissolved Congress and suspended the Constitution. His position strengthened by support from the military, the chief-of-state also announced several months later that Peru was withdrawing from the Inter-American Convention on Human Rights signed in 1969.

The OAS response was relatively rapid. In conformity with Resolution 1080, the foreign ministers of member states met in Washington, to call for a return to representative democracy and to recommend the dispatch of a mediation mission. They also demanded that the Peruvian government commit itself to respecting human rights, and agreed to maintain the *ad hoc* group in order to monitor the evolution of the Peruvian crisis. Several governments in the region also manifested their disapproval with measures ranging from the suspension of aid to the suspension, in the case of Venezuela and Panama, of diplomatic relations. For its part, the Rio Group immediately expelled Peru from its ranks.[34]

The combined pressure of the OAS, regional groups, and OAS member states — the United States included — finally forced Fujimori to yield. At the OAS meeting in Nassau, he promised the return of democracy to Peru, announcing that elections for a Congress charged with elaborating a new Constitution would be held shortly. These commitments were honoured during the course of 1993, and President Fujimori was reelected in the Spring of 1995.

Opinions as to the success of the OAS intervention in Peru are mixed. Some consider that the operation was successful, but that the OAS could have demanded further concessions from the Peruvian president. However, the reluctance of several neighbouring countries to further constrain political authorities struggling with enormous internal problems and enjoying considerable popular support made it difficult to go any further.[35] In contrast, others are more severe, and conclude that OAS action was, in sum, relatively inefficient.[36]

To evaluate the true impact of the OAS intervention, it is necessary to take into account the general context of the intervention. In theory, the OAS could have demanded much more of President Fujimori. However, such demands would have undoubtedly been largely impractical given the weakness of Peruvian democratic tradition, the scope of internal problems, persistent and wide-ranging popular support for the president, and the attitude of several neighbouring countries reluctant to support tougher measures that they feared might have consequences in their own backyards. It is important, then, to consider the regional response to the Peruvian case as a further infringement on the traditional principle of nonintervention and, consequently, as a significant step toward the establishment of a process of regional collective action for the protection of democratic institutions in the Americas.

The regional cooperative security response to the Haitian situation was the first, chronologically speaking, to be undertaken within the framework of Resolution 1080. The initial reaction of the OAS to the Haitian *coup d'état* of 30 September 1991 was surprisingly rapid and unusually firm in comparison to traditional OAS behaviour. The immediate OAS Permanent Council reaction to the coup was the adoption of Resolution 567, which condemned the overthrow of the democratically elected government, and demanded the reinstatement of the ousted president. One week later, the OAS urged its members to freeze Haitian assets within their borders and to impose a trade embargo.

However, the failure of the first OAS mission to Haiti in September 1992 quickly revealed the constraints imposed upon the organization in its reaction to the Haitian crisis by the opposition of certain member states (including Brazil, Mexico, Peru, and Uruguay) to any armed intervention. Only UN action undertaken at the formal request of President Aristide and the OAS Secretary-General allowed some progress to be made toward resolving the deadlock. It was the UN-imposed embargo on arms, oil, and capital that made the July 1993 Governor's Island Agreement possible, although the accord went unheeded despite the efforts of UN and OAS negotiator Dante Caputo.[37]

The repeated failures of multilateral UN-OAS action forced the UN Security Council to declare a total embargo on Haiti in May 1994. Then, on 1 August, the Security Council went one step further with the adoption of Resolution 940,[38] creating the multinational force that was deployed in mid-September 1994.

The Haitian crisis was resolved with minimal loss of life, but revealed all of the limitations of a collective regional response in support of democracy in the area. Indeed, an end to the crisis only became possible when the Americans decided, after several months of hesitation, to intervene militarily under the terms of Resolution 940 in order to reinstate President Aristide. It should be remembered, however, that Brazil abstained from the Security Council vote. Mexico and Uruguay also expressed reservations as to the appropriateness of an armed intervention, whereas Chile, Colombia, Ecuador, Peru, and Mexico refused to participate in the multinational force. Several days after the intervention, most of these same countries were complaining about the American presence in Haiti.

Although certain journalists have described the OAS record in the three cases reviewed above as a victory (Guatemala), a draw (Peru), and a loss (Haiti), analysts' opinions are much less definitive. Most unhesitatingly recognize that the OAS response to the Haitian crisis was not a success. As for Guatemala and Peru, although the return to democracy was relatively swift in both cases, resolution of the crises cannot be attributed exclusively to OAS action. In the following pages, we will examine what this means for cooperative security and support for democracy in the Americas.

In the field of democratic institutions, inter-American cooperation undeniably depends on the establishment of what Bloomfield has called "Defence-of-Democracy Regime." Such a regime assumes a certain degree of consensus with regard to values, regulations, and behaviour. Moreover, it is difficult to conceive that the principal forum for the development of such a regime in the

Americas be anything other than the OAS. What do regional events of recent years have to teach us in this regard?

First of all, it is difficult to deny the emergence within the OAS itself of a truly regional initiative for the promotion and support of representative democracy, at least at the doctrinal level. From the Protocol of Carthagena (1985) to the Summit of the Americas (December 1994), we have effectively witnessed the emergence of a regional consensus with regard to the values and certain practices of representative democracy. The key documents that, taken together, embody this crucial stage in the evolution of the OAS are probably the Declaration of Santiago (1991), Resolution 1080 (1991) and the Protocol of Washington (1992). Their contents represent a highly significant breach both in the traditional regional juridical order and in the conscience of regional actors. The documents corrected a certain imbalance by reducing the weight accorded by the OAS to the previously immutable principles of sovereignty, territorial inviolability and nonintervention. Political circumstances within member states were henceforth declared to be a pretext for collective action[39] as the OAS saw its obligation to intervene in support of democracy recognized.

The phenomenon is all the more significant because it now extends beyond the confines of the OAS. Indeed, most governments in the region are prepared to support the democratization process in neighbouring countries, and several have had occasion to clearly express that support over the past 15 years with gestures ranging from condemnation to the breaking off or suspension of diplomatic relations. Furthermore, subregional forums have added their voices to that of the OAS in support of democracy, as was the case when countries of the Rio Group reiterated their commitment to democracy in the Americas in the Declaration of Buenos Aires (1992).

If support for democracy and human rights seems to have made notable progress in the region, at least as far as doctrine is concerned, what is the situation in practice? Opinion is divided over this question, and answers often depend upon the significance accorded to the terms "success or failure."

Over the past six years, it would appear that sufficient consensus has emerged in the Americas to give the OAS the legitimacy necessary to take charge of cooperative security operations not involving situations where democratic institutions are in crisis. With the creation of the Unit for the Promotion of Democracy the OAS effectively gave itself a permanent instrument for electoral supervision and assistance. The unit also participated in processes of national reconciliation in Nicaragua and Surinam. However, additional financial and organizational efforts on the part of member states are necessary if the Unit for the Promotion of Democracy and the Inter-American Human Rights

Commission and Court are to become the principal structures of OAS intervention in cooperative security operations involving the promotion of democratic practices, prevention of threats to democratic institutions, and peaceful resolution of disagreements.

There also exists a consensus that allows the OAS to carry out certain cooperative security operations in crisis situations. By adopting Resolution 1080, member states effectively endowed the OAS with an important instrument for placing actions undermining democratic institutions squarely on the regional agenda. In addition, there is unanimous support for OAS intervention in the area of mediation.

The imposition of sanctions, however, raises many more difficult questions from the point of view of successful cooperative security in the Americas, given that OAS-decreed sanctions are nonbinding on countries outside the region. Furthermore, as the Haitian case demonstrated, the OAS does not have the means to enforce respect for sanctions amongst its own members.[40]

Armed intervention, for its part, is even more problematic given the numerous constraints involved. Until very recently, all OAS actions were based on the fundamental principles of state sovereignty and noninterference in the internal affairs of a member country. These principles have always had the strong support of Latin American countries as a result of both the asymmetrical distribution of power between the United States and the region and a history of US-Latin American relations frequently marked by unilateral interventionism on the part of Washington.

Despite what some observers consider a new US approach more favourable to solving certain regional problems multilaterally,[41] there still exists sufficient heterogeneity of interests, culture and points of view to make the establishment of any consensus on measures such as multilateral armed intervention very difficult. And this does not even take into account other constraints of a financial or organizational nature.

That said, the results of this study do show that there has been significant progress toward the development of a regional initiative for the promotion and support of representative democracy in the Americas. Member states must, nonetheless, demonstrate stronger political will, notably by providing the OAS with greater financial and organizational support. The arrival of Canada and the Anglo-Caribbean nations could prove to be a positive factor in this respect.

Under present conditions, however, it is premature to conclude that cooperative security in the Americas could go so far as to include military sanctions and armed intervention. MacFarlane and Weiss[42] are correct in arguing that a division of labour between the UN and the OAS is preferable at this stage, and that the UN should be favoured when cooperative security for the protection of democratic institutions requires such drastic measures as military sanctions or armed intervention.[43]

Conclusion

Using this to infer that the region of the Americas does not offer the political and institutional foundations necessary to the implementation of a cooperative security initiative is a step we are not prepared to take. Recent experience shows that the dilemma that confronts the pursuit of diplomatic initiatives in favour of democracy in the region is the following. There is a clear risk in engaging the still fragile capital of legitimacy of the Pan American system in democratic salvage operations whose chances of success within a strictly regional framework are limited. At the same time, the defence of democracy appears to be an essential normative element of the new American regionalism, the consolidation of which can be seen as a guarantee of sorts for the maintenance and development of democratic momentum in the hemisphere. In other words, regionalization and democratization are linked in a fragile relationship of interdependence. Any action that might sacrifice one to the short-term advantage of the other could well endanger both. It is in taking this context into account that we have defined the shape of the threat to regional security represented by the state of development of democratic institutions in each country. Not only have we observed the general fragility of democratic gains and the incompletion of the democratization process, but we have also emphasized the relatively uncertain internal situation of powers that, because of their strategic importance, will determine the future of a regionalism whose shape can no longer be unilaterally dictated from Washington. The difficult emancipation of independent civil authority from military power thus takes on a particular significance in a country such as Brazil, the principal Latin American power, which is probably destined to occupy a Security Council seat in a reformed UN, not to mention the situation in Mexico, a driving force behind the movement toward the regionalization of trade crucial to the future of the inter-American system. These two examples alone suffice to measure the fragility of any regional cooperative security initiative that seeks the development of democratic institutions in the Americas.

Not only is it legitimate to question the capacity of the region to apply the measures provided for in case a disruption in the democratic process affects a

TABLE 4: SYNTHESIS

Attitude Towards Cooperative Security Initiatives

	Activist	Temporizing	Noninterventionist
Weak	Panama	Peru Bolivia El Salvador Guatemala Haiti Honduras Paraguay	
Intermediate	Argentina Venezuela	Chile Colombia Ecuador Uruguay	Brazil Mexico Dominican Rep.
High	United States Canada	Costa Rica Nicaragua	

Democratic Development (vertical axis label)

major player on the regional political scene (e.g., Brazil or Mexico); it is also necessary to recognize the limits on the regional system arising from the fact that certain actors whose support is vital for the implementation of cooperative security objectives in the area of democracy must evaluate the risk of someday facing measures similar to those presently being applied to smaller countries. In order to gain a precise idea of the regional dynamic, then, it is necessary to simultaneously take into account both the domestic situation within states *and* their attitude toward recent regional initiatives in the area of democratic development, all of this a function of their political importance. These elements are represented schematically in Table 4 above.

This classification scheme has no scientific pretensions, but appears useful in summing up the above discussion. States listed are regrouped in function of their level of democratic development, as established in the first section of the article, and in function of their attitude toward regional initiatives in cooperative security (collective action, institutional developments, etc.), as discussed in the second section. Since the attitude of each state with regard to the latter point is not constant, the classification takes into account the general tendency observable since 1985. The table also illustrates the position of each country within the regional hierarchy of power by varying the character size with which names are printed.

A quick glance at Table 4 shows that the fragility of the regional base for the deployment of a regional security system is amplified by the resistance offered by Brazil and Mexico. It should be noted that there is not a perfect correlation between the internal level of democratization within states and their attitude with regard to cooperative security applied in defence of democracy. But there are still no strongly democratic regimes that fall in the noninterventionist category, or democratically weak states in the activist category, Panama excepted. Most noticeable is a certain polarization of the intermediate powers into the activist (Argentina, Canada, Venezuela) and noninterventionist (Brazil and Mexico) categories, whereas the vast majority of weak states opt for a wait-and-see attitude. In other words, despite the progress of recent years, important regional tensions over the issue of democratic development definitely exist.

In view of the overall situation, and above and beyond the simple question of institutional capacity, it is vital not to interrupt the process of regionalization by exposing it to the still perilous trials of crisis intervention, such as recourse to sanctions. At the same time, the development of the regional system must continue to be closely associated with the development of democracy. At this stage, it would thus be preferable to avoid developing a comprehensive cooperative security apparatus in the Americas, and to favour UN intervention for the resolution of crises provoked by disruptions to the democratic process. The UN has legitimacy, credibility, and resources which Pan American institutions have not yet developed, and which it would be premature to give them at this juncture. Without renouncing the gains represented by Resolution 1080, those same institutions should be encouraged to act at the preventive level by improving regional standards and cooperation in this area along the lines suggested in the Declaration of Managua, and by extending their scope beyond the strict framework of OAS action by, for example, linking democracy and trade liberalization.

Notes

This chapter presents the results of research funded by the Department of Foreign Affairs and International Trade of Canada under the auspices of the "Cooperative Security" programme. The authors wish to thank the department for its financial assistance, as well as François Jubinville, Isabelle Martin and Martin Roy for their help with the research.

1. See R. Rosecrance, "Regionalism and the Post-Cold War Era," *International Journal,* 46:3 (1991): 373-93; Andrew Hurrel, "Latin America and the New World Order: A Regional Bloc of the Americas?" *International Affairs,* 68:1 (1992):121-40; J. Whalley, "CUSTA and NAFTA: Can WHAFTA Be Far Behind?" *Journal of Common Market Studies* 30:2 (1992): 125-41; M. S. Soroos, *Beyond Sovereignty: The Challenge of Global Policy* (Columbia: University of South Carolina Press, 1986); S. W. Gill and D. Law, *The Global Political Economy* (Baltimore: Johns Hopkins University Press, 1988).

2. See, for example, Richard H. Ullman, "Redefining Security," *International Security,* 8:1 (Summer 1983): 129-53. See also Pierre Lizée and Sorpong Peou, "Cooperative Security and the Emerging Agenda in Southeast Asia: The Challenges and Opportunities of Peace in Cambodia," Centre for International and Strategic Studies, Occasional Paper no. 21 (Toronto: York University, 1993).

3. Augusto Varas, "From Coercion to Partnership: A New Paradigm for Security Cooperation in the Western Hemisphere," in *The United States and Latin America in the 1990s: Beyond the Cold War,* ed. Jonathon Hartlyn, Lars Schoultz and Augusto Varas (Chapel Hill: The University of North Carolina Press, 1992), pp. 46-63; Viron P. Vaky and Heraldo Munoz, *The Future of the Organization of American States* (New York: The Twentieth Century Fund, 1993); Thomas M. Franck, "The Emerging Right to Democratic Governance," *American Journal of International Law,* 86:1 (1992): 46-91. S. Neil MacFarlane and Thomas G. Weiss, "Regional Organizations and Regional Security," *Security Studies,* 2:1 (Autumn 1992): 6-37. Harold Molineu, "The Inter-American System: Searching for a New Framework," *Latin American Research Review,* 29:1 (1994): 215-26; Richard J. Bloomfield, "Making the Western Hemisphere Safe for Democracy? The OAS Defense-of-Democracy Regime," *The Washington Quarterly* 17:2 (Spring 1994): 157-69; and Peter Hakim, "The OAS: Putting Principles into Practice," *Journal of Democracy* 4:3 (Summer 1993): 39-49.

4. Raymond Aron, *Paix et guerre entre les nations* (Paris: Calmann-Lévy, 1982), p. 285 (our translation).

5. Data employed to describe the situation in countries mentioned in this section are drawn from a variety of sources: Amnistie Internationale, *Rapport Annuel* (1992 and 1993); *The Economist* (April and May, 1994); Economist Intelligence Unit, *Country Report* (various countries) (1992 to 1994); *Europe World Yearbook* (1992-1993); *Facts on File* (1992 to 1994); Jack Child, *The Central American Peace Process 1983-1991* (Boulder: Lynne Rienner Publishers, 1992); *Keesing's Record of World Events* (1992 to 1994); *L'État du monde* (Montreal/ Paris: Boréal/La Découverte, 1991 to 1995); Thomas Sanders, *Field Staff Reports* (1990-1992); G.J. Schmitz and D. Gillies, *Le défi du développement démocratique* (Ottawa: L'Institut Nord-Sud, 1992).

6. Gordon Mace, Louis Bélanger and Jean-Philippe Thérien, "Regionalism in the Americas and the Hierarchy of Power," *Journal of Interamerican Studies and World Affairs,* 35:2 (Summer 1993): 115-57.

7. B. Droz and A. Rowley, *Histoire générale du XXe siècle, Volume IV (since 1973)* (Paris: Seuil, 1992), pp. 445-60.

8. J.S. Fitch has established an ordinal classification of relationships between civil and military authorities, ranging from military domination to tutelary military power, conditional military subordination, consolidated democratic control and finally institutionalized democratic control. J.S. Fitch, "Democracy, Human Rights, and the Armed Forces in Latin America," in *The United States and Latin America in the 1990s,* ed. Hartlyn, Schoultz and Varas, pp.181-213.

9. M. Garreton, "Human Rights and Processes of Democratisation," *Journal of Latin American Studies* 26 (1994): 221-34.

10. Data for this section are drawn for the most part from: Freedom House, *Freedom at Issue* 22:1 (1991); Human Rights Watch, *Human Rights Watch World Report* (1994); Observatoire de l'information, *L'information dans le monde: 206 pays au microscope* (Paris: Seuil, 1989); Reporters sans frontières, *Rapport 1994: la liberté de presse dans le monde* (Montpellier: Reporters sans frontières, 1994).

11. A. Alvarez Béjar et al., *Amérique latine. Démocratie et exclusion*, coll. "Futur antérieur" (Paris: Éditions L'Harmattan, 1994), VIII (our translation). Interviews in Washington, 23-24 March 1995.

12. The *World Report on Human Development* published by the UNDP includes a human development index (HDI) established for all countries, as well as incomplete data on the distribution of wealth both within individual nations and between nations. Programme des Nations Unies pour le développement, *Rapport mondial sur le développement humain* (Paris: Economica, 1990 and 1993).

13. Ibid. The UNDP report gives percentages for 1975 to 1986 and for 1985 to 1989. In order, the available data for each country and each period are: Argentina, 14/-; Bolivia, 12/-; Brazil, 7/8.1; Columbia, -/12.7; Costa Rica, 12/11.6; El Salvador, 15/-; Guatemala, -/14.1; Mexico, 10/-; Panama, 7/-; Peru, 7/12.9; Venezuela, 10//13.9.

14. A. Alvarez Béjar et al., esp. P. Salama, "La pauvreté en Amérique latine: y a-t-il une voie d'issue équitable?" *Journal of InterAmerican Studies and World Affairs*, 141-62.

15. John Williamson and Stéphan Haggard, "The Political Conditions for Economic Reform," in *The Political Economy of Policy Reform,* ed. John Williamson (Washington, DC: Institute for International Economics, 1994), pp. 527-96.

16. Within the OAS, democracy and human rights are considered two independent sectors, each calling for their own specific policies, structures, and actions. For certain countries in the region, the United States and Canada among them, the two sectors call for a common approach. This is the conceptual stance adopted here.

17. See Bloomfield, "Making the Western Hemisphere Safe for Democracy?" pp.157-69.

18. Union panaméricaine, *Charte de l'Organization des États américains*, Documents officiels, OEA/Ser. A/2 (French) (Washington: OEA, 1965).

19. General Secretariat, *American Convention on Human Rights* "Pact of San José, Costa Rica," Official Records, OEA/Ser.A/16 (English) (Washington: OAS, 1969).

20. For one of several Latin American viewpoints on this subject, see Alonso Aguilar, *Pan-Americanism from Monroe to the Present, A View from the Other Side* (New York and London: Monthly Review Press, 1968). See also Pierre Queuille, *L'Amérique latine. La doctrine Monroe et le panaméricanisme* (Paris: Payot, 1969), pp. 252-59.

21. On the impact of the economic crisis in Latin America, see, among others, Miguel S. Wionczek (ed.), *Politics and Economics of External Debt Crisis. The Latin American Experience* (Boulder: Westview 1985).

22. Inter-American Dialogue, *The Organization of American States: Advancing Democracy. Human Rights , and the Rule of Law. A Report of the Inter-American Dialogue Commission on the OAS* (Washington, September 1994), p. 12.

23. Ibid., pp. 12-13. See also Erskine Sandiford, "Preserving and Strengthening Democracy," *North-South* 3, 6 (April/May 1994): 3-7.

24. Interview, Washington (DC), March 1995.

25. Bloomfield, "Making the Western Hemispere Safe for Democracy?" p. 162.

26. Interview, Washington (DC), 24 March 1995. The texts of both the Santiago Declaration and Resolution 1080 appear in the appendix in Vaky and Munoz, *The Future of the Organization of American States.*

27. On the Protocol of Washington, see Heraldo Munoz, "The OAS and Democratic Governance," *Journal of Democracy,* 4, 3 (July 1993): 29-38.

28. Inter-American Dialogue, *The Organization of American States*, p. 12.

29. Ibid., p. 15.

30. The text of the Declaration of Managua can be found in Vaky and Munoz, *The Future of the Organization of American States.*

31. Above and beyond statements of principle, the first section of the Plan of Action accompanying the Declaration of Principles commits member states to a series of concrete measures for the reinforcement of democracy in the region. Among the more notable elements are the commitment by those governments who have not yet done so to ratify the protocols of Carthagena, Washington, and Managua, as well as clear support for the strengthening of the Unit for the Promotion of Democracy.

32. The text of the Mexico Agreement is contained in Foreign Broadcast Information Service, *Daily Report: Latin America*, 29 April 1991, p. 16. For more on this subject, see Jack Child, *The Central American Peace Process, 1983-1991: Sheathing Swords, Building Confidence* (Boulder: Lynne Rienner, 1992), 139ff.; as well as Alain Rouquié, *Guerre et paix en Amérique centrale*, coll. Libre Examen (Paris: Seuil, 1992), 375ff.

33. Bloomfield, "Making the Western Hemisphere Safe for Democracy?" p. 158.

34. Ibid., pp. 30-40.

35. See, ibid., p. 161.

36. See, for example, Gustavo Gorriti, "The Unshining Path: Fujimori and the Ruin of Peru," *The New Republic,* 208, 6 (February 1993): 19.

37. For an account of the Haitian crisis, see, among others, Pamela Constable, "Dateline Haiti: Caribbean Stalemate," *Foreign Policy, 89* (Winter 1992/93): 175-90; and Ian Martin, "Haiti: Mangled Multilateralism," *Foreign Policy, 95* (Summer 1994): 72-89.

38. The text is quoted in the *New York Times*, 1 August 1994.

39. Inter-American Dialogue, *The Organization of American States*, p. 12.

40. On this point, see Domingo E. Acevedo, "The Haitian Crisis and the OAS Response: A Test of Effectiveness in Protecting Democracy," in *Enforcing Restraint: Collective Intervention in International Politics*, ed. Lori Fisler Damrosk (New York: Council on Foreign Relations Press, 1993), pp. 119-55.

41. See, for example, the analysis of Augusto Varas, "From Coercion to Partnership."

42. Ibid., pp. 34-35.

43. In a recent article, Stephen Baranyi reached an identical conclusion. Contrary to certain more conservative opinions, he also expressed moderate optimism with regard to the future role of the OAS in building peace in the grand regions of the Americas. See Stephen Baranyi, "Peace Missions and Subsidiarity in the Americas: Conflict Management in the Western Hemisphere," *International Journal,* 50:2 (Spring 1995): 364ff.

PART III
Europe

Albert Legault

Euro-Atlantic Multilateral Regimes

Introduction

This chapter is based on various earlier studies that dealt with two particular aspects of regime theory. The first area was arms control[1] and the second, more encompassing, was that of collective security.[2] The approaches taken to the study of international relations vary frequently, depending on what seems fashionable or appropriate at the time. Thus, although theories of systems and subsystems and of interstate and intrastate relations were the basis of study during the Cold War, today the two predominant approaches are multilateralism and regime theory. Beyond these fashions, large theoretical debates have resulted between both neorealists and functionalists, and rationalistic institutionalists and reflective institutionalists.

My purpose here is not to produce an epistemological work. I do not intend to defend what we have previously presented on regime theory, but rather to situate this approach in the current debates surrounding multilateralism.

The Grand Theoretical Paradigms

The current debate about multilateralism and regime theory reflects the three large disputes that have been evident since the end of the Cold War. In the first place, Barry Buzan correctly reminds us that regime theory and the theory of international society are rooted in the same tradition, but, because of the particularities of academic discourse, they have become disassociated.[3] The fundamental question that Buzan poses is at what point does an international system become an international society? The argument is based on the distinction between the development of an organic and traditional (in terms of shared common culture) clvil international society (*gemeinschaft*), and a contractual society (*gesellschaft*), which is knowingly embodied in some sort of cooperative project. The question could be perceived as academic, but it touches directly upon the diverse interpretations of cooperation.

Without entering too far into the debate, I think that international society will remain heterogeneous, if only because of the multiplicity of actors. To put it another way, international society is composed of units of *gemeinschaft,* that define themselves, at least in international relations, by their nationalism, religion, language and other state or nation-state characteristics. If these premises are correct, an international system can be nothing but a *gesellschaft* composed of particular *gemeinschaften.* In other words, in as much as and so long as no social contract links the states together, and in the absence of an authoritative international order, international society will remain a *gesellschaft*. This hints at the type of international system in which we live; any multilateral or international association cannot function, intervene or regulate the flow of cooperation except in the manner according to which the contracting parties have defined the rules. I will return to this point.

Secondly, if we accept these distinctions that Barry Buzan would undoubtedly not fully embrace, it becomes easier to demonstrate the subtle distinction of Robert Keohane between rationalistic institutionalists and reflective institutionalists.[4] Tsuyoshi Kawasaki summarizes the debate on institutional cooperation well:

> Rationalistic institutionalists see these institutions as a device to reduce uncertainty in international anarchy. Norms embodied in inter-state agreements, which form the core of such institutions, can function as a framework within which states can predict others' behaviour. Without institutions, guessing others behaviour would be more costly. By complying with the norms even at the expense of sacrificing its short-term, myopic interest, a particular state can enhance its reputation as a reliable partner in the long run and can expect other states to reciprocate, which will lead to the emergence of an information-rich, highly predictable international environment. Thus, it is logical for states, acting rationally and egoistically, to establish and comply with international institutions.

> Rationalistic institutionalists see international institutions as instruments of foreign policy. In the final analysis, states manipulate them to advance their national interest. In sharp contrast, reflective institutionalists such as Friedrich Kratochwill and John Ruggie regard international institutions not as policy instruments but as social reality, to use Durkheim's terminology, which constrains and even changes national interests. States internalize norms embodied in international institutions, and such norm-governed behaviour is qualitatively different from state behaviour purely driven by short-term, myopic self-interests. A particular institution whose member states behave in such a manner is an interstate community governed by

its norms. In the view of reflective institutionalists, therefore, the essence of international institutions lies in shared norms, which cannot be reduced to a sum of short-term, myopic self-interests.[5]

These distinctions are valid only when one accepts the different endpoint of the two schools of thought. To put it another way, in both cases, institutional cooperation adds an element of predictability to the system. It allows a harmonization of expectations of each actor and perhaps also the maximization of their benefits from cooperation and minimization of the disadvantages of noncooperation. However, the outcome is dissimilar: the internalization of rules external to a system responds to moral and social criteria (i.e., a *gemeinschaft* resulting from free consent) different from those of a simple maximization of return from cooperation (or a simple rational calculus of gains).

In an earlier publication,[6] I retraced the origins of the paradigms of "peace by force" and "peace by law" in terms of their intrinsic outcomes. I evoked the paradox of the strategist who can be simultaneously a nationalist or an internationalist at the same time. That is to say, an international strategist whose job it is to calculate the costs and benefits of the state's behaviour is and will remain *internationalist nationalist* if his objective is to maximize the gains of the state. By contrast, an *international internationalist* will maximize the benefits of the international community. In institutional or multilateral cooperation, the same criteria are applicable. He who strives only for the maximization of his own gains is a rationalist in the pure tradition of neorealism. However, he who strives for the good of the international community is a citizen of this world, communitarian in the sense of an international *gemeinschaft*. Thus the framework for cooperation can be seen as belonging either to structural realism or to a more sociological and institutional approach to cooperation, based on the respect for common rules designed to serve the good of the community.

These approaches are related to the old dispute between realists and idealists, or to the distinction between the "is" and the "ought." It is here that our third theoretical proposition intrudes. Despite everything that has been written about regimes, a regime's most noble and important aspect is exactly that which deals with the metaregulation of the system or the definition of the rules of the game. Metaregulation includes the norms and the principles of the regime that I shall define below. In reality, this corresponds to the "ought" — what should be or what should be done — as opposed to what "is" or what happens. In the domestic political order or in the theoretical study of political regimes, the metaregulation of a system corresponds to the regime's function, well developed in Gérard Bergeron's work.[7]

Multilateralism, Regimes and Systems

If neorealists concentrate on the "deductive logic of international anarchy," in contrast to classical realists who base these arguments on the "inductive notion of equilibrium of force," both nonetheless conclude that multilateralism plays a weak role in the evolution of the international system. Kawasaki defines multilateralism as, "a particular state's participation in *ad hoc* or routinized inter-state meetings, which involves at least two other states, and which may result in agreements with at least two other states."[8] Brian Job, however, recasts the Keohane and Ruggie definition and suggests that it means nothing but the "practice of coordinating policies in groups of three or more states."[9]

The minimum of three is clearly the key to the concept of multilateralism. Two other concepts are grafted onto this quantity: the notion of *a process of dialogue* and the eventual *institutionalization of cooperation* through the establishment of an institution of multilateral or international character. Kawasaki distinguishes global organizations like the UN from other regional, or *ad hoc* institutions. In general, all authors agree that multilateralism originates in the cooperation of several states (a minimum of three), and that it can proceed from formal international organizations or international nongovernmental organizations, from simple regimes or from duly negotiated international conventions.[10]

According to Brian Job, the formal institutional character of cooperation is neither a necessary nor a sufficient condition for the existence of multilateralism.[11] In Job's opinion, the operative concept of multilateralism rests in the "structure of attitudes" (sic) underlying multilateralism. In terms of security, Job distinguishes between three approaches: "collective defence" — which presupposes a community of shared interests; "collective security" — which implies a profound transformation of the security dilemma (how to maintain sufficient dissuasive capacity without provoking the war one sought to avoid) for a large number of actors; and "security community" — which implies the disappearance of threat, and the establishment of common and shared values.

Institutional support and actors' attitudes with regard to the problems that multilateralism seeks to manage are obviously important criteria that I will return to later. I now want to introduce in parallel the notion of the deepening and widening of multilateralism that Brian Job has analysed along two axes. The first axis reflects the actors' attachment to multilateralism and ranges from "profound to superficial." The second axis reflects the extent of articulation of multilateralism and ranges from "narrow" to "broad."

I have alluded to similar concepts in the past in order to define the structural dimension of a regime, as well as its dimensions of deepening or widening. The first idea that I wish to repeat here is that the structure of a regime that can span the spectrum from a global or international dimension (i.e., the Non-Proliferation Treaty or the Convention on Chemical Weapons) to a regional dimension (i.e., the Treaty on Conventional Forces in Europe), or even to a national one (i.e., the national dispositions of the Convention on Chemical Weapons which attempt to harmonize national regulations with international texts). As soon as we speak of the deepening or widening of a regime, it is necessary to borrow these concepts from systems theory which is distinct from the concept of regime in two ways.

The first criterion for defining a system is the definition of actors and boundaries of the system. Regime theory and multilateralism do not have to face these kinds of problems. All those who subscribe to the rules of a regime or to the multilateral forum in which they participate, are part of the regime or the multilateral structure. Regimes and multilateralism are situated within structural functionalism, which is related to the older functionalism of David Mitrany. They are social constructs conceived with a view to regulating particular forms of cooperation. We have resolved these semantic problems by noting that one of the necessary conditions for the existence of a regime is the definition of a public space for expression or cooperation, an idea evident in the English concept of "public policy."

Concerning the deepening or widening of a regime, the difficulty results from the fact that cooperation can be just as easily conceived within either the concept of regime or system. For example, the European Union (EU) is both a system — if we define it as an ensemble of cooperations from the harmonization of policies to the elaboration of a Common Foreign and Security Policy (CFSP) — and a regime — if it is seen as a deepening of rules in the area of fiscal and monetary policy, to cite but one aspect of EU cooperation. Therefore, the term "deepening" of a regime has been reserved for the improvement and reinforcement of norms and principles that govern a particular form of cooperation, while the term "widening" concerns the addition of new actors or new public spaces within a particular form of cooperation.

One example suffices as an illustration. In matters of the nonproliferation of weapons of mass destruction, the addition to the London Nuclear Suppliers Group of the Missile Technology Control Regime (MTCR), and the Australian group, that defines the rules of the game dealing with the transfer of dual technologies and chemical know-how, constitutes a double extension of the

TABLE 1: METAREGULATION AND REGULATION OF THE COLLECTIVE SECURITY REGIME

Process of Regime Formation (Regime Metaregulation)			The Organizational Processes of the Regime (Regime Regulation)		
Subregimes	Definitions of Principles and Norms		Rules	Procedures	Verification of Regime Coherence
	Principles	Norms			
Peacemaking	The principles are understood in the sense of general or functional objectives of each dimension of collective security.	By norms are meant the general legal arrangements supporting the definition of codes of conduct for actors in each dimension of the collective security regime.	The totality of criteria for actions allowing principles and norms to become operational. The rules can be generated by an international or regional organization, or by other actors involved in the organizational processes of a collective security regime.	By procedures we mean the specific modes of action contributing to the application of norms and rules. Procedures can differ at the universal and regional levels, but regional procedures can only be legitimate if they respect the principles and norms of universal rules.	By this we mean the monitoring and control mechanisms established by universal or regional organizations with the objective of verifying the application of rules and procedures.
Preventive diplomacy					
Peacekeeping					
Humanitarian Intervention					
Peace enforcement					

Source: «La théorie des régimes et don utilité pour l'étude de la sécurité collective», dans *La redéfinition des politiques de sécurité: le cas yougoslave* (en collaboration avec Charles-Philippe David), Québec, Centre québécois de relations internationales, 1995, pp. 27-74. Le tableau est tiré de la page 67.

nonproliferation regime (the addition of new subscribers to the rules of cooperation and the expansion of subjects included). The concept of deepening a regime, however, is reserved for the amelioration of the norms and principles that govern the broader nonproliferation regime.

To enter into the heart of the subject, a definition of regime must be provided. Although we accept Krasner's definition, ("an ensemble of principles, norms, rules and decisional procedures, implicit or explicit, around which converge the expectations of actors in a given domain of international relations,"[12]) we do not necessarily use his definitions of these constituent terms. To avoid any ambiguity,

> **Principles** *have to be understood more in the sense of general objectives or functional objectives sought within the regime;*

> **Norms** *must be understood in the sense of general legal dispositions that assist in defining the codes of conduct for actors within the regime;*

> **Rules** *indicates essentially what the regime adds to fundamentals in order to render norms and principle operational; and*

> **Procedures** *mean specific modes of action that contribute to the application of the norms and rules.*

Table 1 indicates fairly well what has just been said. In fact, our analysis of Euro-Atlantic multilateralism applies the analytical grid that we have developed above for the analysis of problems of collective security. Peacemaking, peacekeeping and peace enforcement were incorporated into the definition of collective security. So were the new domains of preventive diplomacy and humanitarian aid, which fall between "peacemaking" and "peacekeeping," in the case of humanitarian action and preventive diplomacy, between "peacekeeping" and "peace enforcement."

The table distinguishes between what has been previously called metaregulation of the regime and its regulation. The norms and principles derive from metaregulation or the "ought," that is to say from the noble part of the regime, while rules and procedures came from the organizational aspect of the regime, to which we have added the notion of the congruence of the regime. This notion is borrowed from the sociological aspect of systems theory developed by Talcott Parsons.

We are now in a position to define the conditions necessary and sufficient for the existence of a collective security regime. These include:

■ the existence or definition of a space for public expression;

■ the existence of a multilateral consensus regarding norms for intervention;

■ the legal codification of norms;

■ the existence of clear and coherent rules of application; and

■ the existence of procedures for regulation of differences within the public space.

On the institutional level, it is clear, for example, that the institutionalization of a regime is not a sufficient condition for the effective operation of a regime, but it is improbable that a regime can become truly operational if it is not sustained by organizational rules and procedures. Furthermore, an institution or an international organization that functions on the basis of clearly defined principles and norms, and that is equipped with organizational procedures that are also clear, is not a sufficient guarantee of a regime's effectiveness. In other words, the existence of a capacity for action or intervention does not signify the automatic execution of earlier commitments, since this will depend on the clear will of the regime members. Yugoslavia is ample evidence of this.

Euro-Atlantic Multilateralism and Collective Security

Collective security, as defined earlier, is the type of regime that this study focuses on. For purposes of illustration, I will touch only upon the domains of the establishment and keeping of peace. At this stage of analysis, we should provide a supplementary indication of the regime's norms and principles. The principles and norms are generally taken from the practice of the United Nations or its Charter. This speaks eloquently of the universal character of the principles and norms embedded in the metaregulation of the regime in question. The Europeans are attempting to create on a regional level what was done on a global level with the UN. A more intensive study would probably indicate that the Europeans have done a little better in this regard than other regional security organizations like the Organization of African Unity (OAU) or the Organization of American States (OAS), but that the resurgence of regional multilateralism is only a reflection of what is happening at a global level. Some authors, like MacFarlane and Weiss,[13] maintain that regional organizations, are less well equipped than the UN to resolve conflicts. Michael Pugh, for his part, underlines the fundamental weakness of regional organizations which are "neither sufficiently coherent nor sufficiently strong institutionally" to deal with problems of military security.

However, on the level of responsibilities and competence, all the European institutions reacted to the end of the Cold War by emphasizing new tasks and functions in the areas of peacekeeping and preventive diplomacy. At the meetings in Oslo (June 1992) and in Athens (July 1993), NATO accepted the principle of putting logistical means, information, and alliance forces at the disposal of the UN or the then CSCE for peace-related operations undertaken by these organizations. In January 1994, the Partnership for Peace Program (PfP) called for the development of military cooperation (planning, joint exercises, personnel training, and the development of common doctrine) with East European countries in particular to prepare for peace-related operations.

One month later, the UN gave NATO the task of enforcing exclusion zones around Sarajevo, where the placement of heavy artillery was prohibited.

The use of NATO's capabilities in conjunction with other European institutions is familiar ground. In the Petersburg Declaration of June 1992, the Western European Union (WEU) took on responsibilities relating to humanitarian missions, peacekeeping and crisis management. In addition, the WEU can assume a logistical support role for peace-related operations. In accordance with paragraph four of the Maastricht Treaty, the WEU is responsible for the elaboration and the execution of the EU's actions that have defence implications. This might lead one to suppose that it has a decisionmaking power just as important as that of the EU Council. The WEU has a strategic planning group and maintains close relations with NATO through exchanges of information, documents, and observers. The WEU participated with NATO in the surveillance operations related to the embargo declared against the former Yugoslavia in the Adriatic Sea.

As for the CSCE its mandate permits it to freely intervene in all directions and in any domain in Europe. The OSCE has improved its decisionmaking structures and affirmed its competence in areas of peacekeeping, conflict resolution, preventive diplomacy (notably throughout the numerous observation missions) and the protection of minority rights (with the creation of the position of High Commissioner for National Minority Rights). In virtue of the decisions made at the Helsinki Conference in July 1992, the OSCE can now take on peacekeeping missions, or can give a mandate for such actions to other international organizations. It can also call on the resources of other organizations to implement its peacekeeping functions.

It is noteworthy that each organization has adopted principles and norms compatible with the UN Charter, and that each is dedicated to resolution of particular problems related to collective security at the level of metaregulation. Yet, experts' judgements on the efficiency of the organizations are rather sober.[14]

If we review the principal criticisms, it seems that they can be regrouped into four categories: the competition between organizations is destructive; the decisionmaking process of the organizations renders some less effective than others; the organizations have different capacities and therefore cannot play the same role, and lastly, a consensus has not been reached about the utility of regional organizations regarding the regulation to the peaceful settlement of conflicts.

The first argument does hold some weight, but it can hardly be considered as a key element in relation to theory. The competition in which these organizations are engaged is linked to factors external to the crises they are attempting to resolve and can only affect indirectly the modes of cooperation within the regime. In other words, certain countries desire that an organization have an exclusively European mandate, while others emphasize pan-European institutions, and still others seek to work within NATO, but this factor has no significance in relation to the type of conflicts being addressed. This means that all these institutions are passing up the option of inserting themselves into regimes in formation, something that in itself is not reprehensible. One can denounce the dispersion of effort when there is so much to do, but this does not affect the intrinsic quality of the collective security regime.

Also, it is relatively easy to dispose of the decisionmaking argument. It is true that the OSCE possesses complex decisionmaking rules which would permit the planning of peacekeeping operations: it is obviously more difficult for the representatives of 53 countries to decide on an issue rather than 16 (within NATO) or five (within the UN Security Council). However, these quarrels had no impact on conflict resolution in Yugoslavia and no organization, whether universal, global or regional, came close to solving the problem.

The argument about regime capacities is more important if it focuses is on the advantages of dissuasion. Yet, here too, the capacities of NATO, which are infinitely superior to those of the OSCE or other European institutions, were little help in managing the Yugoslav conflict. All that can be said here is that one organization equipped with powerful military capabilities has more of a chance of deterring or halting hostilities than does an organization that, because of its lack of arms, has no credibility. The security dilemma or paradox, *si vis pacem para bellum,* is and will always be an equation not to be ignored in the search for conflict resolution. This said, it must nevertheless be acknowledged that NATO was the only organization that could have an impact on the Yugoslav conflict.

The fourth argument is the most difficult to address. It is true that the UN is overworked and financially malnourished and that the desire of the Secretary-

General of the UN to decentralize peace by appealing to the regional organizations was closely linked to the absence of material and financial resources. It is also true that the OSCE is the only European organization to have obtained standing as such under Chapter VIII of the United Nations Charter. The decentralization of peace is, however, an increasingly common phenomenon. Russia seems to have taken onto itself responsibilities for the security of the "near abroad" within the borders of the Commonwealth of Independent States. The same thing could, for all intents and purposes, be said of the Western Hemisphere, the Haiti question constituting but one example of a larger process.

Regional organizations can only have a role if the subsystem's dominant powers show leadership and if their willingness to intervene is clearly affirmed.[15] How is this argument different than this about the UN with which we are familiar? The UN has indirectly intervened in two important peace operations in its history: in South Korea in 1950 and in the Gulf War in 1990. In both cases, the United States extracted the decision and brought its allies along to participate in the operations. Two other cases of humanitarian intervention and the reestablishment of democracy under the UN auspices are also indicative. One was in "Operation Turquoise", where the French leadership was crucial in the Rwanda mission. The other, "Operation Support for Democracy" in Haiti, would have never taken place without the American military presence.

The absence or presence of consensus within a regional organization is certainly an important qualifying factor, for without consensus there cannot be a decision. But, this argument carries little weight with regard to the theoretical issues we are discussing. So one must look elsewhere if one wishes to provide a preliminary treatment of these questions.

The Conditions of a Coherent Regime

Among the necessary and sufficient conditions for the existence of a regime listed above, note that the first three have already been fulfilled in Europe. The collective security domain constitutes a well-defined public space; there exists a large multilateral consensus on the norms and principles that could sustain peace missions; and the legal codification of principles of intervention is largely present in the texts that are for the most part inspired by UN principles. There certainly exists some decisionmaking weakness, notably within the OSCE, but this does not create major problems at the level of regime theory.

The two final conditions are less evident on the organizational plane: the existence of applicable rules and procedures that are clear and coherent, and procedures for regulation for disagreements within the defined public space. NATO is in the process of developing procedures and doctrines for peacekeeping and is probably more advanced than the UN in this area; the UN finds itself obligated to start practically at zero each time a new operation is envisaged. A planning cell exists within the WEU and important exchanges of information happen between NATO and the WEU. The OSCE is without a doubt the weakest institution in this area, and it is probable that it will choose to turn to the WEU or NATO, or eventually the EU, for certain future operations. This leads one to suppose that its role will be limited to preventive diplomacy and observer missions, as in the past.

Here, there are hardly any examples, save the negotiations leading to the embargo in the Adriatic, and those which took place between NATO and the UN regarding the enforcement of the exclusion and no-fly zones in the former Yugoslavia. These operations revealed enormous problems of coordination between the affected organizations, but the actual content of these negotiations was always kept secret. It can be concluded, however, that the organizational procedures for coordination were resolved on a more or less satisfactory basis for all participating parties.

Concerning the regulation of differences, in earlier work we derived three criteria of regime coherence: the existence of credible information, respect for commonly accepted procedures (i.e., consent of the host state, respect for ceasefires, and impartiality of intervening parties); and the existence of obligatory procedures for resolution of disagreements. In this area, the functions of negotiation and conciliation were largely shared, at first, between the EEC and the UN, and subsequently between the Contact Group, the EU and the UN. Meanwhile NATO continued to assume important functions in matters of information. One cannot maintain that the Yugoslav experience invalidates regime theory in any respect.

Almost all the ingredients for a regime are in place, despite of the multiplicity of actors and organizations involved. The only case that has not been discussed is that of subregimes of peace enforcement. France's ex-president François Mitterrand always claimed that it was necessary to make war in order to stop the war in Yugoslavia. Despite this, the "Yugoslavian knot" does not invalidate regime theory in matters of peacekeeping and peacemaking, for numerous reasons.

The first is that this case does not to conform the first two categories. The Yugoslavian case is not one of peacekeeping, except possibly the first UNPROFOR mission in Croatia. Instead, it was a case of multilateral observation of a war in progress. The international community contented itself with the provision of humanitarian aid to Bosnia. It is true that the Macedonian case is a frequently cited example of preventive diplomacy, but this success may be explained more in terms of American willingness to prevent the extension of the conflict than of the concerted action of the international community within the context of multilateral cooperation.

The second reason is equally evident. The affected parties never respected their commitments. The Security Council compensated for its helplessness with an accumulation of resolutions of declaratory character, the implementation of which was impossible or ill-advised. In so doing, the international community resigned itself little by little to the *fait accompli*. The passage of time has only reinforced the entropic character of this conflict and few observers believe in a viable peace for this region as long as the conditions for conflict resolution have not matured.

In reality, neither studies of regimes, which are a refined form of multilateralist theory, nor regional studies oriented to a greater extent toward conflicts furnish answers to the questions we are asking. It is necessary to turn to the theory of conflict in order to obtain the beginnings of an answer.

Multilateralism and Conflict Resolution

If it is true, as Brian Job maintains,[16] that humanitarian aid and population protection represent an extension of the basis of multilateralism and multilateral engagements, it is probably equally true that what the external actors or multilateral actions can accomplish is also limited. There are four ideal conditions for conflict resolution:

1. Great powers must be willing to establish such a concert.

2. The initial caution that the actors mutually entertain concerning others' strategic intentions must be weakened to the extent that each participant believes that the others share the same values regarding their mutual security and cooperation.

3. Expansionist tendencies must be repudiated by all parties.

4. Wars must be regarded as too costly to wage.[17]

To return to the Yugoslav case, it is probable that the second and fourth conditions above were hardly achieved, since none of the Yugoslav parties has yet to give up the option of war, and it is also doubtful that the Russians, subject to internal pressures in favour of the Serbs and to the other forces of

Russian nationalism, think like the Americans on this matter. The ideals that sustain the promise of Greater Serbia do not improve the prospect for the repudiation of Serb expansionist tendencies. This calls the third condition into question. Therefore, there is little room left for moving forward.

If the problem is considered from the other end of the stick, through an examination of domestic conditions conducive to conflict resolution, John Sigler — drawing on the work of Zartman and Berman — reminds us that there are four: a "hurting stalemate" for both parties; an imminent catastrophe; an exit door; and legitimate representatives.[18]

Contrary to the situation in the Middle East in 1994, which Sigler uses to illustrate his proposition, there was in the Yugoslav case neither an imminent catastrophe nor a hurting stalemate, except perhaps for the Bosnian government, whose survival was at stake but which had the misfortune not to be one of the principal actors capable of changing the situation on the ground. There also appeared to be no exit option unless it were the partition of Bosnia, an outcome that the international community has thus far sought to avoid, but which may eventually have to be exercised. Finally, it is difficult to maintain that the internal negotiators are really "legitimate representatives," when some of them are being pursued for crimes against humanity.

The internal and external conditions necessary for conflict resolution seem not to exist in Yugoslavia. Note that the only parameter we have not covered is that of peace enforcement. For this to be implemented, an agreement between great powers is needed. As well, their national interest would have to be affected by the conflict, which is manifestly not the case. Moreover, their publics would have to support intervention. They do not, since very few are willing to die for Sarajevo.

Conclusion

Reality suffers little by being structured into concepts, for these latter are but pale reflections of societal categories. Theoretical constructs are used for understanding things, but they often raise questions that the man in the street has no difficulty in answering. For example, the question of knowing whether multilateralism is a new source of transformation of the international system remains academic. It is evident that growing interstate interdependence, due to commerce, exchange, and information is and will remain an important source of rapprochement between states. But such a tendency will never render the international system homogeneous. The Waltzian conception, of international relations whereby transformations of the system generates "similar units" appears obvious so long as the state exists. But to pass from this view to Buzan's belief that a particular international society corresponds to a specific international system seems to lie in the realm of abstraction. In reality, the international system has never achieved the homogeneity and probably the integration between Eastern and Western Europe that was present on the eve of the Second World War. In this respect, as noted at the beginning of this chapter, if one maintains that the system is organized around a particular *gemeinschaften*, the international system as a whole will always remain a *gesellschaft*, because the rules of the game are constantly evolving and actors are constantly attempting to redefine them. This is what the Euro-Atlantic debate teaches us.

In these conditions, the quarrels between rational and speculative institutionalists will remain a Pascalian enigma. Beyond this, a more general question arises: whether regimes and multilateralism can be explained in terms of the neorealist school's argument that states cooperate because it is in their interest to do so, or whether we are speaking of a new and important phenomenon that will produce a qualitative transformation of the international system. In such an order, the quest for stability in the system would be relegated to secondary importance in the face of the growth of cooperation. In response to this, one can retort that there has always been cooperation in conflicts, and there have always been conflicts within cooperation. The argument may be transposed as follows: is there a limiting threshold beyond which the system would be noticeably transformed by cooperation?

Elements of a response are presented in this text. Progress in cooperation and, more precisely, in the domain of collective security is surprising if we compare the current situation to what existed in the 1960s or during the Cold War. The same can be said for a multitude of specific sectors, notably the question of the nonproliferation of arms of massive destruction, although expert opinion is directed in this respect. Whatever the case, what is important is that the more cooperation exists, the more that multilateralism and regimes are affirmed, and the more order and information there is in the system, the more certain sectors of activity become "manageable." In reality, there are no international politics, except in the regulation of certain sectors of the system. This does not mean, however, that the overall system is becoming manageable or susceptible to regulation.

Three final conclusions can be drawn from the analysis of regimes. The first, and most evident is that this theory permits us to define the social reality of "public space" within which cooperation is generated along two axes: one sectoral and the other according to the attribute of metaregulation (the principles and norms) and the rules and procedures developed within the regime. In this sense, regime theory provides us with an excellent tool for comparative analysis of existing regimes. Second, the criteria for assessing the effectiveness of a regime should be analyzed as a function of the internal criteria of the regime in question (the existence of credible information functions, respect for commonly accepted procedures and the existence of obligatory procedures of regulating disputes within the regimes). These are the only instruments that can be used to verify the coherence and the effectiveness of a regime. The question of knowing how a regime can regulate a conflict becomes a factor external to regime theory. This is the third and last conclusion, for the study of regimes allows us to examine modes of cooperation within a regime, but it possesses no predictive power with respect to the resolution of conflicts outside the regime. This problem arises from what we know about conflict, and not from the cooperative or institutional character of a regime.

Neither multilateralism nor regime theory constitute a solution for the regulation of conflicts. All that can be said is that regimes regulate cooperation within a forum of cooperating states, but that they are incapable of bringing a recalcitrant state to act as the majority of the regime's participating states wish. In reality, all theories are social constructs. One must, therefore, live with these constraints.

Notes

1. See Michel Fortmann, *Proliferation et non-proliferation nucléaires, strategies et contrôles*, (Québec et Paris: International Relations Centre of Quebec and the Foundation for national Defence studies, 1993), p. 469.

2. The appropriateness of the regime theory for the study of collective security is described in Charles-Philippe David and Albert Legault (in collaboration with Isabelle Desmartis, Julie Fournier and Charles Thumerelle), *La redéfinition des politiques de sécurité: le cas yugoslave,* (Québec: Centre québécois de relations internationales et Foundation pour les études de défense nationale, 1994), p. 27-74.

3. Barry Buzan, "From International System to International Society: Structural Realism and Regime Theory Meet the English School," *International Organization*, 47:3 (1993): 327-52.

4. Robert O. Keohane, *International Institutions and State Power: Essay in International Relations Theory* (Boulder: Westview Press, 1989), pp.158-79.

5. Tsuyoshi Kawasaki, *The Logic of Japanese Multilateralism for Asia Pacific Security* (Vancouver: Institute of International Relations, UBC, 1994), pp. 10-11.

6. Albert Legault, "Towards the Twenty-First Century," in *Building a New Global Order Emerging Trends in International Security*, ed. David Dewitt, David Haglund and John Kirton (Toronto, Oxford, New York: Oxford University Press, 1993), pp.401-15.

7. Gérard Bergeron, *La gouverne politique* (Paris and Quebec: Mouton et les Presses de l'Université Laval, 1977).

8. Kawasaki, *The Logic of Japanese Multilateralism for Asia Pacific Security*, p. 9

9. Brian Job, *Multilateralism: The Relevance of the Concept to Regional Conflict Management*, (Vancouver: Institute of International Relations, UBC, 1994), pp. 3-4.

10. Kawasaki, *The Logic of Japanese Multilateralism for Asia Pacific Security*, p.10.

11. Job, *Multilateralism,* p. 6.

12. Stephen Krasner, *International Regimes* (Ithaca: Cornell University Press, 1983), pp. 1-2.

13. S. Neil MacFarlane and Thomas G. Weiss, "Regional Organizations and Regional Security," *Security Studies*, 2:1 (1992): 6-37.

14. See Victor-Yves Ghebali and Brigitte Sauerwein, *European Security in the 1990's: Challenges and Perspectives* (New York and Geneva: United Nations, 1995), pp.154-155. Josef Joffe, "Collective Security and the Future of Europe: Failed Dreams and Dead Ends," *Survival*, 34 (Spring 1992): 36-50.

15. What Brian Job called "aspiring regional powers."

16. Job, *Multilateralism,* p. 30.

17. Shannon Selin, *Asia Pacific Arms Buildups; Part Two: Prospects for Control* (Vancouver: Institute of International Relations, UBC), p. 47.

18. John Sigler, "Conflict Resolution in the Middle East," in *Les conflits dans le monde*, ed. Albert Legault and John Sigler (Quebec: Centre québécois de relations internationales et Foundation pour les études de défense nationale, 1994), pp. 79-114.

David Long

The CFSP and Beyond:
The EU's Territorial and Functional
Conceptions of Security

Introduction

Security and security policy are part of the agenda of the European Union (EU) as never before. The inclusion in the Maastricht Treaty of a Common Foreign and Security Policy as a second pillar of the European Union is evidence. In the defence arena the proposed relationship of the EU to the Western European Union (WEU) appears to show that the EU is grappling with security policy in earnest, though the results have been decidedly mixed. War in the former Yugoslavia has served to heighten the sense of urgency to effect a security profile to the EU, as conflict in the Balkans has dispersed refugees across the continent of Europe and threatens to spread beyond its present confines. The EU's Common Foreign and Security Policy and its relationship to the WEU are likely to feature prominently on the agenda of the upcoming intergovernmental conference reviewing the Maastricht Treaty.[1]

This chapter argues that, in dealing with security issues beyond its borders, the EU can draw on two traditions of thought from its own development, but that recently it has predominantly focused in practice on one, a military, territorial conception of security.

The other approach, the functional route to security manifested in the origins of the European Coal and Steel Community, has progressively been relegated to second place in the public pronouncements of the Community/ Union on peace and security.

I took inspiration for this essay from David Mitrany's critique of the European Economic Community (EEC) in his article, "The Prospect of European Integration: Federal or Functional," to advance a critique of the EU's approach to security from a functional perspective and to suggest an alternative. The chapter is in three parts. The first describes the current security discourse of the EU, especially the establishment of the Common Foreign and Security Policy (CFSP), outlining territorial assumptions and the notion of excluding external threats as the basis for security policy in the EU. The second part outlines Mitrany's critique of the EEC as an exclusive regional organization and relates this to the origins of security policy in the EEC/EU (notably in the establishment of the European Coal and Steel Community) and also to current security politics in the EU. The third part considers the example of the EU's relations with Central and Eastern Europe (CEE) in the context of the two traditions of security policy for the EU.

The functional approach discussed in this chapter is multilateral in form. It highlights multiple channels between states, different patterns of state and nonstate interaction in different issue areas, and implies an integrative, cooperative approach to security. On the other hand, Mitrany's functional approach, while predating the more recent conceptual development of multilateralism by Ruggie by half a century, differs from multilateralism in its nonstate focus, its close attention to the satisfaction of material need, and its assertion that the most profitable avenues for international cooperation are found away from the usual channels of diplomacy and international politics.

Security Policy in the EU: Maastricht and After

While hedged around with "if's, but's and maybe's," the CFSP displays a major change in the status of security policy of the EU. Unfortunately, the development of the CFSP has drawn on a traditional notion of foreign and security policy, particularly in its institutional focus on security policy as the responsibility of Ministries of Foreign Affairs and of Defence. While this might simply be explained by bureaucratic infighting and turf-wars, there is no doubt that baggage comes with the association of security and security policy with departments that have traditionally been understood to deal with it as an external threat to national security, national interest, or (more broadly) international order. I will present a brief outline of the origins and development of the CFSP and then examine its underlying assumptions.

The Development of the Common Foreign and Security Policy

Any account of the CFSP must begin with a discussion of the development of European Political Cooperation (EPC). CFSP developed from the EPC. The history of the CFSP, as it is related by the EU itself and in texts about the EU, can be briefly summarized as follows: the Treaty of Rome created a community whose focus was economic. The external relations of the member states, for which the EEC itself was responsible, were also largely economic. As the

EEC grew in wealth, power, size, and stature, it had more weight internation-ally — both economically and politically. However, the coordination of external economic relations by the European Commission were not matched with a common foreign policy stance of the EEC. This led to confused positions of EEC member states and a feeling that the EEC's potential power in the inter-national system was not being sufficiently exploited. There was also a perception within the EC and outside that it lacked focus in its relations with the rest of the world.

EPC was partly a response to these developments, though it never over-came the problems from which it was created. It emerged in the early 1970s as a mechanism whereby the member states of the EEC consulted on and coordinated their foreign policies through regular meetings of their foreign min-isters. EPC remained outside the treaty framework of the EEC: it was intergovernmental, political, ad hoc and voluntary. Despite the EEC's growing economic power, EPC remained declaratory rather than effective; that is, it entailed consulting EEC states on foreign policy issues and issuing statements on the situation in South Africa or the Middle East. When significant issues appeared, especially those implicating national security interests, EPC fell more or less by the wayside, as was the case of the Falkland Islands conflict, where the British government merely sought an EPC rubber stamp for its own unilat-eral actions.[2] The progressive development of the EPC and its routinization within the business of the EEC ultimately led to its institutionalization in Title III of the *Single European Act* (SEA), though it remained an intergovernmental political framework.

The development of foreign policy coordination and consultation was one thing, while the discussion of security and defence policy within the frame-work of the European Community was another. Security was always something of a problem for EPC and defence matters were so controversial as to be explicitly excluded from consideration. Article 6 of Title III of the SEA refers to security policy. The High Contracting Parties (the EC member states) were "ready to coordinate their positions more closely on the political and eco-nomic aspects of security," for instance, within the framework of the CSCE and on issues that required the application of trade sanctions. The SEA also refers to the need to keep up with others technologically, the US and Japan presumably, to ensure security in Article 6(b). By contrast, cooperation on "hard" security matters — defence cooperation — was expected to continue within the framework of NATO.

Even with the development of the CFSP, although military and strategic dimensions of security were not excluded, political and economic aspects of security policy remained the primary focus.[3] Procedural changes were as important as the change in substantive focus. While the defence and security aspects of the CFSP conjured up visions of previous attempts at defence cooperation in Europe, such as the Pleven Plan of 1952 that aimed to create a European Defence Community,[4] at a practical level it is clearly a reaction to the frailties of EPC, its voluntary and declaratory nature and the lack of significant policy output.

Title V of the Maastricht Treaty envisages "systematic cooperation" on foreign and security policy which codifies the procedure of EPC once again, with the possibility of the Council of Ministers defining a common position. Member states are expected to "inform and consult each other within the Council" and exert "combined influence" through "concerted and convergent action" (Article J.2.1). The range of issues covered by the CFSP under Maastricht include coordination and consultation of EU members on arms control negotiations in Europe, on nuclear nonproliferation issues, and on economic aspects of security, particularly the control of the transfer of military technology to third countries, arms exports, and the creation of a common positon in the Organization for Security and Cooperation in Europe.[5] These provisions are within the political and economic aspects of security, the traditional concern of EPC.

According to Maastricht, joint action is to be implemented on matters determined by the Council of Foreign Ministers with general guidelines set by the European Council. Majority voting applies to joint action (Article J.3.2), and "joint actions shall commit the Member States in the positions they adopt and in the conduct of their activity" (Article J.3.4.). That it was to be "gradually implement[ed]" suggests that this article is quite weak. Furthermore, following the difficult negotiations of Maastricht, the CFSP has become what is now known as the second pillar of the Union (with Justice and Home Affairs as the third). The practical implication of the "Pillar" formulation is to keep CFSP an intergovernmental, political, consensus mechanism, not formally coming under the scrutiny of the European Court of Justice or the European Parliament, let alone the direction of the Commission.

The joint actions that have taken place under the CFSP are exemplified by EU actions to provide humanitarian assistance in Bosnia-Herzegovina and to provide observers for the parliamentary elections in Russia. Joint actions are for the most part within the usual bounds established by EPC, though the extreme situation in Bosnia has led to a more active approach than typifies most EC/EU decisions.[6]

The EU addressed the military aspects of security at Maastricht. But the operative Article (J.4) is hedged around with qualifications even greater than those that apply to the development of the CFSP. Three of the six parts of it concern what the Article does *not* do. Specifically, it is not subject to the majority voting provision of joint action. It is not prejudicial to participation in NATO or to bilateral relations with third countries (Article J.4.3-5). Furthermore, the main instrument of defence cooperation is to be an already existing international organization, the Western European Union (WEU), which is described as "an integral part of the development of the [European] Union," notwithstanding the fact that the treaty creating the WEU expires in 1998 (Article J.4.2) and that the memberships (of the EU and the WEU) are not consonant, requiring the creation of WEU associate member and observer status.[7] We must wait until the 1996 Intergovernmental Conference that is set to review the timetable and prospectus set out by the Maastricht Treaty to see if anything further is going to be put in place regarding defence cooperation.[8] The development of the Eurocorps — defence cooperation initially between France and Germany, but now also including other (but by no means all) EU member states — holds both potential advantages and problems for the EU-WEU defence identity. On the one hand, if it is at all successful, it would signify a greater cooperation on defence matters. On the other hand, the Eurocorps promises to create a second tier in CFSP, just as the EU is trying to cope with centrifugal tendencies in other policy areas such as economic and monetary union. These problems only arise, however, if the Eurocorps becomes an effective vehicle for defence cooperation rather than the paper agreement it appears to be at present.

The Character of the CFSP

The chapter has so far described the historical development of the CFSP and its limitations. This section will look at some of the guiding principles of the CFSP and its underlying assumptions. The CFSP might not be as strong as some of its proponents would like. On the other hand, this section suggests that there may be reasons to question the goals and methods of the CFSP as currently presented.

To put it very bluntly, the aim of security policy in the EU as manifested in EPC and the CFSP is premised on the territorial exclusion of threats to security; the exclusion is ultimately performed through coercive measures, in the final analysis military force. Security policy in the EU, then, is essentially a state-centred perspective writ large onto the proto-European state. As I noted above, security and security policy have been narrowly conceived as the business of defence and foreign ministry apparatus. This creates and reinforces the "history" of security policy as an addendum to the development of European political cooperation; it can be read against the backdrop of past abortive attempts at creating a European defence community that have culminated rather naturally in the Common Foreign and Security Policy of the Maastricht Treaty.[9] The problem here is an evacuation of the substance of security: security policy is what foreign and defence department officials do and security is what security policy provides. Besides the reductionism of this position, there is the serious question of whether revival plans for European defence is appropriate at all given the changed international context.

More fundamentally, security policy in the EU implicates identity, specifically the identity of the European Union. Indeed, in some ways, what is secured above all is EU identity. The article on EPC in the SEA is premised on the notion that security cooperation would contribute to "the development of a European identity in external policy matters." Security is seen as a route to European identity enhancing the present member states of the EU.[10]

EU identity is being created through differentiation from others. The CFSP implicitly interprets security policy for the EU member states in the face of threats from outside the EU. Despite the initiatives such as the Stability Pact, the CFSP embodies confrontational rather than cooperative security. The creation of outsiders to the EU might be considered inevitable. After all, there are limits to engagement and membership. Yet, the significance of being on the inside or the outside will increase as the EU as a group of states grows more "powerful," as we have seen with the recent defection from EFTA to the EU of Austria, Sweden, and Finland. Unfortunately, the negative implications of the inside/outside distinction are worsened by the view that the EU is some sort of third power. This used to be the view of the EC between the US and the Soviets; today, it is the EU *versus* a North American bloc and an Asian bloc. Furthermore, the third power view of the EU complements and reinforces a unitary vision of the Union by highlighting the need for internal coherence and solidarity in the face of external challenges. In the discourses of the CFSP, the EU's capabilities and modalities of internal cohesion and external expression are implicitly compared to those of a state and also rest on an understanding of power ultimately determined by the possession of military force. Certainly, the development of a security policy suggests that some within the EU hope that it will in future be a great power, though many other Europeans equally fear such a development.[11]

Ultimately, however, the paradox of the security discourse of the EU as found in the CFSP is that it looks for problems and threats. In short, while helping to secure the EU's identity, the CFSP is also posed as a solution to security problems. Regrettably, as it concentrates on security interpreted as defence against threats either directly or indirectly from outsiders, it jeopardizes the EU's openness and the prospects for international cooperation and ironically the EU's own security!

The paradox of the CFSP is a result not of flawed analysis, but of a lack of analysis, however. Security policy has relied rather conservatively on notions of security derived from national foreign ministries and defence ministries. Furthermore, security policy is seen as instrumental to the development of a regional union — it is another part of the federal puzzle alongside Economic and Monetary Union — rather than being valued for the security it could provide.[12] Finally, despite the ferment in security studies in the academic world, the EU has adopted an approach more in tune with the Cold War than the current fluid situation in Europe. Furthermore, the EU has ignored its own history, in which an alternative conception of security and security policy based on cooperative rather than confrontational security features prominently, a conception moreover that underpins the security that is now felt within and between the member states of the European Union.

The Functional Alternative

That the concept of security in the EU's security policy has remained undeveloped is surprising for a number of reasons. First, while the discussion above might appear new, the criticisms of the territorial, military-oriented, and exclusionary conceptions of European security are long-standing. In short, one does not need to be a postmodernist to embrace the criticisms of the territorial basis of the CFSP.

The second reason is that the EU is betraying itself in the attempt to formulate a security policy with a defence emphasis. Clearly, recent circumstances in the former Yugoslavia and the experience in the Gulf have oriented the discussion of security policy in the EU toward the management and settlement/enforcement phases of conflict resolution.[13] It continues to be true, however, that the EU's strongest tools for conflict management are persuasion, based on economic power, as well as some diplomatic procedures. These tools are most appropriate in the preconflict and mediation phases of disputes.

One theoretical account of the role of the EU in conflict management is David Mitrany's functional approach. The functional alternative to the CFSP can be found in an extension of Mitrany's criticisms of the federalism and regionalism of the EEC and his writings on the origin of the European Coal and Steel Community.

Mitrany's Critique of the EEC

Although functionalism has since been hailed as a theory of integration, its originator, David Mitrany, was none too impressed with larger attempts at European regional integration as manifested in the European Economic

Community. His reasoning echoes his wartime analysis of the need for a working peace system. The proponents of European integration who supported the EEC Treaty were aiming for a European federal state, he argued. Mitrany criticized this because it reasserted the territorial basis of political organization; in other words, why should cooperation on all economic issues be constrained by a continental treaty? Why should cooperation with non-Europeans take second place? This had serious implications for the prospects for world peace; why, Mitrany asked rather provocatively, should a European Union "suddenly be guided by sweet reasonableness and self-restraint"?[14]

According to Mitrany, "the very concept of a closed regional union is a contradiction of the historic European idea" — that is, European civilization had prided itself on its openness. Attempts to find a European identity, which would have to be vigorous given the differences between Europeans, would detract from world peace and what today would be called the EU's role as a world partner.[15] Mitrany argued that creating loyalty to this new regional bloc would foster international discord.

> To build up a cohesive loyalty, national movements have often had to disinter or invent all sorts of historical, social, and emotional affinities, above all to keep alive the fear of some common external danger. Regionalism, starting with more differences than affinities, would have to go even further in that.[16]

He also noted that the precarious balance necessary to keep together the diverse interests within the EEC, especially turning to foreign policy and defence, would expend energy on internal matters that could otherwise be devoted (more profitably) to advancing the general cause of international peace and security.

At the heart of Mitrany's critique is his view that the supporters of the EEC were hoping to create a federal state and that the EEC was indeed a proto-federal state at the regional level. As such, the EEC was based on territorial assumptions about authority and jurisdiction rather than functional assumptions. Mitrany contrasted the new regional economic bloc with the other European Communities, arguing that the EEC would hinder international cooperation:

> The ECSC and Euratom are straight functional bodies and can get on with their allotted task without offending the position of other countries, while remaining open to link up with them. The point is that for service units like the ECSC and Euratom, as for all the specialized agencies of the UN and any future functional bodies, wider association means more points of co-

operative contact; for a self-inflating organization like the EEC, more fields of control must mean internationally more points of competitive contact.[17]

According to Mitrany, the argument for a federal union of Europe relied on a view of international economic interaction that was faulty. Quoting an American jurist, Mitrany argued that "geographical association no longer corresponds to the actual interests of neighbours."[18] Regional organizations cut across international cooperation, hindered economic progress, and jeopardized peace.

Mitrany's final criticism of the development of the EEC was that a regional bloc is inherently undemocratic and bureaucratic. In an argument that anticipates the recent criticisms of the "democratic deficit" in the European Union, he attacked the idea of direct elections to the European Parliament (EP). He suggested that there was an inexorable process in modern politics that increased the power of the executive over the legislature. The EP, he reasoned, was unlikely to overcome this tendency. He maintained that the distance of the EP from its constituents and the nature and complexity of EEC business made for a complete lack of accountability:

> While ... it is a fair claim that the present communities ... fall short in democratic content as long as they lack a representative assembly, it is an illusion to think that in a "more perfect union" an elected parliament will gather unto itself more power than is now left to national parliaments even in the best of democratic states. It is likely to be less. It will have neither the cohesion nor the acquired traditions of a national parliament, while the executive will be under greater pressure of public business but also less exposed to the watchfulness of parties and press and popular opinion.[19]

One can only note that the distance and the relative lack of control by national parliaments of foreign and security policy — as contrasted with other policies — are magnified still further in the EU as Mitrany indicated it would be for a whole range of "European" policies.

Mitrany's criticisms of the EEC are directly applicable to recent attempts to forge the Common Foreign and Security Policy. For Mitrany, the EEC as a regional federation is not a route to peace in Europe. His reasoning is that whatever functional activities the EEC might pursue, the territorial and constitutional focus of a regional federation promotes the arbitrary division of Europe. Meanwhile the real security issues and the needs of the people of Europe, within the EEC but especially beyond, would be ignored. By extension, the Common Foreign and Security Policy is not a route to European security as currently configured within the EU. It reflects the constitutional and territorial attitude to European integration that Mitrany so disliked. What Mitrany might have preferred will be discussed in the closing sections of the chapter.

The European Coal and Steel Community — A Functional Alternative?

As was demonstrated above, at the same time as he was criticizing the EEC as a regional bloc, Mitrany was a fervent supporter of the ECSC. Indeed, Mitrany not only supported the creation of a Coal and Steel Community as a functional organization in the heart of Europe, but he prescribed it as a solution to security in Europe. In the 1944 *The Road to Security*, Mitrany called for reconstruction efforts in Europe to be built around cooperation on steel and coal by France and Germany. He cited this as a potentially more fruitful route to international peace and security than the reestablishment of a League of Nations arrangement, that is, the UN. Mitrany emphasized that economic welfare and security were closely linked; there was no question of the priority of one over the other. He argued that "it is generally agreed that [preventing German rearmament] involves control not merely of the actual armament industries, but also of the heavy and chemical industries, as well as other industries and services." Mitrany noted that some had, therefore, argued that

> the only effective means of prevention is joint control over the whole sector of an industry. That means a willingness to accept also for ourselves, in the common interest, such joint control as would prevent the use of a particular industry or material for aggressive purposes.

Concluding this line of argument, Mitrany stated that this method did not oppress the Germans as much as the Versailles Settlement had at the end of World War I, because "the controls would be part of an equally effective service to the German people, and would apply to other countries as well."[20]

Mitrany's argument about the difference between the ECSC and the EEC can be illustrated by an interesting contrast between the preambles of the ECSC and the EEC Treaties. The security rhetoric of the ECSC Treaty contrasts with the predominantly welfare-oriented EEC Treaty and also with the EU's subsequent self-image as a unitary regional union, predominantly but not exclusively focusing on economic matters. The Treaty of Paris mentions peace three times, and peace is generally given high priority in terms of the aims of the new Coal and Steel Community. It opens as follows:

> Considering that world peace can be safeguarded only by creative efforts commensurate with the dangers that threaten it ... Convinced that the contribution which an organized and vital Europe can make to civilization

is indispensable to the maintenance of peaceful relations ... Recognizing that Europe can be built only through practical achievements which will first create real solidarity...

By contrast the Treaty of Rome creating the EEC mentions peace once and it relegates that reference to the last clause. Instead, references to prosperity, standards of living and union are promoted:

Determined to lay the foundations of an ever closer union among the peoples of Europe ... Resolved to ensure the economic and social progress of their countries by common action to eliminate the barriers which divide Europe ... Affirming as the essential objective of their efforts the constant improvement of the living and working conditions of their peoples...

While there is clearly the influence of historical context to take into account, it is nonetheless significant that economics and security are increasingly divorced in the EEC as compared to their integration into the ECSC.

There were many reasons for the establishment of the European Coal and Steel Community. However, in the realm of ideas at least, the functional approach to security was a contributor to the way in which the community was created. Following Mitrany, the functional approach to security undertaken, even if imperfectly, in the ECSC stands as a clear, practical functional alternative to the tradition of EPC/CFSP.

Given the position of the ECSC within the EU today, however, it is understandable that for the most part the ECSC Treaty is discussed in terms of the treaty it begat, the Treaty of Rome, or in its contribution to energy or industrial policy.[21] The ECSC is a victim both of its own success as a mechanism for security and of the increasing bifurcation of economic welfare and international security within the EC/EU. While Mitrany contrasted the ECSC and the EEC, it is not clear to me that he would still defend the ECSC today — nor, given the developments in the ECSC, whether Mitrany was entirely correct in his estimation of the ECSC as a functional organization or as a guarantor of security in Europe in the way he intended. It is arguable, at least, that the symbolic value of the ECSC and subsequently the EC was more significant for the peace of Europe than their functional value.

The Functional Alternative for the EU: Limits and Prospects

What does the alternative tradition of functional security and David Mitrany's articulation of it mean for security policy in the EU? I will address this in two parts: first in terms of the substance of security policy and then in terms of institutional design.

Security from the functional perspective is integrative rather than exclusionary, community-oriented rather than externally-focused, and concerned with economic and social interaction besides high political and military affairs. It also implies not only that security policy must integrate economic aspects of security but that trade policies must include elements of security. The example of security in Central and Eastern Europe might be helpful at this point, as it offers a scenario for highlighting the differences between territorial and functional security in action in the EU.

The EU and Security in Central and Eastern Europe

Along with the prospect of a resurgent and nationalistic Russia and a potentially volatile Southern flank, Central and Eastern Europe (CEE) is the area of greatest security concern to the EU member states because of proximity, current instability, and its history of weapons build-up, of which the nuclear arsenal is only the most notable aspect. The challenges in Central and Eastern Europe are immense: ethnic conflict both within and across state boundaries, economic decline and transition, border disputes, the sudden demise of international coordination, migration, etc. Yet, it is unclear how the CFSP can be of any practical utility either in providing security for the EU itself or for the Central and East Europeans. Indeed, the debate over Eastern enlargement, over the terms of the Europe agreements and over assistance to the fledging democracies and market economies, has served to alienate Central and Eastern Europeans. In sum, notwithstanding the Stability Pact, the CFSP is irrelevant or worse for European security.

The EU is developing a wide range of relationships with Central and Eastern Europe either as separate member states or in wider international fora such as the EBRD and the World Bank. Aid and trade are being facilitated by such contacts, though there is some dispute about the efficacy of the measures being taken.[22] However, the economic objectives and principles underlying the projects in Central and Eastern Europe have not been linked to security. Instead there are free market rules: improving market access, retraining of workers, and assisting with economic, technical, and financial help constitute major planks of the Europe Agreements. In its report to the European Council for the Summit in Edinburgh, (11-12 December 1992), the Commission proposed further measures to promote creating a Europe-wide free trade area and to overcome obstacles to investment in Central and Eastern Europe.

There is a hint of what the functional alternative would require in the above quote from the Treaty of Rome. The EU's security policy above all should be ensuring "the economic and social progress ... by common action to eliminate the barriers which divide Europe." Unfortunately, the territorial and threat assumptions of the CFSP make this difficult. One proposal that follows from Mitrany's functional approach would be to open to the EU trade with Central and Eastern European countries in order to meet needs most effectively and to cooperate across Europe.[23] Unfortunately, Mitrany's fears regarding the EEC have purchase as we see the entrenched interests within the member states of the EU blocking concessions to the CEE countries or demanding/extorting compensation from the wealthier member states for their cooperation. The result has been a set of European agreements that exclude the key commodities that the CEE countries would trade and concessions on items that are of marginal significance and whose level of trade will never reach the level of the concession!

It is not clear in any event that a glorified free trade area rather like the EEA is integrative enough to guarantee security. Delors has expressed his dissatisfaction with the "soulless" aspect of economic integration.[24] This is transplanted into relations with the CEE countries. While a 1992-style programme fits the "spirit of the age," there is a lack of connection to security, even in the broadest sense. The institutionalized insecurity of the global market is hardly a robust basis on which to create European security. It has been argued before that economic interdependence in trade and investment makes war less rational and therefore less likely. Yet, this has proved a flimsy argument in the past and looks no more likely to work in the future.

At the level of personal security, though, there can be little doubt that EU openness to agricultural trade, as an example, would be likely to give farmers in the CEE region at least the prospect of some elemental form of material security that would otherwise be difficult to obtain. Such an argument accords, of course, with the "trade not aid" school of development theory. It also resonates with the EU's own approach to its farmers in the Common Agricultural Policy, where security for farmers was one of the primary goals of the policy.

What other prescriptions derive from the functional alternative? In the ECSC, security was provided through functional cooperation in militarily as well as industrially significant sectors. Heavy industry is arguably less important in Western economies, but still largely so in the East. In any event, the task is to find the area in which functional cooperation could most completely integrate industrial and military activities. This might today be in certain dual (civil and military) technologies. However, the EEC Commission report to the European Council for the Edinburgh summit gives us a hint into the idea of Trans-European Networks involving transport, telecommunications, and energy. Infrastructure projects would give a large infusion of needed investment and would result in a relief of the bottlenecks to further economic development and growth. From a financial standpoint, they look a distant prospect. It is not clear that infrastructure projects to improve communications across Europe are as central to common security as was coal and steel to postwar Germany and to Franco-German relations. What is evident is that the absence of such integrating initiatives makes the likelihood of a failure of economic transition and development in the CEE countries greater because of the lack of physical connection and by a failure to bridge the psychological gap between the CEE countries and the EU.

The experience of the ECSC suggests another approach: functional cooperation between previous adversaries in production central to civilian industrial development and military power. The post-Cold War version of this scenario suggests a pan-European consortium on nuclear technology, informatics, and biotechnology.[25] The aim would be to bring together the technical knowledge and the specialists in an area of increasing significance to advanced economies, as well as to the development of weapons of mass destruction. The critical aspect of this proposal would be to bring in Russian scientists; it is the former adversaries who need to cooperate. This is, of course, a very ambitious proposal and in that sense is rather out of tune with Mitrany's concerns with the more mundane, technical functions. The proposal fits more easily with neofunctionalism. The proposal has value, nevertheless, in that it sets parameters for the achievement of genuine security in Europe, or as Mitrany would have it, a working peace rather than a protected peace.

The Institutional Form of the EU

The functional alternative is suggestive not only of the orientation of EU security policy. It also indicates that the EU should be more flexible in its institutional development. Intriguingly, this accords with recent developments within the Union and in the Union's relations with other European states.

There is a large and growing literature on the extension of the EU into East-Central Europe and further.[26] The EU has a number of different links with Central and Eastern Europe, including the development of trade and cooperation agreements, the Europe agreements, as well as the Commission's part in coordinating the aid programmes PHARE and TACIS, and the majority shareholding of member states in the European Bank for Reconstruction and

Development. The matter of future membership of CEE countries is also being actively discussed.

At the same time, the EU is considering ideas for a multispeed or variable geometry Europe. Instead of all member states adhering to the same set of policies, variable geometry suggests that different states will take different packages of common policies. This has certainly been a pragmatic response on the part of the member states of the EU to difficulties with advancing to deeper integration involved in, for instance, Economic and Monetary Union or the Common Foreign and Security Policy. Such pragmatism and the form that it has taken suggests that, despite the rhetoric of the CFSP, the European Union is less and less a singular structure and more a multiplicity of overlapping activities and processes that vary according to function.[27] Such developments would have been applauded by Mitrany as functional reactions to the realities of international life, though the modalities — political dialogue, the Stability Pact, the various trade and aid packages — need to be taken much further in the way that they give Central and Eastern Europeans both a stake and a say in the exchange.

To summarize, in terms of the institutional form of the EU, both internally and in relations with the CEE countries, there are indications that a functional approach is reasserting itself, despite the conception of security found in the CFSP. However, Mitrany would tell us that the problem of European security is far from solved since there is no integrated, cooperative approach to security evident in EU policy toward the CEE countries, but rather an irrelevant security policy and a set of economistic trade and aid policies that fail to deal adequately with the fundamental security questions at stake in Europe. Further, while EU bureaucrats and representatives of member states shudder at the idea of the complexity of institutional structure introduced by such functional developments, it is worth noting that diversity can be a strength rather than a weakness as it contributes to flexibility and to the range of options available for conflict resolution or avoidance.

One final implication of the functional approach follows from the insight that international institutions should be organized according to specified functions and that international security is enhanced by the plurality of such international functional institutions. In the current context, it is clear that the EU should concentrate on economic security matters. Rather more controversially, it seems at least plausible that other institutions can address other security functions: the existence of other fora for cooperation on defence and "hard" security issues means that this need not be an area left uncared for; there is still a role for NATO, even from the functional perspective.

The proposition that there can be international institutions performing a security function appears in Mitrany, *A Working Peace System,* but it is problematical because it reimports concepts of military and territorial security that were supposed to be transcended by other functional arrangements. On the other hand, the functional approach does provide a useful rationalization of an already emerging or established division of labour.

Conclusion

The EU has unfortunately chosen to emphasize traditional exclusionary, territorial and military-oriented notions of security in the development of its Common Foreign and Security Policy, despite its own access to, and comparative advantage in, a functional alternative concept of security and security policy. The Common Foreign and Security Policy relies on a narrow meaning of security, ill-suited to the region of greatest security concern to EU relations, Central and Eastern Europe. Mitrany's critique of the EEC applies nicely to the CFSP. Analysis of the origins of the EU in the ECSC also points to some directions for security policy guided by the tradition of the functional approach, such as openness in trade with the CEE countries and technical cooperation with Russia. This chapter is not a condemnation of the EU itself as a route to peace and security. It is incontrovertible that the EU has over its existence contributed to peace, stability, and prosperity within its borders. But the last three words of that sentence highlight the problem with the CFSP; the EU's international relations and particularly its security policy must reflect its internal character more closely if it is to contribute to peace on the continent of Europe as a whole.

Notes

Previous versions of this chapter have been presented at a workshop on "Functionalism and Conflict Management," Ottawa, March 1995, and at the European Community Studies Association Biennial Meeting, Charleston, South Carolina, May 1995.

1. Fraser Cameron, "The 1996 IGC-A Challenge for Europe," *ECSA Newsletter,* 8:2 (1995): 9-13.

2. Stephen George, *Policy and Politics in the European Community* (Oxford: Oxford University Press, 1991), pp. 218-20.

3. Jacques Delors, "European Integration and Security," *Survival,* 33:2 (1991): 104.

4. John Pinder, *The European Community: The Building of a Union* (Oxford: Oxford University Press, 1991), pp. 6-7; Neill Nugent, *The Government and Politics of the European Community* (London: MacMillan Press, 1991), pp. 39-41. The plan for a European Defence Community failed, of course, because of concerns about German rearmament and British hesitancy and ultimate reluctance to join in the project.

5. Commission of the European Community, *European Union* (Luxembourg: Office for Official Publications of the EC, 1992), p. 31. European Council declaration was annexed to the Maastricht Treaty.

6. Commission of the European Union, *Bulletin of the European Union 1/2-1994* (Office of Official Publications of the EU, 1994), p. 66; Commission of the European Union, *Bulletin of the European Union, 10-1994* (Office of Official Publications of the EU, 1994), p. 47.

7. The WEU has ten full members, comprising all EU states that are also members of NATO, with the exception of Denmark which has opted for observer status. Additionally, there are three associate members, the non-EU members of NATO: Turkey, Norway, and Iceland.

8. Lawrence Martin and John Roper, *Towards a Common Defence Policy* (Paris: Institute for Security Studies of the WEU, 1995).

9. George, *European Community*, p. 29.

10. Delors, "European Integration and Security," pp. 104-7.

11. Christopher Hill, "European Foreign Policy: Power Bloc, Civilian Model - or Flop?" in *The Evolution of an International Actor*, ed. R. Rummel (Boulder: Westview, 1990), p. 54; and John Galtung, *The European Community: A Superpower in the Making* (London: George Allen and Unwin, 1973).

12. Delors, "European Integration and Security," pp. 104-5.

13. Ibid., pp. 102, 106-8; and Trevor Salmon, "Testing Times for European Political Cooperation: The Gulf and Yugoslavia, 1990-1992," *International Affairs*, 68:2 (1992): 250-52.

14. David Mitrany, *A Working Peace System* (Chicago, IL: Quadrangle, 1966), p. 187.

15. Ibid., pp. 184-86.

16. Ibid., p. 186.

17. Ibid., pp. 109-10.

18. Ibid., p. 182.

19. Ibid., pp. 196-97.

20. David Mitrany, *The Road to Security* (London: National Peace Council, 1944), p. 17.

21. Nugent, *The Government and Politics of the European Community*, pp. 34-9; and Pinder, *European Community: The Building of a Union*, pp. 3-6; George, *European Community*, ch. 7.

22. Robert Keohane, Joseph Nye and Stanley Hoffmann (eds.), *After the Cold War: International Institutions and State Strategies in Europe, 1989-1991* (Cambridge, MA: Harvard University Press, 1993).

23. I am indebted to Robert Wolfe for this suggestion.

24. Delors, "European Integration and Security," p. 104.

25. Craig Murphy made this point in the "Functionalism and Conflict Management" workshop, Ottawa, March 1995.

26. Finn Laursen, "The EC and Its European Neighbours: Special Partnerships or Widened Membership?" *International Journal,* 47:1 (1991): 2; and Anna Michalski and Helen Wallace, *European Community: the Challenge of Enlargement* (London: RIIA, 1992); and John Pinder, *The European Community and Eastern Europe* (London: Pinter/RIIA, 1991); Neill Nugent, "The Deepening and Widening of the European Community: Recent Evolution, Maastricht and Beyond," *Journal of Common Market Studies,* 30:3 (1992).

27. Edward Mortimer, "European Security after the Cold War," *Adelphi Paper*, 271 (London: IISS, 1992); and Peter Wilson, "The 1940's Debate on a New Europe and Thinking About the New Europe in the 1990's," London School of Economics, unpublished manuscript, 1992, pp. 25-26.

Allen G. Sens

Cooperation under Neorealism: Bringing in the Small States (of Eastern and Central Europe)

Introduction

Few items on the international security agenda have received the degree of attention currently devoted to regional security issues. There are two related explanations for this focus on regional security: the absence of a clearly identifiable, single actor threat to international peace and stability and the relatively high profile of contemporary regional conflicts; and the identification of regional security issues as threats to international peace and stability. "European" security issues have received considerable attention because of the high profile of the Yugoslavian débacle, and because the future of Europe is a key element in the evolution of the global post-Cold War security environment. One of the pressing issues in European security is the future of the Central European countries in the political and economic life of the continent. The debate over the "enlargement" of the North Atlantic Treaty Organization (NATO) and the European Union (EU) to include Central European states has been front and centre in Europe for some time.

Of particular concern in studies of regional security is the future of cooperation among regional actors after the withdrawal of the Cold War overlay.[1] For "neoliberals," the preservation or development of regional cooperation, especially multilateral cooperation and institutions, is regarded as a bulwark against increasing tensions, conflict, and warfare. Multilateralism means peace and stability, or at least a good shot at it. For "neorealists," regional cooperation is far less meaningful. There is little evidence to suggest that multilateral frameworks and institutions significantly affect the behaviour of states in an anarchic, self-help environment. These two approaches also differ on the nature and future of multilateral cooperation. "Neoliberals" are optimistic, arguing that states have learned the value of cooperation and institutions and will maintain and strengthen them. "Neorealists" are sceptical, doubting the ability of such cooperative enterprises to develop or even survive beyond the conditions that prompted their formation.

With respect to these issues, most of the attention has been focused on the policies, interests, and motivations of the most powerful regional actors. The smaller states in these regions have often been neglected in examinations of regional security and regional cooperation. There is a need to bring the small states into such discussions, for any truly representative, universal multilateral effort must of necessity include the small states. It follows that there is a need to understand the motivations behind the behaviour of small states with respect to cooperative behaviour. This chapter intends to make three contributions to the study of regional security and regional cooperation:

- first, the chapter asserts that small states have been neglected in neorealist theory. It seeks to make a "first cut" at enhancing the explanatory power of neorealism by "bringing the small states in" to existing neorealist theories of cooperation;

- second, the paper asserts that the case of the small states of Eastern Europe provides an illuminating example of the utility of a neorealist explanation of small state behaviour with respect to multilateral cooperation; and

- third, the paper seeks to make a contribution to the enlargement debate in light of these perspectives. The evidence strengthens the case for an early enlargement of NATO and the EU.

Cooperation under Neorealism and its Critics

In response to both the persistence of many Cold War institutions and the critics of neorealism's alleged inability to offer any positive prospects for the international system, neorealists have recently begun to remind everyone — including themselves — that a wide variety of cooperative behaviour can occur in an essentially anarchic international environment. The motivation for this cooperation originates with one of the core assumptions of neorealism: states exist in a self-help world. Simply put, states will cooperate if it is in their interests to do so. This cooperation is, of course, inherently limited by concerns over cheating and relative gains, two symptoms of an international system that is fundamentally competitive in nature. International institutions, in turn, are reflections of the distribution of power or are the instruments of dominant states.[2]

Some neorealists have offered complementary explanations that seek to improve neorealism's ability to account for cooperation. Charles L. Glaser, for example, attempts to reorient realism away from an overdeveloped focus on competition and proposes "contingent realism" as a solution.[3] For Glaser, states seeking security will often find it in their interests to engage in cooperative policies to signal peaceful intentions to other states. In another example, Joseph M. Grieco proposes what he calls the "voice opportunities" thesis, which suggests that states will cooperate in order to secure opportunities to voice their concerns and gain some influence over the issues and events that are of concern to them.[4] Implicit in such arguments is the belief that states are often more interested in the maintenance of power and the status quo than they are in power maximization and revisionism.

Opposing the neorealist conception of cooperation is a spectrum of theories that seek to find explanations for cooperation based on something other than pure self-interest. Neoliberals, or liberal institutionalists, argue that multilateral cooperation and multilateral institutions create a commitment to cooperation that acts as a deterrent against the payoffs of cheating and relative gains. States will sacrifice short-term gains for the advantages of long-term cooperation, reinforced by the logic of punishment in iterated situations. In this way, the behaviour of states becomes bounded and more disposed toward cooperative behaviour.[5] Closely related are theories of interdependence, which suggest that state behaviour is modified by patterns of sensitivity or vulnerability to the actions of others. In such situations, cooperation in a variety of "regimes" is a logical state response.[6] Functional theorists argue that cooperation can develop from modest initial experiences, either at governmental or sub-governmental levels, into broader or deeper forms of cooperation.[7] Still others suggest the importance of ideological, cultural, and social or class commonalities as explanations for cooperation and the persistence of cooperation. For these alternative perspectives, cooperation becomes a self-perpetuating value, a force in its own right, rather than purely a reflection of self-interest derived from a particular distribution of power.

Small States and Neorealist Theory

As suggested in the introduction, small states have not been subjects of close examination by neorealists. The reason for this is simple; for neorealists, it is the most powerful units that are the most important. The attitude of Kenneth Waltz is typical: "the theory, like the story, of international politics is written in terms of the great powers of an era ... in international politics, as in any self-help system, the units of greatest capability set the scene of action for others as well as for themselves." And furthermore: "Concern with international politics as a system requires concentration on the states that make the most difference. A general theory of international politics is necessarily based on the great powers."[8]

As a result, the bulk of thought about small states in neorealism has focused on their role in the strategies of the great powers or on the fate that has befallen them in a great power world. Small states are subjects only to the extent that they serve as junior allies, buffers, satellites, bases, battleground and bargaining chips.[9] There is little understanding of the unique security dilemmas facing small states, and therefore a lack of appreciation for the perspectives and perceptions behind small state behaviour. The emphasis on power politics in the neorealist approach also de-emphasizes the small states, which by definition have less power. Furthermore, when attention is paid to small states, it is usually when they are threatened by a traditional military or political (i.e., coercive) threat. The helplessness of small states in these situations only serves to confirm both the importance of power (and the importance of those that have it) and the assertion that small states have little or no significance independent of their relationship with the great powers.

It is not the purpose of this chapter to oppose fundamentally this assertion, but rather to suggest that small states are more important in the international system and to theories of international relations than neorealism suggests. Neglecting small states leaves a gap in our theoretical and practical knowledge of the international system and regional subsystems. Such neglect also ignores the insights that the peculiar security dilemmas of small states can bring to our understanding of international cooperation. The first task of this section is to explore how small states can be brought into neorealist theory in a more sophisticated fashion; the second task is to illustrate the relevance of small states with respect to explanations and incentives for cooperation.

Small States and the Assumptions of Neorealism

The first assumption of neorealism is that states are the primary unit in the international system and that they are essentially unitary, rational actors. A greater appreciation of small states is in no way inconsistent with this assumption. There are, after all, far more small states than great powers, and a theory that holds the state as the dominant unit of analysis would do well to understand those states that form the greatest number of the units in the system. And small states may in fact be excellent examples of the unitary, rational actor model. Small states have been accused of irresponsible behaviour, particularly in balance of power systems where their alleged tendency to bandwagon with growing powers contributes to the system being thrown out of balance.[10] Despite these accusations, small state actions which appear irresponsible from a great power, or systemic, perspective are quite rational from the perspective of the small state, which is often forced into rapid policy changes based on shifts in alignment or the power balance. Therefore, accusations of irresponsible behaviour should not prejudice appraisals of the "rationality" of small states.

Furthermore, in their relations with great powers, small states frequently do surprisingly well in negotiated settlements. This is because while great powers often have their attention divided between many issues and actors, small states can often concentrate all of their diplomatic and political resources on an issue that may be of paramount importance to a small state but of peripheral importance to a great power.[11] This diplomatic "power of the weak" has another dimension; small states can, under certain conditions manipulate great powers in a phenomenon known as the "tail wagging the dog." In such situations, the commitment a great power makes to the security of a small state becomes a symbol of that great power's prestige and strength. Small states may employ this as an instrument of leverage to extract favours or concessions from their patron. The ability to employ such strategies assumes a high degree of strategic calculation and a unity of effort on the part of small states. Finally, smaller entities may be more rational as actors in that they possess fewer domestic intervening variables which can interfere with assessments of interest. As Raymond Aron has suggested, the "defensive power" of a state is a function of *"la cohésion de la collectivité, l'adhésion des masses au régime, l'accord entre les membres de l'élite gouvernementale sur l'intéret national."*[12]

The implication for neorealist theory is that small states can have an impact in the international system.[13] Instead of maintaining the standard assumption of the inconsequential role of the small states in their relations with the great powers, neorealism would do well to acknowledge that the less powerful units in the system may under certain conditions be very significant. In addition, the relationship between small states and great powers is more of an interlinked, as opposed to a one way, relationship than neorealism acknowledges; it is this linkage that has had serious consequences for system stability in the past, not the behaviour of the small states in isolation. Again, the point is not to challenge the weaker position of the small states, but to argue that the small states are more important beyond the significance they have been accorded.

The second assumption of neorealism is that states exist in an anarchic, self-help system. No states are more aware of this than are the small states. Their inherently weak power position places them at a disadvantage in a system where the maximization or maintenance of power is a fundamental goal.

In an anarchic system, small states do not have the capacity to ensure their own security. As a result, they must seek help from others to do so, and seeking help in a self-help system is a dangerous endeavour. Furthermore, in a world of security competition one's strength is not only important for self-protection, but also for one's attractiveness as an ally. The ability of a small state to obtain help, and any influence it might have in such a relationship, is based on what assets can be brought to a collective effort. Small states do not have much to offer in a relative sense; often they are valued more for their geopolitical location or the nature of the terrain they occupy.

None of this is inconsistent with neorealist assumptions, but what has to be recognized in any greater incorporation of small states into neorealist theory is the need to highlight the security dilemma faced by small states. For small states, the reality of requiring help to ensure their security carries with it an additional set of dangers, namely, the risks associated with cooperation with a great power or a number of great powers. Another dilemma confronting small states is the reality that while conflict between the great powers can have dire consequences for small states, excessive cooperation among the great powers can also be a threat to the security of small states, for such cooperation may come at the expense of the interests and security of small states. Small state security options are thus double-edged. Such security conundrums, while fundamental to the strategic reality of small states are rarely, if ever, felt by great powers.

The third assumption of neorealism is the primacy of military power in relations between states. Although the prominence of this assumption has faded somewhat and constitutes one of the primary lightning rods for critics of neorealism, it remains an essential component of a body of theory based on self-help in an anarchic environment. For small states, military potential is a reflection of power potential; their military potential is limited and their capacity to combat great powers is very circumscribed. This is due to the limited endowment of small states with respect to militarily relevant assets, such as population base, economic and fiscal resources, industrial base, strategic minerals, and the costs of military research and production. However, this does not mean that small states are inconsequential in military terms. Some small states have proved extremely difficult opponents for great powers, such as Vietnam, while the surprising level of resistance of others has upset the war plans of the great powers, as was the case with Belgium. Furthermore, small states made significant military contributions in larger conflicts, as did the Dominions in the Second World War.

The fourth assumption of neorealism is that states are preoccupied with concerns over their independence and sovereignty. This is felt with particular intensity in small states, where the threat of submergence of one's economic and cultural independence under a larger political, cultural, or social entity is a constant concern. As a result, issues of political independence, economic sovereignty, and cultural protection have long been a component of the security calculations of small states. As Paul Sharp points out, the security threat perceived by small states is much broader in scope:

> From the point of view of the governments of many weak states, however, the problem is neither one of how to achieve an impact on the international system, nor one of being ready to deter or defeat specific external military threats. Rather, it is the more generalised difficulty of maintaining both the internal and the external credibility of their claims to be acting for sovereign, independent states which are capable of ensuing the cultural identity and material propensity of their people.[14]

The concern of more and more great powers with similar issues suggests that there is some value to exploring the small state experience with a broadened security agenda.

The fifth assumption of neorealism is that the external environment exerts tremendous pressure on the conduct of states. Again, the experience of small states is sharply revealing, for the shape of the international environment is of enormous significance to small states and informs the avenues they have open to ensure their security. Considerable detail is required here, for these points capture most of the motivations behind the behaviour of small states, and can inform explanations of current and possible future behaviour. What is evident is that small states do have security preferences, and the most desirable of these centre on multilateral options. However, in the absence of such options (or in the absence of the credibility of such options) small states will resort to other, albeit less preferable options.

Historically, small states have been caught in "cycles of insecurity," which are characterized by shifts in the distribution of power and the rise and decline of dominant states. In the period after such shifts, small states are compelled, as are all states, to evaluate their security policies and adjust them to new security environments, new centres of power, new patterns of amity or enmity, and new threats. However, balance-of-power systems are not kind to small states. In such situations, small states are confronted with the dilemmas inherent in their security options: each option is double-edged. Small states are trapped in a perpetual "search for security," and hope for the evolution of a qualitiatively different environment which might satisfy their security needs.

Small States and the "Search for Security" in a Balance-of-Power World

In balance-of-power systems, small states have most frequently relied on bilateral alliances as a security mechanism.[15] However, the bilateral alliance option is laden with risks. An alliance with a great power may create new enemies — those of its great power ally. In addition, a reversal in the fortunes of its security guarantor can have dire consequences for the small state. An alliance with a great power may also prove unreliable, for a great power may be unwilling to risk war over a smaller (and perhaps expendable) ally. Finally, bilateral alliances with a great power may lead to a loss of autonomy over military affairs and freedom of political manoeuvre. There is a very real risk that a bilateral alliance with a great power could erode domestic policy autonomy and national sovereignty, and in extreme cases, there is the risk of outright domination. As Robert Rothstein has offered: "The small power may move not from insecurity to security, but from insecurity to the status of a satellite."[16]

Multilateral alliances are held in high regard by small states and for good reason. Multilateral alliances offer a number of advantages in terms of security potential, including a greater deterrent effect, a greater military capability, and a greater legitimating "weight." Multilateral alliances also alleviate some small states' concerns with respect to bilateral alliances: great powers neutralize each other in a multilateral alliance; there is less likelihood of one dominant power with a national interest who dictates alliance direction and policy; and there is less chance that the small state will become submerged by a single dominant threat to its independence and sovereignty. Furthermore, in multilateral alliances small states have an opportunity to obtain a voice, or a seat at the table, with attendant hopes for some influence over collective decisionmaking and intra-alliance politics. Small states may also establish roles within multilateral alliances as mediators or bridgebuilders. However, there are two drawbacks to the multilateral alliance option. First, it is not always available because such alliances may not exist. Second, multilateral alliances may evolve into concert systems, which would imply the exclusion of small states from consultation and decisionmaking input.

The alliance option is thus laden with conundra, although multilateral alliances are certainly highly favoured by small states. In an attempt to avoid the drawbacks associated with alliances small states have often turned to neutrality as an alternative. Pursuing a policy of neutrality in response to insecurity has been appealing to small states.[17] Neutrality offers deliverance from potential conflicts, and freedom from direct attack and the destruction of war. Should war break out, aggressors will be engaged against a number of opponents, and as a consequence will be disinclined to attack a neutral. And should an aggressor attack in the context of a wider war, it would be unable to bring its full military potential to bear against the neutral state.[18]

However, the success of neutrality relies heavily on prevailing conditions.[19] Neutrality requires the agreement or approval of great powers to act to underwrite or guarantee a policy of neutrality. Several neutrality treaties conducted before the outbreak of the Second World War were rendered superfluous when Nazi Germany chose not to honour them. Swedish and Swiss neutrality survived, largely due to special strategic and geographic reasons. Neutrality policies also suffer from the "affinity paradox" — that neutrality satisfies a potentially hostile power more than a friendly one.[20] Finally, a credible neutrality policy is costly; a neutral must convince the other actors in the system that its commitment to neutrality is unshakable. The maintenance of credible defences to underwrite a neutrality policy can be an unbearable burden for small states.

The security alternatives for small states in traditional, balance-of-power systems are therefore laden with risks and undesirable implications or consequences. Small states have been repeatedly forced to endure these dilemmas while formulating security policy. This "cycle of insecurity" can be summarized as follows:

Change in Security Environment
(Shift in Distribution of Power or Change in Dominant State)

|

Obsolescence of Old Security Mechanisms
(Erosion of Old Alliances or Faith in Neutrality)

|

Adjustment to New Conditions
(Multilateral Alliance, Bilateral Alliance, Neutrality)

Escaping the Cycle of Insecurity

It is for this reason that small states have been leading advocates of alternative global and regional security "systems." The hope is for the establishment of a system that will ameliorate the security dilemmas they confront in balance-of-power systems by reducing the intensity of competition and developing cooperative norms and mechanisms. Not coincidentally, multilateralism figures prominently in these hopes. However, multilateralism is not enough; the kind of multilateralism matters enormously. To satisfy the concerns of small states, multilateral mechanisms must be as inclusive (globally or within a region) as is possible, must offer formal equality with respect to commitments extended to member states and rights within decisionmaking structures, and protect diplomatic and political sovereignty. Integrative and collective security systems offer many of these qualities, or at least have the potential to offer them.

Integrative systems offer much to small states. They are by definition "security communities," in which warfare is no longer regarded as a serious policy option among member states. Therefore, an integrative environment offers a high level of security from traditional threats. Integrative systems also possess joint economic and diplomatic frameworks and institutions in which small states can operate. As these systems are heavily concerned with economic cooperation, they also offer economic rewards to the participants. For small states this means access to large markets for their products and an improved opportunity to specialize. However, integrative systems do entail high levels of vulnerability affecting economic and social autonomy; that is, they threaten the very claim of small states to act as distinct political, economic, and social entities. Integrative systems provoke the ever present fear in small states of political marginalization and submergence. Nevertheless, such systems offer much in the way of an escape from the security dilemmas that haunt small states.

Collective security systems also ameliorate some of the security anxieties of small states. In collective security systems, potential aggressors are deterred by the preponderance of force implied by the "all against one" provision. To the extent that cooperative frameworks and mechanisms are developed in such systems, the inclusive nature of collective security (as opposed to the exclusive nature of concert systems) enables small states to be involved in joint decisionmaking and consultation. The collective security future provides, in principle, a measure of physical security and nonconflictual norms, locks the great powers into a multilateral arrangement, allows for small state input and participation in the system, and reduces concerns over sovereignty and national identity which would attend an integrative Europe. However, a transition to a collective security system raises anew for small states the issue of reliability. Small states cannot be entirely confident that the system would come to their aid in the eventuality of aggression from inside or from outside the system.

From this discussion of small states, the security mechanism preferences of small states can be presented as follows (in order of preference):

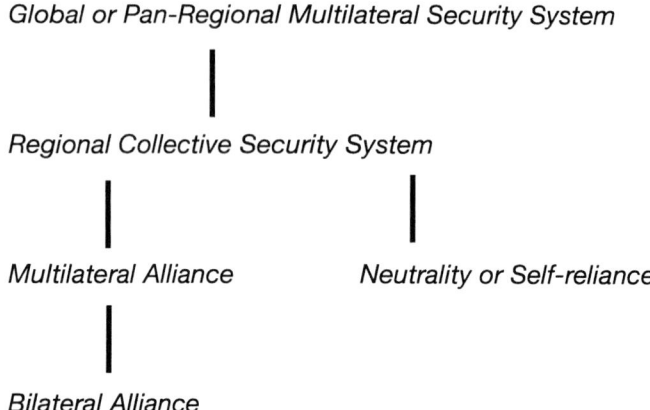

Global or Pan-Regional Multilateral Security System

Regional Collective Security System

Multilateral Alliance   *Neutrality or Self-reliance*

Bilateral Alliance

Small states are attracted to multilateral options and their attendant institutions because they can satisfy the concerns of small states with respect to:

1. security interests
    – protection from potential threats external to region
    – protection from potential threats within the region

2. diplomatic interests
    – access to decisionmaking procedures
    – voice
    – influence
    – consultation
    – the creation or maintenance of a cooperative environment
    – the definition of a foreign policy niche and its role

3. economic interest
    – access to markets
    – opportunity to specialize

There are a number of conclusions that can be drawn from this discussion. The first is that the security concerns of small states can be accommodated within the neorealist conception of international relations. This accommodation serves to make neorealism more sensitive to the perceptions and behaviour of the larger part of the state membership of the international system. Second, this accommodation highlights many of the incentives for states to engage in multilateral cooperation within the neorealist model, and so strengthens the ability of neorealism to explain and account for cooperation. Third, this discussion goes a long way to explaining the preoccupation of small states with multilateral forms of cooperation and their attendant institutions over other forms of cooperation. Finally, accommodating small states into neorealism explains the reasons why many small states do not cooperate in some endeavors, for there may be doubts about their effectiveness, and about the threat these endeavors pose to other concerns of small states, such as the fear of loss of sovereignty, the fear of domination by great powers, or the fear of a lack of commitment or equal access to the benefits of multilateral cooperation. Small states do not favour multilateral cooperation because they are more moral, altruistic, or better international citizens. The central interest of small states in multilateralism is their desire to see the development of an international or regional environment which ameliorates their greatest security fears and anxieties.

If small states have an interest in multilateral cooperation, why should great powers have any interest in cooperating with small states on a multilateral basis? How might neorealist theories of cooperation account for this phenomenon? Some of the explanations are familiar to traditional realist conceptions of the role of small states in the strategies of the great powers. Great powers may wish to engage in multilateral security cooperation with small states to prevent an opponent from adding their strength to its own, or to employ the small states as buffers, satellites, or future battlegrounds. However, if small states are of more consequence than they are generally given credit for, then great powers may see real value in cooperative arrangements with them. Great powers may also desire the involvement of small states for purposes of prestige, to symbolize their attractiveness as an ally or the appeal of the principles for which they stand. Furthermore, a larger membership in a multilateral effort may enhance the moral "weight" of that effort.

There are also disincentives to seeking the participation of small states in multilateral enterprises. More states means more centres of decision, and the consequent difficulties of maintaining cohesion and effective decisionmaking. Great powers risk becoming entangled in multilateral arrangements that may weaken their capacity to act. In addition, a larger membership is likely to include a greater number of internecine rivalries and hostilities, which can erode the cohesion of a multilateral arrangement. The security perceptions and anxieties peculiar to small states can also cause a rift in cooperative arrangements between small states and great powers. Finally, the inclusion of small states may be problematic due to a lack of compatibility between the ideological, social, or economic systems of other participants and potential newcomers.

Bringing in the Small States of Central Europe

The small states of Central Europe are experiencing a resurrection of some of their traditional geopolitical quandaries.[21] The security problems facing these countries after the Cold War would not be entirely unfamiliar to an observer of the 1920s or 1930s. Despite some very real differences from past periods, the Central European countries are once again caught in a "strategic limbo."[22] To the West lies the European Union (EU), a strong united Germany, and the "lucky, well organized end" of the continent.[23] To the East is Russia and the successors to the fractured Soviet empire: Belarus, Moldova, and the Ukraine. For countries that have belonged to a subregion denigrated as "the other Europe," "the crisis zone of Europe," and the "Warsaw Pact countries," the response to the current environment has been unequivocal.[24] The fundamental aim of the Central European countries has been to join the economic and political life of "Europe" through formal unity with the multilateral institutions and frameworks of Western Europe.

It is my contention that a neorealist explanation for cooperation that accommodates the security condition of small states provides the strongest explanation for the behaviour demonstrated by the Central European countries. The motivations for Central European states lie with their "search for security" after the Cold War. In terms of motivations, these countries are seeking to:

■ protect the integrity of their territories and boundaries against the threat of external aggression or irridentism;

■ protect their political sovereignty and independence, including their cultural autonomy, against domination or submergence by a single great power or a group of great powers;

■ develop their economic strength and modernize their economies; and

■ further the consolidation of their democratic transition, and strengthen domestic stability.[25]

The Central European states have been presented with a number of potential avenues to pursue these security goals. Consistent with the experience of small states, multilateral options have figured prominently in the foreign policy aims of Central European countries. One available avenue was to join Global or Pan-European frameworks, specifically the UN, the CSCE/OSCE, and the Council of Europe. Another available avenue was to establish a multilateral framework within Central Europe. The most attractive avenue available was to seek membership in the multilateral institutions of Western Europe. Other non-multilateral (and less preferential) options included establishing bi-lateral security arrangements with great powers, or to try to go it alone, by adopting a policy of self-reliance or neutrality. Developing close political or economic relations with Russia or the Commonwealth of Independent States (CIS) was, at least initially, unthinkable.[26] The preferred option of the Central European states — participation in the multilateral life of Europe — is informed by the viability of other options and their historical experience.

Avenues of Security for Central European States

Global multilateralism and Pan-European multilateralism. In the interwar period, the countries of Central Europe invested considerable hope in the League of Nations. The League offered three attractive promises: security cov-erage from a supranational body; opportunities to have a voice in such a forum; and a conflict resolution mechanism. However, the League became a hollow institution. The capacity of the organization to protect its weaker members was exposed in Abyssinia and Manchuria. The relevance and value of the League as a "voice of opportunity" for the small states eroded along with the League itself. Finally, after some early success — the League was successful in managing a crisis between Bulgaria and Greece over border incursions into Macedonia in 1925-26 — the ability of the League to act as a mediator de-clined as its reputation eroded.

At present, neither the UN nor the Organization for Security and Coopera-tion in Europe (OSCE) offers a satisfactory answer for the security concerns of small states. Although membership in the UN is valued for its own sake, there are few illusions about the relevance of the UN as a security guarantor. Many Central European states had high hopes for the then CSCE, but these hopes have largely faded as the conflict resolution mechanisms of that organization proved to be inadequate in dealing with the Yugoslavian crisis. The OSCE lacks the concrete capabilities and institutional structure required for effec-tiveness, and in any case the OSCE has not been given that kind of role in the institutional mix in Europe. Finally, while the Council of Europe has provided a useful diplomatic outlet, it does not have the capacity to act on behalf of the security of Central European states either.

Central European multilateralism. The history of multilateral collaborative efforts within Central Europe is not a particularly positive one. Efforts to estab-lish such cooperation have been characterized more by their limitations than by any progress toward multilateral security structures. Prior to the First World War, the Balkan alliance of Greece, Bulgaria, Serbia, and Montenegro fell apart over the division of the territorial spoils gained by the dismemberment of the

Ottoman Empire in Europe in 1912-13. This dispute resulted in the Second Balkan War of 1913. In the interwar period, the Little Entente was formed by a series of treaties between Czechoslovakia, Yugoslavia, and Romania in 1920-21. In 1926 it was strengthened to include mechanisms for the arbitration of disputes, and in 1933-34 a permanent council, economic council, and a permanent secretariat were created. The Little Entente was employed as an instrument to strengthen foreign policy cooperation and the collective voice of its membership; however, it was formed primarily as a mechanism to defend the territorial provisions of the Treaty of Trianon and to oppose Hungarian revanchism and any effort to restore the Habsburgs or their legacy. In 1934 the Balkan Entente was formed by Greece, Turkey, Romania, and Yugoslavia. While a series of conferences had led to agreement on mechanisms for settling disputes and on the creation of a customs union, the Balkan Entente never attained the unity required for more ambitious programs of cooperation. The terms of the Entente were directed at potential Balkan aggressors, either members of the Entente itself or Bulgaria. The Baltic Entente was also formed in 1934, based on the Latvian-Estonian alliance of 1923. Like the Balkan Entente, its provisions were very modest, and no momentum toward greater cooperation was achieved.

Expansion of existing multilateral frameworks was consistently raised as a possibility. The Little Entente was envisioned as an eventual pan-Central European organization, a "Great Entente" stretching from the Baltics to the Aegean. However, no close links were ever established to the Balkan Entente, and there was no extension northward because of the Polish-Czech conflict over the Teschen District and Poland's close relationship with Hungary. Other multilateral efforts in Central Europe centred on agriculture and trade. Building on an earlier effort by agricultural parties to coordinate their policies, there was a governmental effort in 1930 to form an agrarian bloc that would cooperate to secure preferential treatment for agricultural exports from Central Europe. However, this effort was undermined by the depression. Despite the prevalence of protectionist economic policies in Central Europe, there were efforts to create a regional customs union. In the early 1930s, France proposed the Tardieu Plan, designed to progressively lift trade barriers in the Danubian region. The plan failed due to political tensions among the Central European states and the opposition of Germany and Italy.[27]

After the Cold War, countries in Central Europe sought to establish multilateral cooperative arrangements. The emphasis of these regional initiatives has been on increased economic and political cooperation. This is the rationale behind arrangements such as the Visegrad Agreement between Hungary, the former Czech and Slovak Federal Republic, and Poland, and the Pentagonal Initiative, now known as the Central European Initiative (CEI). The Visegrad Agreement was formed out of concerns over Russia, instability in the East and consequent refugee flows, and coordinating the foreign policies of member countries in their relations with the West (especially Germany) and the East (especially Russia).[28] Built around the idea of a "Mitteleuropa"[29] the CEI is based on the view that "regional cooperation means contributing to the creation of a European economic and cultural area based on common roots and interests, which will be achieved more easily if developed as a process which, starting from the bottom — namely regional realities and priorities — can be completed progressively."[30] Such regional multilateral efforts perform reassurance roles, building confidence between partners in an uncertain political and economic situation, and stabilizing the democratic process. They also have the additional function of facilitating the participation of their members in the economic and political life of Europe by developing links to larger European institutions. Both the Central European Initiative and the Visegrad Agreement were formed with one eye on forging regional cooperation, a second eye looking to participate in the institutional life of Western Europe, and a third eye looking to obtain security guarantees to reduce fears of a resurgent Russia.

However, the impact of these organizations should not be overestimated. While these organizations may relax tensions and improve the political climate between the small states of Central Europe, they do not, and cannot, solve the fundamental security dilemmas of Central European countries. They do not possess the military or political power to advance the interests of the Central European countries or ensure their security against traditional or nontraditional threats. Furthermore, the scope and depth of cooperation within these multilateral efforts is limited, and, as early optimism has faded, they have acquired a largely symbolic character. The CEI has been largely moribund and was damaged by the outbreak of conflict in Yugoslavia. The Visegrad Triangle, now the Visegrad Four, has fallen into some disrepair as the immediate threat from Russia and the mass movement of refugees did not appear, and as Czechoslovakia dissolved itself and tensions between Slovakia and Hungary intensified. The Czech Republic, for example, has refused to coordinate with other Visegrad states on strategy for obtaining membership in NATO and the EU, arguing that the Visegrad mechanism is for matters internal to the Visegrad. This conception extended to Czech insistence that each Visegrad country meet separately with Bill Clinton during his visit in 1994. The Visegrad has also not served to resolve the tensions between Slovakia and Hungary over the Hungarian minority in Slovakia, or the mutual recognition of the Slovak-Hungarian border.

The reasons for the limited success of Central European multilateralism. On the surface, one would expect some significant multilateral cooperation to emerge in Central Europe. These countries do share some commonalities: a fear of an ascendant and revisionist Germany or Russia; a fear of close cooperation between Germany and Russia; and predominantly agrarian economies and a need for markets for their produce and for economic modernization. However, the past and current record of multilateral efforts within Central Europe inspires little confidence in the future of this avenue as a security mechanism in Central Europe. In the first place, the power potential of Central European multilateralism is limited, and, on its own it is incapable of ensuring the security of these states against threats. In 1926, the members of the Little Entente felt they had to strengthen their security by linking the Entente more closely with France through a series of understandings. The Little Entente did not have the power to resist the political and economic pressures placed upon it by Germany in the mid- to late-1930s. Nor was there any agreement on the great power threat; most Central European countries were concerned with different great powers. Instead, to the extent there was any shared threat perception, it was directed against other Central European states, usually Bulgaria or Hungary.

In the second place, the potential for closer multilateral cooperation was constrained by rivalries between Central European states. These rivalries centred on territorial and minorities' disputes, which were more the norm between Central European states than were stable, uncontested borders. Poland, for example, had border conflicts with the Soviet Union, Lithuania, Germany, and Czechoslovkia. Hungary had conflicts with Czechoslovakia, Yugoslavia, and Romania. Bulgaria had disputes with Romania, Yugoslavia, Turkey, and Greece. In the late 1930s, territorial revisionism in Central Europe was pursued not only by Nazi Germany but by Poland and Hungary as well.[31] Today, there remain serious territorial and ethnic minorities' disputes in Central Europe, from the tensions in Albania and Macedonia through to the issue of ethnic Hungarians living in Romania, Slovakia and the Rump Yugoslavia. In the past, multilateral efforts of Central European states yielded minimal results with respect to the nationalities and territorial questions and the political violence often associated with it. Today, it is doubtful whether multilateral mechanisms in Central Europe are capable of responding effectively to ethnic conflict, irridentism, terrorism, or other potentially destabilizing forces.

Third, economic nationalism has circumscribed the coordination of economic policies. In 1929, the Depression led to the collapse of the Central European banking system. A conference in Warsaw in 1930 failed to arrive at a collaborative response and each state turned to unilateral, protective policies that not only exacerbated the impact of the Depression, but also facilitated the increasing economic penetration of Central Europe by Germany. Today, despite efforts to create a free trade environment, economic cooperation in Central Europe has a long way to go before approaching the levels that exist in Western Europe. In light of this experience, the states of Central Europe will not acquire sufficient payoffs (either in terms of enhanced security or economic wealth) through cooperation amongst themselves.

Looking to Western Europe. For the small states of Central Europe, only membership in the institutions of Western Europe can address their security concerns in contemporary Europe. However, that membership has not been forthcoming in the form desired by Central European states. For in the West, the question of how these countries and their political and economic "space" will fit into the institutional structure of Europe remains unresolved. Western Europe had hoped that membership in what was then the Conference on Security and Cooperation in Europe (CSCE) and reassurances in the form of the May 1991 decision to establish multinational rapid reaction forces, the 6 June 1991 declaration at Copenhagen that any coercion aimed at Central Europe would be of "direct and material concern" to NATO, the creation and subsequent extension eastward on 10 March 1992 of the North Atlantic Co-operation Council (NACC), the January 1994 establishment of the Partnerships for Peace (PfP) Program, and the creation of "associate partnerships" to the Western European Union (WEU) would be a sufficient level of engagement for Central Europe in lieu of full NATO, WEU, and EU membership.[32]

However, these mechanisms have not proved satisfactory for Central European states, particularly since they did not offer full membership or tangible security guarantees.[33] Because the small states of Central Europe are motivated primarily by security and developmental concerns, half measures which fall short of the full benefits of membership are unsatisfactory. Hopes for inclusion in NATO continue to rise and fall with the political climate, and in any case only some countries — namely the Visegrad countries — are considered as serious candidates for membership. Increasingly, Central European countries are focusing on membership in the EU. Given the nature of some of the issues confronting Central Europe — crime, migration, the environment, economic progress, and stability — membership in the EU may be more relevant to some of these countries' concerns.[34] However, they continue to regard NATO membership as crucial, as there is no substitute for NATO in three critical respects: The EU does not have the military or foreign policy strength, cohesion, or record of NATO; the EU does not have the US as a member; and Germany is stronger in the EU than it is in NATO.

If all else fails: bilateralism or self-reliance. If multilateral mechanisms fail, or are unavailable, the small states of Central Europe have other security mechanisms available: the establishment of bilateral ties to great powers of self-reliance. Bilateralism was the policy of choice after the breakdown of the Balkan Alliance, and the interplay of regional rivalries in the Balkans and great power involvement led to the end of any pretense that the Concert of Europe still existed in any meaningful sense. Bilateralism became the policy of last resort in the interwar period, as the small states, faced with the rise of Germany in the West and the recovery of Soviet Russia in the East, abandoned their multilateral mechanisms for bilateral security ties. There was an attempt to strengthen mechanisms such as the Little Entente, and efforts to establish a Central European axis against Germany. These efforts failed, and multilateral cooperation began to break down. In 1932, Poland concluded a nonaggression pact with the Soviet Union, and in 1934 signed a nonaggression pact with Germany. In 1935 Czechoslovakia signed a nonaggression pact with the USSR, a move that intensified Polish-Czech tensions. Yugoslavia improved relations with Germany. Romania pursued ties with the USSR until the coup of 1936, after which King Carol attempted to pursue a policy of balance. Later, Marshal Antonescu, along with King Boris' Bulgaria, signed the tripartite pact with Germany. The multilateral frameworks of Central Europe had faded away in the face of rising threats.

The danger today is that this pattern might repeat itself. In the absence of any meaningful global or pan-European security organization, and with multilateralism within Central Europe unable to address the security concerns of these states, the only realistic multilateral avenue available to the Central European small states is ties with the multilateral frameworks of Western Europe. Should such ties not be forthcoming, the only option available for these states will be to seek security arrangements with individual countries on a bilateral basis, or to depend on a policy of self-reliance. Thus far, the large number of bilateral arrangements signed between Central European countries and great powers have differed from those signed in the 1930s in two important respects: they reject territorial claims and uphold minority rights, and agreements are now signed in the context of the multilateral environment that prevails in Western Europe. However, these agreements have been signed in an environment characterized by the lack of an immediate threat. The test of the spirit of these agreements (and any multilateral arrangements) will come when or if such a threat emerges, or when and if ethnic minorities become mobilized and agitate for greater rights or territorial revision. Should some Central European states adopt a policy of self-reliance, it is unlikely that this would improve matters. Adoption of self-reliance policies could lead to rising tensions over territorial and minority disputes, and to regional arms races, and would likely compromise internal economic and political reforms.

The Enlargement Conundrum: Bringing In Central Europe

What contribution can this discussion bring to the current debate over the enlargement of NATO and the EU?[35] This is a case of existing multilateral institutions seriously debating the desirability of expanding their membership to include more small state members. The enlargement debate is a complex one, involving consideration of timetables and prospective members, the future shape of these institutions, the reaction of Russia, and the impact on the operational capabilities of the institutions themselves. In this context, the preceding discussion on small states and cooperative incentives within neorealism, and the case of the security problems confronting the Central European states, suggests that there is another, heretofore unmentioned, arrow in the pro-enlargement quiver.

At the core of the arguments presented against enlargement is the view that bringing some or all of the Central European states into NATO or the EU will weaken these organizations and aggravate the Russians. Enlargement would bring more rivalries and tensions into organizations that must already deal with their own internal conflicts (i.e., the Greek-Turkish situation in NATO). Expanding NATO and the EU would create political and institutional problems associated with a greater number of decisionmakers and could compromise the cohesion, capability, and effectiveness of both organizations. Expansion might provoke Russia or strengthen the hand of nationalists in the Russian domestic debate. If expansion made the Russians feel insecure, it would offer no solution to the security of Central European countries in any case. Furthermore, there are questions about the internal qualities of these countries in terms of democracy, human rights, civil-military relations, socio-economic stability, and development needs.

The core of the argument in favour of enlargement is that expanding NATO and the EU will impart stability onto the region of Central Europe. Expansion would hopefully contain regional rivalries and ethnic or minorities' disputes (the third attempt to do so since Versailles and Yalta/Potsdam). The mechanisms that suppressed the combative nationalisms of Western Europe would be allowed to work their magic in Central Europe. Furthermore, enlargement would strengthen the democratic transition in these countries, a foundation of hopes for long-term peace and stability in the area. Enlargement would also provide a boost to the economies of Central European states, which in turn would buttress domestic stability by reducing the ability of extremist factions to capitalize on large numbers of poor and alienated people.

However, there may be another compelling argument for early enlargement, based on an improved understanding of the behaviour of small states in general and the Central European states in particular. If enlargement is not forthcoming and these states are not brought in to the multilateral security structures of the West, then they may be compelled to fall back on other options, and adopt bilateral arrangements or self-reliance strategies. This replay of the earlier intertwined relationship between great powers and small states in this area raises the spectre of the combative rivalries of the region — based on minorities and territorial questions — once again sparking tensions among European great powers and Russia, which could compromise the efficacy and the future of multilateral cooperation, and even peace, on the continent:

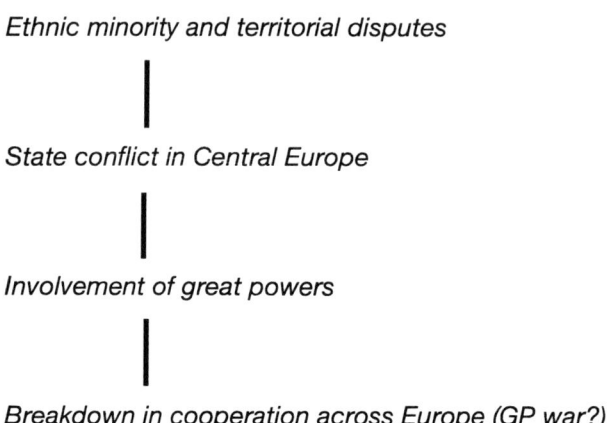

Ethnic minority and territorial disputes

State conflict in Central Europe

Involvement of great powers

Breakdown in cooperation across Europe (GP war?)

Early enlargement of NATO and the EU may be the best insurance against this scenario; the hope is that enlargement would provide a firebreak between substate conflict in Central Europe and its spread to Central European states and the wider European system. On the other hand, enlargement may be totally inconsequential. Conflict might not break out if NATO and the EU are not enlarged; and conflict may break out if NATO and the EU are enlarged. However, based on an understanding of the anxieties and concerns of small states, as well as the history of the Central European countries, enlargement would satisfy many of the security concerns of these states and might preempt behaviour that entails the risk of wider conflict should the can of ethnic and territorial worms in Central Europe be opened. For those who would wait until a threat or crisis capable of triggering such small state behaviour manifests itself, by then it might be too late to be meaningful. If it is to play any preventive role at all, enlargement must come sooner rather than later, for confidence in these organizations depends in a large part on a lengthy period of political cooperation and joint operational experience. This does not necessarily invalidate the case against expansion; it does, however, add another argument to the case for enlargement, one based on an understanding of the behaviour and motivations of small states.

Conclusion: Neorealism, Multilateralism and Small States

How well do neorealist theories of cooperation, adjusted to accommodate the peculiarities of small states, explain the behaviour of Central European small states in their drive to join the multilateral life of Western Europe? Quite well, it would seem, although there is a weakness in the application of theory to practice. One of the motivations of these small states to join NATO — their perception of a likely resurgent threat from the East — can be explained by the need for small states to seek external security guarantees in the face of threats in an anarchic, self-help system. As to the question of why these small states are not joining with Russia against the power of Germany or the EU, the great powers of Western Europe, including Germany, are "bound up" like a family of Gullivers in the multilateral institutional structures of Europe. The United States also retains a presence in Western Europe, providing an external balancing element within NATO. Great powers in Western Europe, especially Germany, are therefore less of a threat to the small states. That is the structural explanation; if historical patterns of amity and enmity are included, the fear of the Colossus to the east combined with a tamed Germany make this behaviour all the more understandable.

Neorealist theories of cooperation also provide an effective explanation of the Central European desire to join the EU: that of economic self-interest. Despite attendant concerns about having their economies submerged in a larger Europe and despite lingering concerns over German economic influence, the benefits of entry outweigh the negatives, especially in the context of the dire economic situation of many of these countries. The small states of Central Europe need economic assistance, markets, and modernization more than they fear the loss of economic sovereignty.

Another interest of small states in joining both organizations that can be explained by neorealist theories of cooperation is the desire of these small states to obtain what Grieco calls "voice opportunities." The wish for involvement, influence, a seat, or voice at the table is a consistent theme in the study of small states and this meshes nicely with the voice opportunities thesis. While Grieco speaks in the context of "less powerful" countries, this thesis can, and should be extended as an explanatory variable to the small states as well.

The behaviour of Central European states can also be explained in terms of the desire to avoid domination and loss of autonomy. While the entry into NATO and the EU implies a loss of some of that sovereignty, for these states that result is acceptable in the face of the alternative: the political and economic influence that could be exerted by Russia and FSU countries at some time in the future. Russian actions in the Baltics, Russian "peacekeeping" activities in the CIS, and the military operation in Chechnya have not gone unnoticed by the small states of Central Europe. Once again, the historical experience contributes to this sentiment. When compared to the domination experienced in the Warsaw Pact, how bad could the sovereignty implications of membership in NATO and the EU be?

If there is a weakness in neorealism's explanatory power with regard to the behaviour of these countries, it lies with the desire of these countries to join Western European institutions to strengthen their domestic democratic transitions. One of the strongest criticisms of neorealism is this de-emphasis on the domestic dimension. However, there have been moves away from this restriction. When Stephen Walt and others speak of the importance of ideological affinity for the formation and cohesion of alliances, they are tacitly acknowledging the influence of internal factors on external behaviour, even if they stress that this means they are speaking of like units or "birds of a feather."[36] If neorealism accepts the relationship between external behaviour and internal needs or rationales, then neorealism can incorporate this important element in the cooperative motivation of the Central European states, as well as the issue of the incidence of war between democratic states.

Finally, neorealism can also explain why the multilateral avenue within Central Europe has met with so many obstacles. The modesty of these attempts is due to the fact that Central European multilateralism cannot satisfy the security or economic needs of the small states of Central Europe. To some, it might seem that the small states of Central Europe had a self-interest in multilateral cooperation and therefore should have come together in some stronger arrangement. However, in fact the interest of small states in such cooperation was rather weak, as it could not achieve what the small states desired and therefore attention was diverted to seeking meaningful external security assistance and economic links, and in the absence of multilateral avenues this has meant bilateral relations with great powers.

In conclusion, bringing the small states into neorealism enriches its explanatory power and the coverage of neorealist theory and neorealist theories of cooperation. Indeed, because small states depend so heavily on cooperative mechanisms of all types to secure their basic needs and desires, accommodating the small states in neorealism enhances the ability of neorealism to account for cooperation in the international system. Incorporating small states into neorealism requires no major reorientations of the fundamentals of the school; what it does require is a deeper understanding, and accounting, of the impact small states have and will continue to have in international relations and of the motivations behind small state behaviour. When applied to the case of Central Europe, the continued dissatisfaction with the half-measures offered by the West thus far becomes more understandable; the insecurity of these states will not be satisfied by anything less than full membership. The ability to account for both threat-based and reward-based motivations for Central European governments is also highlighted. With respect to the enlargement issue, examination of the Central European states suggests that the case for enlargement can be made more strongly than it currently is, although it is beyond the scope of this chapter to argue that the debate shifts decisively in one direction or another as a result.

Notes

1. Barry Buzan, "Third World Security in Structural and Historical Perspective," in *The Insecurity Dilemma: National Security of Third World States,* ed. Brian Job (Boulder: Lynne Rienner Publishers, 1992), p. 79.

2. John J. Mearsheimer, "The False Promise of International Institutions," *International Security,* 19:3 (Winter 1994/95): 5-49; Joseph M. Grieco, *Cooperation among Nations: Europe, America, and Non-Tariff Barriers to Trade* (Ithaca: Cornell University Press, 1990); and Grieco, "Anarchy and the Limits of Cooperation: A Realist Critique of the Newest Liberal Institutionalism," in *Controversies in International Relations Theory: Realism and the Neoliberal Challenge,* ed. Charles W. Kegley, Jr. (New York: St. Martin's Press, 1995), pp. 151-71.

3. Charles L. Glaser, "Realists as Optimists: Cooperation as Self-Help," *International Security,* 19:3 (Winter 1994/95): 50-90.

4. Joseph M. Grieco, "The Maastricht Treaty, Economic and Monetary Union and the Neorealist Research Programme," *Review of International Studies,* 21:1 (January 1995): 21-40.

5. For example, see Robert O. Keohane, *After Hegemony: Cooperation and Discord in the World Political Economy* (Princeton: Princeton University Press, 1984); Keohane, *International Institutions and State Power: Essays in International Relations Theory* (Boulder: Westview Press, 1989); and John Ruggie (ed) *Multilateralism Matters: The Theory and Praxis of an International Form* (New York: Columbia University Press, 1993). Because neorealists and neoliberals share some fundamental assumptions (states are rational, unitary actors operating in an anarchic international system), the discourse between the two is essentially an interparadigm debate.

6. See Robert O. Keohane and Joseph Nye, *Power and Interdependence: World Politics in Transition* (Boston: Little, Brown, 1977); James N. Rosenau, *The Study of Global Interdependence: Essays on the Transnationalisation of World Affairs* (New York: Nichols, 1980); and Stephen D. Krasner (ed.) *International Regimes*, special issue of *International Organisation,* 36:2 (Spring 1982).

7. See David Mitrany, *A Working Peace System* (Chicago: Quadrangle Books, 1966); and Ernst B. Haas, *Beyond the Nation-State* (Stanford: Stanford University Press, 1964), esp. ch. 1.

8. Kenneth N. Waltz, *Theory of International Politics* (New York: Random House, 1979), pp. 4-5.

9. For a discussion of these roles, see Trygvie Mathisen, *The Functions of Small States in the Strategies of the Great Powers* (Oslo: Universitetsforlaget, 1971).

10. This allegation is curious in and of itself; why should small states, which allegedly have little impact beyond their relationship with great powers, be so readily blamed for instability in balance-of-power systems?

11. See Erling Bjol, "The Power of the Weak," *Cooperation and Conflict*, 3 (1968): 160.

12. Ibid., p. 160.

13. In regional systems, the activities of small states will be more significant, as small states are more capable of exerting themselves in their localities as opposed to internationally.

14. Paul Sharp, *Irish Foreign Policy and the European Community: A Study of the Impact of Interdependence on the Foreign Policy of a Small State* (Brookfield: Dartmouth Publishing, 1990), p. 23.

15. The alliance dilemma has occupied the attention of students of small state security for some time. See, for example, Robert L. Rothstein, *Alliances and Small Powers* (New York: Columbia University Press, 1968); and Omar De Raeymaeker, *Small Powers in Alignment* (Leuven: Leuven University Press, 1974).

16. Rothstein, *Alliances and Small Powers*, p. 61.

17. As Trygve Mathisen has observed, "Non-alignment and neutrality seem to be almost instinctively desired by small powers." Mathisen, *The Functions of Small States in the Strategies of the Great Powers*, p. 250.

18. In the words of former Swedish Prime Minister, Tage Erlander: "We are building up a defense which has naturally not much of a chance of surviving against a concentrated attack by a Great Power but which, nevertheless, may be rather troublesome to overcome if Sweden is a secondary objective." Cited in William E. Paterson, "Small States in International Politics," *Cooperation and Conflict,* 3 (1968): 121. This hope, of course, did not save Belgium in 1914, or the Netherlands in 1941.

19. Geography, too, can play an important role in the success of a neutrality policy. Physical location on the periphery of major events (Portugal) or terrain (Switzerland) is an important component in the history of European neutralism.

20. Gerald Stourzh, "Some Reflections on Permanent Neutrality," in Schou and Brundtland, *Small States in International Relations*, p. 96.

21. The question: "What is Central Europe?" inevitably bogs down on the issue of boundaries. Are the Baltic states in Central Europe? Is "Central Europe" the Visegrad Four? Or the Six? Where do the Balkans start and Central Europe begin? In this paper, "Central Europe" is the region between Germany and the states of the FSU, with its northern boundary the Baltic Sea and its southern boundary the border of the former Yugoslavia and Greece. Obviously, there is overlap with the region known as "Balkan Europe," which has as its southern boundaries the Aegean and Adriatic Seas. However, "Central Europe" will also refer to much of "Balkan Europe" for the purposes of this discussion. For a discussion of terminological

issues see M. B. Biskupski, "Does the East of Europe have a Modern History?' *Contemporary European History*, 3:2 (July 1994): 217-30.

22. Hans Binnendijk, "The Emerging European Security Order," *The Washington Quarterly,* 14 (Autumn 1991):70. For reviews of this historical period, see Joseph Rothschild, *East Central Europe Between the Two World Wars* (Seattle: University of Washington Press, 1974): and Hugh Seton-Watson, *Eastern Europe Between the Wars 1918-1941*, 3rd ed. (Hamden, Conn: 1962).

23. Brian Beedham, "Look Up, Europe, the Eastern Frontier has Opened," *International Herald Tribune*, 27 February 1992.

24. See E. Garrison Walters, *The Other Europe: Eastern Europe to 1945* (Syracuse: Syracuse University Press, 1988); and Ivan T. Berend, (trans.) Adrienne Malkay-Chambers, *The Crisis Zone of Europe* (Cambridge: Cambridge University Press, 1986). For Central Europeans, the term central, as opposed to eastern, is a symbol of The countries' liberation. There is widespread objection to equating the Cold War period with "stability" in Central Europe and the current period as unstable and insecure. See László Valki, "Security Concerns in Central Europe," in *Central European Security Concerns: Bridge, Buffer, or Barrier?* ed. Jacob Kipp (London: Frank Cass, 1993), p. 1.

25. For a historical account of Central Europe with an emphasis on the democratic dimension see Joseph Held, *The Columbia History of Eastern Europe in the Twentieth Century* (New York: Columbia University Press, 1992).

26. For many Central European countries, closer ties to Russia are still unthinkable. See Steven Erlanger, "East Europe Watches the Bear, Warily," *New York Times*, 21 October 1994, p. 1. Even a train station brawl between Russians and Polish police can lead to angry exchanges between these countries. John Pomfret, "Poland and Russia Struggle With Ties That Don't Bind," *International Herald Tribune*, 5-6 November, 1994.

27. Henry Bogdan, *From Warsaw to Sofia: A History of Eastern Europe* (Santa Fe: Por Libertate Publishing, 1989), p. 212.

28. See Joshua Spero, "*Déjà-vu* All Over Again: Poland's Attempt to Avoid Entrapment Between Two Belligerents," in *Central European Security Concerns*, ed. Kipp, pp. 93-117.

29. Alois Mock, "The Pentagonale," *Austria Today*, 3 (1990): 5-7.

30. "Message of the Five Prime Ministers of Italy, Yugoslavia, Austria, Czechoslovakia, and Hungary to the Thiry-Five Members of the CSCE." Gipfeltreffen Venedig (The Venice Summit), 1 November 1990. There have been some whispers in Central Europe regarding a new Austria-Hungary, and some echoes of the 1930's dream of a United States of Central Europe. See Laszlo Lengyel, "Europe through Hungarian Eyes," *International Affairs*, 66 (April 1990): 291-98.

31. Hungary had fought for the revision of the Treaty of Trianon for most of the interwar period. With the assistance of Germany and Italy, it regained territory from Czechoslovakia in 1938. Poland also seized the Teschen District from Czechoslovakia under the so-called First Vienna Award.

32. The NACC was created in November of 1991, and 18 new states were invited into the NACC on 10 March 1992. See "Declaration and Working Programme of the 'NACC' Meeting

in Brussels," *Europe Documents*, 12 March 1992, no. 1765. The North Atlantic Council also declared on 21 August 1991 that "noting the enhanced concerns of Central and East European states, we reiterate our conviction that our own security is inseparably linked to that of all other states in Europe, particularly the emerging democracies." NATO Press Communiqué, "The Situation in the Soviet Union." Statement issued by the North Atlantic Council Meeting in Ministerial Session at NATO Headquarters, Brussels, 21 August 1991.

33. The level of consultation and "voice" was also a disappointment. At the inaugural NACC meeting, each country had some five minutes to speak, a practical limitation that worsened at the second meeting in which 34 countries participated.

34. Central European countries also want full membership in the EU. Poland's foreign minister Andrzej Olechowski recently stated that Poland wanted to be at the centre of the EU and wished to be fully involved in decisionmaking. See William Pfaff, "The Poles are Moving Closer to the Center," *International Herald Tribune*, 5-6 November 1994, p. 8.

35. For a recent examination of the NATO enlargement debate, see Ronald D. Asmus, et al., "NATO Expansion: The Next Steps," Michael E. Brown, "The Flawed Logic of NATO Expansion," and Dana H. Allin, "Can Containment Work Again?" *Survival*, 37 (Spring 1995): 7-52. See also Ronald D. Asmus et al., "Building a New NATO," and Owen Harries, "The Collapse of 'The West'," *Foreign Affairs,* 72:4 (September/October 1993): 28-40, 41- 53.

36. Stephen M. Walt, *The Origins of Alliances* (Ithaca: Cornell University Press, 1987).

Zoltan Barany

Alone or Together?
Cooperation and Conflict in East-Central Europe

Introduction

After the Warsaw Pact's demise, the states of East-Central Europe (Czech Republic, Hungary, Poland, and Slovakia) found themselves in a security limbo. No longer occupied and "protected" by the Soviet Union, these countries could not realistically expect to join NATO in the immediate future. But how should they ensure their own security and what role, if any, could be played by their neighbours in the region? In other words, how can security be organized after the Warsaw Treaty Organization (WTO), but before NATO, in the shadow of the protracted war in the former Yugoslavia and in an area where Soviet-Russian domination has been a constant for two centuries?

This chapter is not concerned with theory- or model-building but with an empirically based explanation of East-Central Europe's regional security position.[1] More specifically, I am interested in the various (Czech, Slovak, Polish, and Hungarian) conceptions of national interest and relative advantages and obstacles in the way of the creation of institutional security structures. I suggest that these factors can explain why Budapest was replaced as the leading sceptic of the idea by Prague following the breakup of the Czechoslovak federation. The Czech Republic has clearly become the state that would prefer to fly solo, and is intent on presenting itself to the West as the likeliest candidate for immediate entry into NATO and other international organizations. In contrast, the other states of the region seem to believe that, in the ongoing process of European integration, the outcome would be most favourable if they were to stick together and join as members of a relatively cohesive bloc. The basic argument of this essay is that the potential for institutionalized multilateral security is limited in East-Central Europe.

Regional Security and the Long Shadow of the Warsaw Pact

The end of communism in Eastern Europe poses serious questions concerning the military and security future of this traditionally volatile region.[2] From a global viewpoint, at least, Soviet hegemony achieved relative stability in Eastern Europe. Although occasional flareups did occur, the Kremlin and its soldiers, the Warsaw Pact, and the local communist elites managed to extinguish them until 1989. The velvet and not-so-velvet revolutions of that year signalled not only the return of real sovereignty to these long-oppressed lands, but also the reappearance of ethnic tensions and the reemergence of suppressed habitual antagonisms. Along with the abolition of the Warsaw Treaty Organization, a stabilizing and mediating influence disppeared from the region.

Throughout the communist period, the determining characteristic of Eastern Europe's security situation was the Soviet domination of the region. In the wake of the Second World War, and particularly after the formal creation of the Warsaw Pact (1955), the East European satellites had to adopt the Soviet Union's offensive military doctrine without taking into account their own national security concerns. Soviet-made armaments were adopted throughout the bloc, and Moscow's military advisers supervised the comprehensive Sovietization of native military establishments.[3] The WTO had a great deal of political significance for the bloc in that it provided a formal framework binding the communist states together, it limited the sovereignty of the individual member states, and it served as a useful forum for the expression of Eastern Europe's support of various Soviet foreign policy initiatives.[4]

From its inception, and even after its limited reorganization following the August 1968 invasion of Czechoslovakia, the Warsaw Pact remained an alliance thoroughly dominated by Soviet hegemony. The problems of the Pact were symptomatic of the entire "family of socialist nations." The blatant disregard of the East European states' national interests in decisions regarding military doctrine, strategy, expenditures, and armaments were among the most important complaints of dissidents and reformers throughout the communist period.

As a result of the strengthening democratization drive in the East European states — which gradually led to Moscow's increased reluctance to meddle in these states' internal affairs and culminated ultimately in the revolutions of 1989 — by 1990 the WTO had become a defunct military-political organization; it was unceremoniously abolished in the summer of 1991. Negotiations on the withdrawal of Soviet occupation troops were completed expeditiously and the last Soviet soldiers left Eastern Germany in 1994. However, the departure of the Soviet troops presents further dilemmas to the successors of communist leaders in the former Communist bloc. The Soviet army had caused enormous environmental damage and left their former bases in catastrophic condition. The lack of proper maintenance of exercise grounds, buildings, and training facilities gave rise to widespread public protests as well as innumerable unresolved legal cases.

Though the fall of the WTO and the withdrawal of the occupying forces were received enthusiastically in Eastern Europe, much of the region found itself in a precarious security situation. The realization that the former non-Soviet Warsaw Pact (NSWP) states were unable to protect themselves from virtually any external attack came as a shock to most post-communist politicians and their constituents. The occupying troops of the Soviet Union had provided adequate air defence for these states, but once they were gone the newly independent countries were incapable of guarding their airspace. The severity of the situation was demonstrated in late 1991 when Yugoslav fighter jets repeatedly violated Hungary's airspace as Hungarian forces helplessly looked on.

With the Warsaw Pact and Soviet hegemony gone, ethnic tensions, virulent nationalism, separatism, thinly-veiled revanchism, and other troublesome socio-political phenomena — aptly characterized as the "New Tribalism" — once again emerged. Every country in the region has experienced nationalist and racist incidents and most of their governments have not been able to address these issues in a satisfying manner. Attempts to manage these threats have often been frustrated by the turbulent political situation in individual states as well as in the region as a whole.[5] Although the former Yugoslavia was never a Warsaw Pact member, the war there serves as a timely reminder of what might happen between and within former WTO allies if solutions to their problems are not found. Czechoslovakia fell apart in January 1993 with relative civility, but there are no guarantees that traditional antagonisms (Hungarian-Slovak, Polish-Russian, Bulgarian-Turkish, etc.) will be settled or managed in a like manner.

In sum, then, not only has Eastern Europe historically been a highly flammable region, but the security legacies of communism were uniformly negative. Owing to the long-standing Soviet domination of the region, the most important security legacies of the communist era are (i) the lack of a comprehensive regional security structure; and (ii) insufficiently regulated civil-military relations. The relationship between the armed forces and society is also a problem. In the post-communist era, the democratizing East European regimes must reform civil-military relations to ensure that the armed forces are subordinated to constitutional authority and firm civilian control.[6]

Societal views of the military can shift quite rapidly.[7] In the former NSWP states, with the exception of Poland and Romania, the military occupation lost much of its former prestige; officers were generally disdained as the servants of foreign (i.e., Soviet) and ideological (i.e., communist), rather than of national interests. With the withdrawal of the Soviet occupation forces and the demise of the Warsaw Pact, these armed forces have clearly become "national." As the new tribalism began to take hold, the West, and more particularly, NATO, has grown more wary of East Europeans and the "bag of tricks" they might bring along to Brussels.[8] Still, perhaps it is not unreasonable to speculate that the East-Central European four could gain full membership in NATO within the next decade.

In the meantime, politicians and soldiers have sought to enhance their countries' security by negotiating bilateral military cooperation agreements with their neighbours, NATO members, and other European states. The East-Central European countries, especially, have actively explored the possibilities of regional cooperation in a number of different forms. They have become funding members of several regional organizations, including the Carpathian Euro-Region, the Central European Initiative, and the Visegrad Group. The most recent effort of the three, the Carpathian Euro-Region, was formed in 1993 with the participation of the Carpathian regions of Hungary, Poland, and Ukraine. Since then, Slovakia and Romania have also been accepted as members. The fundamental objective of this group is to develop one of Europe's most backward regions (parts of Poland, Slovakia, Ukraine, Romania, and Hungary) and encourage its integration into European political and economic processes. Cooperation between these countries has not always been smooth, given the numerous unresolved issues between them.[9]

The oldest of these regional organizations, the Central European Initiative (CEI) was started in 1989 by four states — Austria, Hungary, Italy, and Yugoslavia. The intention of its two Western members was to counter and balance what was expected to become the overwhelming German influence in Central Europe. At the time of the first meetings, Hungary was still a one-party state and the Warsaw Pact appeared relatively strong. From mid-1989 on, high-ranking officials of these states have studied the possibilities of regional cooperation. The primary goals have been improved cooperation between the member states and a number of ambitious investment projects ranging from an extensive new highway network to the coordinated development of communications systems.[10] Since then, the CEI has been expanded to include the former Czechoslovakia and Poland as well.

From the perspective of this chapter, the most important of the emerging regional organizations has been the Visegrad Group, which embraces the four East-Central European states.[11] The balance of this chapter will be devoted to this organization.

The Visegrad Group

The first trilateral — and since January 1993 (i.e., since the breakup of Czechoslovakia) quadrilateral — relationship, known as the "Visegrad Group," emerged as an unexamined proposition and one of the most interesting and encouraging initiatives in the post-communist region.[12] The initiative to establish some sort of organized cooperation suggested that the post-communist elites in these states had already cleared an obstacle characteristic of the region in earlier eras. The new political elites in Budapest, Prague, and Warsaw did not wait for advice and guidance from Washington, Moscow, Paris or London, but started to look to each other in their efforts to improve their international position.[13]

There were five fundamental reasons for beginning this cooperation: (i) Through cooperation and coordination, the three neighbours worked for desired results by returning to the traditional relationships established over the centuries: their cultural and intellectual heritage and commonalities in their religious traditions; (ii) The major challenges before them were similar: how to establish democracies, with all that this goal involved (creating new institutional structures, and demolishing the one-party system), the transformation of their economies from the central plan toward the market, and the solidification of their sovereignty and independence; (iii) The existence of an unstable and slowly crumbling Soviet Union in the initial (1989-91) period of post-communist transitions which demanded some sort of multilateral security arrangement in East-Central Europe; (iv) The international organizations of the West, particularly the European Community, had made it clear by 1990 that the future membership of the East-Central European states depended heavily on their ability to cooperate with each other; and (v) Less tangible, but still important, is the idea of a "Central European consciousness," the notion of "Mitteleuropa" which has long existed as a topic of discussion among the region's intellectuals. With the formation of the Visegrad Group, it was hoped that this idea could be realized in practical results and achievements.

The idea of Central European cooperation was one of the popular issues for Polish, Czech, and Hungarian intellectuals and dissidents in the 1980s. Several dissident groups from these three states were in close contact before the revolutions; most of their intellectual leaders (Vaclav Havel, Adam Michnik, Bronislaw Geremek, Miklos Haraszti, and Gyorgy Konrad) knew each other personally.[14] The fact that several of them had become influential politicians after communism's fall fostered the development of more genuinely cordial relationships between these states.[15]

At the same time, there have also been some very serious obstacles in the way of realizing cooperation. Although there was a great deal in common among these states, the new political elites had only a limited appreciation of their mutual interests. During the communist period — notwithstanding the Soviet bloc's international institutions and the multidimensional interaction between these states — there was little genuine cooperation and inadequate knowledge of each other even in elite circles. International ties in the bloc focused on Moscow and were not truly multilateral. Just as importantly, regarding both political and economic matters, each country was trying to evaluate every issue from its own narrow perspective — perhaps a result of the heady experience of regaining independence — often neglecting the advantages to be derived from the creation of long-term, mutually beneficial programs and projects. Furthermore, a number of bilateral issues raised problems for multilateral cooperation. The most important of these have undoubtedly been the treatment of the Hungarian minority in Slovakia, as well as the issue of the Danube dam (Gabcikovo/Nagymaros), but contentious issues have also existed between Poland and the former Czechoslovakia.

The idea of multilateral cooperation between these states first surfaced during Poland's Prime Minister Tadeusz Mazowiecki's January 1990 visit to Prague. An ill-conceived and improperly prepared trilateral meeting in Bratislava (where Hungary and Poland sent lame-duck representatives: Matyas Szuros and Gyula Horn on the one hand, President Wojciech Jaruzelski on the other) three months later was followed by high-level negotiations between the East-Central European leaders. Finally, the summit in Visegrad, Hungary in February 1991 between the leaders of the three states (Presidents Havel and Lech Walesa, and Prime Minister Jozsef Antall) resulted in a joint declaration pledging mutual support for the process of integration into Western Europe's international institutions.[16] Eight months later (October 1991), the three states held a summit in Cracow, Poland where their intentions to help each other join European economic and political organizations were confirmed. For the time being, however, the suggestion of a free-trade zone within the group was not received with the necessary level of support.[17] The free-trade zone, which to date has been the most tangible result of the Visegrad Group's political and economic cooperation, finally took effect in March 1993 and customs duties between the member states should be eliminated by the year 2001.[18]

Regional Cooperation Versus National Interest

From the beginning, the fundamental problem hindering the achievement of deeper cooperation was the conflict between national interest and regional integration. This conflict was reflected in the member states' dissimilar perspectives and desires concerning the framework and ultimate character of their cooperation. In this aspect, the chronological dividing line was 1 January 1993, the breakup of federal Czechoslovakia. Until this time, the least enthusiastic member of the Visegrad Group was probably Hungary. Following the June 1992 national elections which propelled Vaclav Klaus to the Czech prime ministership, and especially after the "velvet divorce" of Czechoslovakia, the Czech Republic replaced Hungary as the state most sceptical about the rewards of regional cooperation. Until 1993, Hungary's prime minister had repeatedly emphasized that "any action institutionalizing our triangular cooperation would be a major mistake," arguing that institutionalization might actually slow down the process of integration into West European institutions. He and his Cabinet members had continuously stressed the informal nature of the triangle, frequently describing it as a "political club" and emphasizing the loose nature of its structure.[19]

The reason for this Hungarian stance remained in concert with contemporary notions of Budapest's national interests. Until January 1993, Hungary was the undisputed frontrunner in Eastern Europe in terms of political stability and attraction to the West. This point is well illustrated by the fact that Hungary had received more foreign investment than the rest of the region combined. Thus, Hungarian elites thought that their chances of joining international institutions by themselves were just as good, and perhaps better, than if they were part of a group of states. In Poland, on the other hand, the opposite view emerged. Poland was the original backer of the idea of East-Central European cooperation, and more specifically, of the goal of establishing some sort of trilateral council in the region. Subsequently, several leading Polish politicians pressed for institutionalization, arguing — like Stanislaw Puzyna from the Polish Senate's Centre for International Studies — that:

> there is a lack of infrastructure of bilateral and trilateral agreements adequate to the new realities. There are no institutions making a framework for the new forms of cooperation, according to common market principles.[20]

At the Visegrad and Cracow summits, Polish representatives had repeatedly expressed their conviction that integration within Central Europe was essential and supported institutionalization. In contrast, the Hungarian attitude suggested that creating a new international bureaucracy, especially in the wake of the CMEA's and the Warsaw Pact's demise, was not the answer for the relative international isolation of the region.[21]

Initially, Czechoslovakia's approach to regional organizations appeared to approximate that of Poland. As the breakup of the federation neared, and particularly in its aftermath, a different view emerged in Prague. Since January 1993, the Czech Republic's political leadership has become increasingly sceptical about the merits of the Visegrad Group. A few days after the separation, Prime Minister Vaclav Klaus confirmed his view that cooperation within the Visegrad Quadrangle was the result of an artificial process created by a Western desire for a political and economic grouping in Central Europe.[22] Although Klaus suggested that he supported cooperation in the region, he insisted that emphasizing the institutional aspect of cooperation was a mistake.

In contrast, the Slovak position became even more supportive of the Visegrad Group after Czechoslovakia's breakup than before, to the extent that Slovakia has made overtures to countries farther east, such as Ukraine and Russia. Slovak Prime Minister Vladimir Meciar has repeatedly called for greater cooperation among the Visegrad countries in their efforts to join the European Community (later the European Union). In opposition to Klaus, Meciar appears to firmly believe that a more coordinated approach by the four states would lead to fewer policy mistakes and would shorten the time for acceptance by international organizations.[23]

The most important event in the short life of the Visegrad Group has undoubtedly been the breakup of federal Czechoslovakia.[24] In fact, it appears that the international community has underestimated the impact of the partition on both Czech and Slovak and on East-Central European security. In the Czech Republic and Slovakia major conceptual problems emerged concerning national security and a number of experts seem to agree that in these two states "we are back to square one."[25] In both states — as elsewhere in the region — there was (is) very little civilian knowledge of security and civil-military issues. In the Czech parliament, for instance, there were no committees on defence or security and it appears that everyone from Prime Minister Klaus on down, held the same views of: "What is defence good for?" and "Should we not eliminate the military?" Obviously this approach has fostered tensions between civilians and the military.

The split between Slovakia and the Czech Republic has had a major impact on security. The "old" Czech notion of regional cooperation held that it was necessary for westward integration. At least until the fall of 1991 Czechoslovakia wanted to play the role of being a bridge to the West (although what that "bridge" might specifically denote was never satisfactorily explained). The "new" Czech Republic, clearly the "winner" of the breakup, no longer considered itself a bridge to, but instead — for all practical purposes — a part of the West. The country's geopolitical "shift" was accompanied by an important geographical effect with psychological implications: the Czech Republic's longest border is now with Germany and its easternmost part is slightly further to the east than that of Austria. Slovakia, in effect, has become the Czech Republic's buffer to the east, but is no longer a drain on Czech economic resources, nor a political liability. The general feeling in the Czech Republic is that the country is considerably better off (given its low inflation and unemployment rates and inconsequential foreign debts) than Hungary or Poland, let alone Slovakia. Thus, shortsighted as this view may be, turning their backs on the east (and by extension, on the Visegrad Group) seems to be a rational policy decision, especially since most Czechs see their own identity much more closely intertwined with Germany and Austria than with their neighbours to the east.

The split in Slovakia was followed by an identity crisis. Feeling rejected by Prague — an unjustified reaction, since it was the Slovak political leadership that was very much intent on separation — and not trusting Budapest, Bratislava improved its relations with the Ukraine and Russia. Foreign policymakers in Slovakia envisioned a new role for their country; namely to pose as a bridge between Poland and Ukraine. Such a conception was deeply flawed on two counts: first, the role proposed for Slovakia was superfluous, for Warsaw and Kyiv had already established a satisfactory relationship on their own; and second, it left the entire notion of a state acting as "the bridge between regions" in the age of advanced communications unquestioned. Since the breakup, Slovakia has put a great deal of faith in the Visegrad Group, ignoring the reality of its slow demise. If it disappears, it would hit Slovakia the hardest, for Bratislava stands to lose the most. Slovakia could become hostage to Ukrainian-Russian relations, especially in terms of security; particularly given Bratislava's strong ties to both these states.

Some Thoughts on East-Central European Security

One of the pillars of the initial stage of security cooperation in the Visegrad Group was the very existence of the Soviet Union.[26] Two major international events between the Visegrad and Cracow summits (i.e., February and October 1991) the coup attempt in Moscow in August and the eruption of ethnic war in the former Yugoslavia in the summer altered the security thinking of the Visegrad states' political elites. This conceptual shift was reflected in the Cracow Declaration, which revealed the growing realization of the weaknesses of the member states' existing security guarantees. The little enthusiasm that could be detected for cooperation in the security sphere — partly driven by fear that a new Warsaw Pact or something even distantly akin to it should be created — quickly dissipated once the Soviet Union ceased to exist. Nevertheless, political instability in the former USSR, the reality of war in the former Yugoslavia, the possibility of a large wave of migration from the east suggested that some sort of cooperation in the security area had to be considered. It appeared clear to all members of the Visegrad Group, however, that security guarantees should be gained from Western security institutions, especially from, and preferably within, NATO.

But what is to be done before the elusive goal of full NATO membership is realized? The compelling motive for cooperation for the Visegrad Group's members is their shared sense of insecurity in the "no man's land" between a friendly but essentially noncommittal West and an unstable East. Part of the problem is that, as alluded to above, perceptions of insecurity are certainly the lowest in the Czech Republic, while the other three member states all have some very real security concerns. But one potential enemy for Slovakia is Hungary, whereas Hungary's other traditional foe, Romania, is a valued partner of Bratislava. Similarly, Poland's potential concerns regarding Belarus, Germany, Lithuania, and Russia are not shared by either Slovakia or Hungary.[27] Politicians in Bratislava, Budapest, Prague, and Warsaw intend to protect their own national interests and appear not to see a new regional security organization as offering a net gain to them. Some security concerns are clearly unique to the individual states; they also seem to view their national interests in dissimilar terms. Furthermore, keeping the Visegrad Group alive to apply concerted pressure on Western institutions may not be a convincing reason, considering that states that do not belong have thus far gained the same institutional affiliations (the North Atlantic Cooperation Council and the "Partnership for Peace" Program, for instance, include all former WTO states).

In a January 1994 meeting, the leaders of the Visegrad states agreed that the group would fade away unless a major effort were made to revive it.[28] Those present blamed the Czech Republic, and particularly its prime minister, for the probable death of the organization, although tensions and unresolved issues clearly existed between most participants. Since then, the members of the Visegrad Group have acted on their own. Bilateral agreements on a number of issues have been signed between most member states but not within the framework of the group. For instance, during a lengthy and contentious process that led to the conclusion of the basic treaty between Hungary and Slovakia no reference was made to the Visegrad Group, much less any attempt by other members of the group to help mediate in the negotiations.

In April 1995 Hungary and Poland, the two countries enjoying the best relations within the group agreed to cooperate in their efforts to join NATO and the European Union.[29] Budapest and Warsaw are optimistic that their NATO membership is not far off. Such cooperation is not unexpected, particularly in view of Russian opposition and Ukrainian uneasiness concerning NATO's proposed expansion. In the meantime, leaders of the Czech Republic have become more interested in joining the European Union (a policy that has been supported by the findings of a number of recent public opinion polls), while Slovakia has increasingly turned its attention toward the East. Still, even given these recent changes, the fundamental foreign policy objective of all four East-Central European states retain membership in both the European Union and NATO. They are hopeful that the United States will be true to its word and not allow NATO's expansion to be vetoed by any "third party" (i.e., Russia).

The states of Eastern Europe (particularly the Czech Republic) have different ideas about international organizations, regional security, and their own relative advantages *vis-à-vis* each other. Since 1989 they have acted, for the most part, as if they were rational actors, trying to maximize their interests. Regional cooperation, as perceived in East-Central Europe (again, especially in Prague), would deliver small benefits, particularly in comparison to integration with Western Europe. Since January 1993 the Czech Republic, the country that would have the least to gain from a regional organization like the Visegrad Group, has been the most reluctant to promote it; in contrast, Slovakia, which would have the most to gain, has been its most ardent supporter. In the security context of contemporary East-Central Europe, the requirements of cooperation — either well-developed institutions or a clear external threat — are undoubtedly missing. Consequently, the capacity for cooperation in the region, especially in the security area, is very limited and thus the establishment of an institutionalized security structure seems highly unlikely.

Notes

The author is indebted to Scott Parrish and Peter Rutland for their insightful comments on an earlier version of this chapter.

1. For recent theoretical treatments of these issues, see Joseph Grieco, *Cooperation among Nations* (Ithaca: Cornell University Press, 1990); Helen Milner's "International Theories of Cooperation Among Nations," *World Politics,* 44:3 (April 1992): 466-96 provides a good overview of the recent theoretical literature on cooperation. For articles dealing specifically with the region, see the special issue on "Central European Security Concerns: Bridge, Buffer or Barrier," *European Security,* 1:4 (Winter 1992).

2. This section draws on Zoltan Barany, "The Military and Security Legacies of Communism," in *The Legacies of Communism in Eastern Europe,* ed. Zoltan Barany and Ivan Volgyes (Baltimore: Johns Hopkins University Press, 1995), pp.101-17.

3. These points are developed in more detail in Zoltan Barany, "Soviet Takeovers: The Role of Advisers in Mongolia in the 1920s and in Eastern Europe After World War II," *East European Quarterly,* 28:4 (January 1995):409-33; and "Soviet Control of the Hungarian Military under Stalin," *Journal of Strategic Studies,* 14:2 (June 1991): 148-64.

4. Zbigniew Brzezinski, *The Soviet Bloc: Unity and Conflict* (Cambridge: Harvard University Press, 1967), pp. 458-59.

5. On these issues, see Zoltan Barany, "Mass-Elite Relations and the Resurgence of Nationalism in Eastern Europe," *European Security,* 3:1 (Spring 1994): 162-81.

6. See Zoltan Barany, "The Military and Political Transitions in Eastern Europe," *Comparative Politics*, forthcoming.

7. For instance, the South African Defence Forces, long despised as "terrorists in uniform," recently became popular among the country's blacks for pacifying the rival factions in their communities during the spring of 1994. See *The New York Times*, 11 April 1994, pp. A1, A4.

8. Ivan Volgyes, "Military Security in the Post-Communist Age: Reflections on Myths and Realities," *Studies in Comparative Communism,* 25:1 (1992): 89-95.

9. See, for instance, Ivan Illes, "The Karpatok Euroregio," *Valosag*, no. 6, June 1993, pp. 12-19.

10. *Nepszabadsag*, 13 November 1989.

11. For an excellent examination of the Visegrad Group, see Valerie Bunce, "Regional Cooperation and European Integration in Post communist Europe: The Visegrad Initiative," unpublished manuscript, June 1995.

12. This section benefited from my long conversations with Pal Dunay, Bogdan Goralczyk, and Istvan Gyarmati in Budapest in May and June 1993.

13. Joshua Spero, "The Budapest-Prague-Warsaw Triangle: Central European Security after the Visegrad Summit," *European Security,* 1:1 (Spring 1992): 58-83.

14. See, *The Independent*, 6 November 1989.

15. *The Independent*, 26 January 1990; *Frankfurter Allgemeine Zeitung*, 8 February 1990; and *Süddeutsche Zeitung*, 9 November 1990.

16. Jan B. de Weydenthal, "The Visegrad Summit," *Report on Eastern Europe*, (1 March 1991): 28-32.

17. Jan B. de Weydenthal, "The Cracow Summit," *Report on Eastern Europe*, 25 October 1991, pp. 27-29; and Roger East, *Revolutions in Eastern Europe* (London: Pinter, 1992), p. 106.

18. See Karoly Okolicsanyi, "The Visegrad Triangle's Free-Trade Zone," *RFE/RL Research Report*, (15 January 1993), pp. 19-22; Harald Zschiedrich, "Die Freihandelszone der 'Visegrad-Staaten': Neubeginn einer intraregionalen Kooperation?" *Sudosteuropa*, 42:9 (September 1993): 491-511; *Neue Zürcher Zeitung*, 10 March 1993; and *The Prague Post*, 5-11 May 1993.

19. See, for instance, *Pesti Hirlap*, 13 February 1991; *Magyar Hirlap*, 7 October 1991; *Uj Magyarorszag*, 17 July 1992.

20. Bogdan Goralczyk, "Visegrad Group: Is Cooperation in Central Europe Possible?" unpublished manuscript, February 1993, p. 5.

21. For a more detailed discussion of these points, see Rudolf L. Tokes, "From Visegrad to Krakow: Cooperation, Competition, and Coexistence in Central Europe," *Problems of Communism*, (November-December 1991): 100-114.

22. See CTK (Czech Telegraph Agency), 11 January 1993. In early January 1993, Klaus expressed the same views in an interview with the French daily *Le Figaro*.

23. See Meciar's news conference in London, NCA/John Henderson, 9 March 1993.

24. For excellent articles along these lines, see Jeffrey Simon, "Does Eastern Europe Belong to NATO?" *Orbis*, (Winter 1992): 21-35; and, by the same author, "Central Europe: 'Return to Europe' or Descent to Chaos?" *Strategic Review*, (Winter 1993): 18-25.

25. Author's telephone conversation with Jeffrey Simon, May 1993.

26. I am indebted for some of these points to Bogdan Goralczyk. For more detailed discussions of these issues see Richard Weitz, "Pursuing Military Security in Eastern Europe," in *After the Cold War: International Institutions and State Strategies in Europe, 1989-1991,* ed. Robert O. Keohane, Joseph S. Nye, and Stanley Hoffmann (Cambridge: Harvard University Press, 1993), pp. 342-380; and Jeffrey Simon, *Central European Civil-Military Relations and NATO Expansion*, McNair Paper, no. 39 (Washington, DC: National Defence University, April 1995).

27. See, for instance, Joshua Spero, "*Deja Vu* All Over Again: Poland's Attempt to Avoid Entrapment Between Two Belligerents," *European Security*, 1:4 (Winter 1992): 92-117.

28. NCA (Munich), 14 January 1994.

29. OMRI Daily Digest II, no. 81, 25 April 1995.

S. Neil MacFarlane

The CIS and Regional Security

I am clearly and fully aware that a shapeless organization like the CIS has no future.

Leonid Kuchma, February 1995.

Introduction

In this chapter I examine the evolving role of the Commonwealth of Independent States (CIS) as a multilateral[1] organization with regional security responsibilities.[2] Since the end of the Cold War, and in the context of the growing burdens placed upon the United Nations, there has been increasing interest in the potential of regional organizations in the prevention, management, and resolution of local conflict. Yet, there are important reasons to question the capacities of regional organizations to produce regional security. Tom Weiss and I explored these issues in two recent articles,[3] and came to the following general conclusions:

- regional organizations tend to lack the material and financial resources to "produce" regional security;

- the members of these organizations generally have stakes in the outcome of local conflicts and ties to the principals in these conflicts that make it difficult for organizations to achieve and sustain impartiality. To put it another way, the shared interest of regional actors in the "public good of regional stability is often accompanied by unilateral interest in obtaining specific favourable outcomes";[4]

- often the capacity of regional organizations to enhance regional security is circumscribed by the noninclusive quality of their membership. They often do not include major players in local conflicts, particularly nonstate actors; and

■ regional organizations often replicate within themselves power imbalances within their regions. They have a tendency, consequently, to become foreign policy instruments of regionally dominant powers.

As such, although there is logic to "regionalizing" the management of international security, there are also pitfalls of sufficient width and depth to draw into question the wisdom of excessive reliance on such organizations.

I examine to what extent these conclusions apply in the former Soviet region, with particular reference to the CIS. In addition to providing a useful empirical application of the generalizations enumerated above, the subject has direct policy relevance. Notably, the Russian Federation has put forward the CIS as a potential Chapter VIII regional organization and has sought the international community's recognition of this status. In addition, they have sought financial support from the international community for peacekeeping forces operating under CIS mandate. A sensible response to these démarches presumes an understanding of the performance of the organization in those regional security issues where it has become involved. In this chapter, I hope to provide such understanding.

The first section of the chapter provides a brief historical account of the development of the CIS and its activities in the realm of regional security and analyzes the role of the organization in conflict management and resolution up to 1993. The second looks at the evolution of Russian perspectives on its place in the region, and considers the evolution of the CIS peacekeeping role from the end of 1992 to the present, with particular reference functionally to peacekeeping and geographically to Georgia. The conclusion summarizes findings and relates them to the broader corpus of our research on the role of regional multilateral organizations in the area of regional security. It also considers how other organizations — such as the OSCE and the UN — might complement Russian and CIS activities in enhancing regional stability in the former Soviet Union.

The Early History of the CIS as a Multilateral Regional Security Organization

The Commonwealth of Independent States was created at the time of the dissolution of the Soviet Union in December 1991. It was originally conceived as a looser replacement to Soviet structures, allowing the newly independent states to manage the problems associated with the collapse — and notably the legacies of a single military structure and a highly integrated economy.

By the end of 1992, some 250 agreements on various aspects of coopera-tion were on the books.[5] In the realm of security, most notable among these was the Treaty on Collective Security (Tashkent, May 1992). This document included commitments to refrain from the use or threat of force, to resolve disputes peacefully, to refrain from joining alliances directed against other par-ticipating states, to consult on issues of international security affecting their interests and to coordinate their positions on such questions, as well as to form a Collective Security Council consisting of the heads of state and the commander-in-chief of the CIS Joint Armed Forces. The Council and the commander-in-chief were to be responsible for the coordination of the activi-ties of the armed forces of participating states. Acts of aggression against any member would be treated as aggression against all members. All members were obliged by the treaty to render assistance to members targeted by such acts.[6] In short, it was a fairly standard regional collective security agreement, although with a military institutionalization more ambitious than the norm. If implemented, it would have a significant effect in constraining conflict in the region and would likely make a substantial contribution to international secu-rity.

In addition, for the first eighteen months after the Soviet collapse there existed a CIS Joint Military Command, headed by Marshal Evgenii Shaposhnikov. There was also provision among CIS nuclear states for joint command of the USSR's strategic nuclear legacy.

The first year was perhaps impressive for the number of measures adopted, but less so with regard to implementation.[7] Elizabeth Teague commented in this context that "At their meetings CIS leaders tried to tackle important ques-tions, but the decisions that they adopted were almost universally ignored."[8] She noted further that in April 1993, for example, Islam Karimov asserted that 270 measures adopted by the CIS were unacceptable to Uzbekistan and were, therefore, not applicable to it. Increasing economic differentiation within the former Soviet region rendered efforts to sustain common economic institu-tions unsustainable, as was the case with the unified currency area and the CIS interstate bank.[9] Efforts to sustain a joint military command were short-circuited by the Ukrainian decision to form a national army and subsequent subordination of all conventional units on its territory to the Ukrainian state in January 1992, and by serious Russian-Ukrainian disagreements in 1992 and 1993 over the control of strategic forces. These last ultimately occasioned the collapse of the CIS Joint Command in June 1993.[10] Marshal Shaposhnikov, the CIS commander, commented at this time that "the CIS joint forces had never existed except on paper and it was increasingly clear that they would never be anything more than that."[11] In the meantime, the organization showed little capacity to deal with emergent and existing regional security issues, such as the Transdnestr conflict, the Nagorno-Karabakh dispute, and the outbreak of civil violence in Tajikistan. Where some progress was made in the region's diplomacy, it tended to lie outside the framework of the CIS, as when Yeltsin brokered a durable cease fire in the conflict in South Ossetia in July 1992, and Russia deployed peacekeepers there as part of a broader force that included Georgians and Ossets.[12]

What were the basic problems evident in this less than stellar record? In the first place, from the outset, members differed as to the ultimate purpose of the CIS. Ukraine, for example, saw it as a way to manage the process of transition to full independence, and, so far as one could tell, had little interest in the articulation and development of integrative structures. Vyacheslav Kostikov noted in June 1992 that Ukraine had failed to sign 40 percent of CIS agreements up to that point and had insisted on qualifying another 10 percent. Kazakhstan, by contrast, saw the CIS as a way to perpetuate close integration among former Soviet republics. By late 1992, it was generally observed that the organization's membership was divided into two groups on the issue of integration, with Russia, Belarus, Kazakhstan, Uzbekistan, Kyrgyzstan, Tajikistan, and Armenia favouring a broadening and deepening of CIS activities, and the others (Ukraine, Moldova, Azerbaijan — while it was a member, and Turkmenistan) resisting it.[13]

The membership was incomplete, with Georgia and Moldova refusing to adhere to the organization at the outset, and Azerbaijan departing in 1992. In addition, member adherence to significant agreements was often partial, as with the Tashkent Collective Security Agreement, which Ukraine, Turkmenistan, Belarus, Azerbaidzhan, and Moldova refused to sign. Third, many of the emergent conflicts in the region involved actors who were not members of the CIS and hence not party to it. The Ossets, the Abkhaz, the Tajik opposition, and the Transdnestrian insurgents were not at the table. Had they been invited to CIS conclaves, it would have been as unequal interlocutors.

This reflected two deeper problems. First, much of the conflict in the region was not interstate, but substate in character. The CIS' instruments of collective security could not obviously be brought to bear on issues of domestic jurisdiction within member or nonmember states, and, arguably, of covert intervention. Second, and in a related vein, effective multilateralism presumes effective states. It is difficult to establish and sustain "an institutional form which coordinates relations among three or more states on the basis of 'generalized' principles of conduct" (see note 1) accepted by all members when the states themselves are unconsolidated and have not achieved agreement on generalized principles of conduct within their own societies.

Perhaps most fundamentally, the problem faced by the CIS in its first year of operation was a serious asymmetry of power, with the Russian Federation dwarfing the others in economic capability and potentiality and in military capability. In realist theories of cooperation, this should serve not as an obstacle to, but as a facilitator of, cooperation. The "hegemon" has the power to impose cooperative mechanisms that further the public good of order, and provide an environment of stable expectations that permits mutually beneficial interaction.[14]

The problem in 1992 was that the potential hegemon — Russia — had opted not to play the role. As I have argued elsewhere, in its first year of existence, the Russian Federation underestimated the importance of its relations with other former Soviet states, pursuing instead the "Western orientation" that it inherited from the Gorbachev era.[15] By contrast, there was very little by way of coherent policy initiative *vis-à-vis* the CIS or its member states.

The Evolution of Russian Policy Toward the Near Abroad and the CIS

As 1992 progressed, several things became clearer to Russian policy-makers. First, the expected benefits of orientation toward the West were not forthcoming to the extent anticipated. This relieved the Russians of an important constraint on foreign policy and security activism in the former Soviet space. Second, the potential risks of inattention to problems emanating from contiguous states (e.g., migration, smuggling, the loss of control over monetary and credit policy, illicit arms transfer, the link between political processes in contiguous states and majority-minority relations in the Federation, the issue of "Russian" military units stationed in neighbouring states, to name but a few) became increasingly obvious. Third, even if, in a rational actor calculus, it might have made sense to ignore these issues, they played into Russian domestic politics in such a way as to require action to control events on the Russian periphery.

The result was an embrace by the Russian Federation of the hegemonic role in the CIS in 1993 and 1994. Russian policymakers identified the affairs of the region as the principal priority of foreign policy formulation. The Federation began a sustained effort (employing political, military, and economic means), to restore effective control in the CIS area, as well as to broaden the organization's membership to include non-Baltic outliers such as Georgia and Azerbaijan. Russia began a concerted diplomatic effort to secure international recognition of the CIS as a legitimate Chapter VIII regional organization and observer status for the organization at the United Nations.[16] Of particular significance to the topic at hand was the embrace of CIS-mandated peacekeeping.

The advent of a regional peacekeeping role appeared to add meat to the bones of this otherwise insubstantial organization.

Before examining the empirical side of this question in detail, however, it bears mention that aspiring regional hegemons have at least two general options for the pursuit of their regional objectives. The first is a hub and spokes option, where the central power seeks to dominate its neighbours through the construction of a series of bilateral relationships with them. There are obvious disadvantages with such an approach to regional integration, particularly in the economic sphere. The principal advantage, however, is that this approach minimizes the prospects for less powerful regional actors to balance against the hegemon. The other option is multilateral, in which cooperation is managed primarily through more or less inclusive intergovernmental organizations. Here, there are possible gains in allocative efficiency as well as in the legitimation of policy, but this may occur at the cost of freedom of action.

In most cases, both tracks are pursued simultaneously (viz., US hemispheric policy in the post-Cold War era). The choice is more one of emphasis than a clear embrace of one alternative at the expense of another. This is true also of Russian regional policy. Although the CIS is prominent in Russian rhetoric, the evolution of a more active and assertive Russian policy in the region displays a clear preference for bilateral instruments.

This is evident in diplomacy over a broad range of issues over which the CIS has purview. In the realm of security, for example, the failure of the February 1995 Kazakh effort to have the CIS summit adopt a "peace and security pact"[17] was accompanied by the conclusion of a series of one-sided Russian-Kazakh bilateral agreements transferring to Russia substantial control over the security and defence affairs of the Republic of Kazakhstan. Where the regional organization is employed, it generally acts as a legitimizing instrument for Russian unilateralism. This is abundantly clear in the Russian practice of peacekeeping, the most active area of CIS activity in the security field since 1992.

Peacekeeping, Russian Policy, and the CIS

Peacekeeping has a comparatively long history in CIS documents. The organization took up the question of peacekeeping in March 1992, when it produced the Agreement on Groups of Military Observers and Collective Peacekeeping Forces, dealing with issues of status, recruitment, structure, and procurement, as well as provisional rules for the formation and deployment of CIS peacekeeping forces. The agreement stipulates that peacekeeping groups are established on decision of the Council of Heads of State of the CIS. It allows for peacekeeping (interposition and observation, monitoring of disarmament, and facilitation of peaceful settlement, with deployment occurring only after a ceasefire is in place) rather than peace enforcement. They are not permitted to participate in combat operations and must retain neutrality and impartiality. Participation is composed on a voluntary basis.

This was followed in September 1993 by an Agreement on Collective Peacekeeping Forces.[18] As Kreikemeyer and Zagorsky note, this agreement was intended not so much as a general document on peacekeeping, but as an enabling instrument for intervention in Tajikistan. The relevance of its expansion of the function to include "collective defence" and of its annex on the establishment of a Joint Command over Peacekeeping Forces to the broader activity of peacekeeping in the CIS region is, hence, questionable.[19] The CIS Council has considered peacekeeping operations in Nagorno-Karabakh (1992 and 1994), Tajikistan (September 1993), Abkhazia (April 1994 and October 1994). In two of these instances — Tajikistan and Abkhazia — the CIS Council authorized the deployment of peacekeeping forces.

The pattern of CIS peacekeeping is one of clear Russian dominance and the manipulation of the multilateral organization for unilateral purpose.[20] As for the first (dominance), it suffices to note that Russia provides the great bulk of peacekeeping personnel and command structures. Although the operation in Tajikistan, for example, was mounted with the promise of units from Kazakhstan, Kyrgyzstan, and Uzbekistan,[21] the bulk of these units either did not arrive or were reasonably quickly withdrawn. The force from the outset has been dominated by units of the Russian 201st Motor Rifle Division stationed in Dushanbe. In the case of Georgia, no non-Russian CIS units have been deployed in either the Osset or the Abkhaz operations.

The Georgian Case

The second (unilateral manipulation of the organization) may be demonstrated by reference to one or two specific cases. The strategic objective for Russia in Georgia since the beginning of 1993 has been the reestablishment of a military presence and political influence in the Transcaucasus. The manipulation of Georgia's civil conflicts has been one among several means of achieving this end. Peacekeeping is one phase in this evolving strategy.

In Abkhazia, Russian forces (if not the Russian government) armed the insurgents, while volunteers from the Russian Federation (notably Chechens and Cossacks)[22] greatly augmented their combat capability. Russia brokered a ceasefire in summer 1993 along the Gumista River, providing observers to ensure that the two sides' obligations were fulfilled. It appears that while the

Georgians did withdraw the bulk of their heavy weaponry from the republic, the Abkhaz side did not disarm. Russian observers failed to report these apparent violations. Nor did they interfere with, or report, the reconsolidation of Abkhaz forces in "demilitarized" zones prior to the resumption of war in September-October 1993. In this respect, Russian behaviour played an important role in the collapse of the Georgian position in Abkhazia and the withdrawal of Georgian forces beyond the Inguri River.

At this stage, Georgia decided after months of resistance to join the CIS, and Russia and Georgia signed a Status of Forces Agreement legalizing the stationing of Russian forces in Georgia. Russian forces then intervened in Mingrelia, providing the Georgian government logistical assistance essential to the defeat of insurgents loyal to the late ex-president Zviad Gamsakhurdia. More to the point, Russian units interposed themselves between Georgian and Abkhaz forces along the Inguri River in late 1993, five months before the peacekeeping mandate was formalized by the CIS in May 1994. Russia also placed sanctions on Abkhazia in order to force the Abkhaz to the table to negotiate a compromise that would retain Georgia's territorial integrity. Russia has created a situation in which the survival of the Georgian state and regime are largely dependent on the presence of Russian military protectors. One can at least sympathize with the widespread view held in Georgia to the effect that Russian policy in Georgia — including that related to peacekeeping — amounted to a steady manipulation of both the Osset and the Abkhaz questions in order to prevent the consolidation of independence in Georgia and to return Georgia to the fold. Some Russian press commentary concurred:

> The Georgian parliament is well aware of the political failure. The country's economy will be revived through Russian money, Russia will set up the Georgian Armed Forces, and Moscow specialists will settle the sovereign state's internal problems. Not for nothing does the old proverb run: "Whoever controls Tbilisi controls the Caucasus." Roughly the same situation is emerging as in the 19th century, and Georgia is acquiring roughly the same status.[23]

This 1994 commentary seems to be confirmed by the conclusion in March 1995 of a comprehensive Georgian-Russian agreement on military cooperation. The agreement extends the arrangement for the basing of Russian troops in Georgia for 25 years and envisages a broad role for Russian military advisers in the training of the Georgian army. Georgian government sources concluded from this development that Georgia had effectively accepted Russian domination.[24] The role of the CIS in this venture was two-fold. First, the granting in May 1994 of a CIS peacekeeping mandate for already deployed

Russian forces legitimized their presence. Second, it served as an (unsuccessful) basis for seeking external financing of Russian operations in the area.[25]

The combination of military assistance to the two sides in the Nagorno-Karabakh conflict and the effort to mediate that conflict has produced similar results in Armenia and Azerbaijan. It is reasonable to expect that if Russian mediation actually gets anywhere, one component of the settlement will be the deployment of a sizeable Russian-dominated peacekeeping force in the buffer zone around Nagorno-Karabakh already cleared by Armenian forces (see note 22).[26] In Tajikistan as well, Russia's peacekeeping efforts have essentially guaranteed the survival of a pro-Russian unreformed communist regime, a government that not only accepts but promotes Russian policing of the frontier between that republic and Afghanistan. Indeed, Tajik government forces were included in the peacekeeping contingent, a fact that hardly encouraged confidence in the force's impartiality.

This apparent pattern has given rise to the accusation that Russia is essentially pursuing a policy of deliberately exacerbating local conflicts in certain CIS states by encouraging local minorities to fight for self-determination at the expense of the territorial integrity of existing states. In turn, governments of the disintegrating states have to request Russian peacekeeping forces to preserve the territorial integrity of the state.[27] Whether or not one accepts this proposition, leading Russian policymakers have acknowledged that the deployment of peacekeeping forces is one important means of exerting influence over historical possessions beyond the current Russian frontier. In an interview in November 1993, for example, Kozyrev noted that after the collapse of the Soviet Union, Russia faced two options. The first was to hold the USSR together as a state, which was hopeless. The second was to pull out of the other republics of the USSR completely. This would have constituted an "unwarranted loss of influence gained over centuries." The compromise was to maintain bases capable of peacekeeping operations throughout much of the former Soviet Union.[28]

In general, it seems reasonable to conclude that CIS peacekeeping — rather than being a genuinely multilateral regional activity directed at stabilization and security — is an integral component of Russian policy in the near abroad, serving the purpose of legitimizing the assertion of the Russian state at the expense of its weaker neighbours.

Conclusion

To summarize, the CIS region has an impressive number of security-related issues that might form the basis for activity by a multilateral regional security organization: nuclear arms control, disposition of forces inherited from the USSR, legal and illegal arms and technology transfer, control of the external borders of the former Soviet space, potential interstate conflicts, and potential and actual civil conflicts within member states, among others. Much ink has been spilt in the negotiation of agreements in many of these areas. Yet the record of implementation is unimpressive. The security-related institutions of the CIS are either empty shells (e.g., the Collective Security Council) or have short and ineffectual lives (e.g., the Joint Command). Where concrete progress on these issues has been made (as on military cooperation), the principal context of negotiation tends to be bilateral rather than multilateral.

On paper, the most substantial activity of the organization lies in the realm of peacekeeping. Here, however, a close look suggests that this is in fact a Russian or Russian-dominated activity, and that it forms one aspect of Russian state policy in reestablishing influence and military presence in the former Soviet region. The organization serves as a legitimizing device in this effort. In this sense, it does not fit the parameters of multilateralism set out at the outset of this chapter.

In many respects, the experience of the CIS in regional security does conform to the generalizations concerning regional conflict and regional security organizations set out earlier. The organization is unimpressive in terms of institutional and financial resources. This inhibits any development of an independent supranational identity, as well as impeding efforts to "produce" regional security. As with many other organizations, the most significant conflicts that it attempts to address are intra- rather than interstate in nature. The consequent problems of domestic jurisdiction would complicate the organization's efforts to define a role for itself even if it had the necessary broad consensus and organizational resources to do so. The record of CIS involvement in regional conflict suggests also that its actions reflect the state interests of its principal members more than they reflect a communitarian interest in the public good of stability. Its state-centric basis, coupled with the acceptance of all members of the principle of territorial integrity, make it a less than ideal venue for negotiation and mediation involving nonstate actors. Most importantly, it reflects also the problem of asymmetry of power. The clear preponderance of Russia in the region impedes organizational development in at least two ways. First, it is not necessary to Russia in the pursuit of its regional objectives, since, as the Russians show on a daily basis in the region, whatever their internal problems, they have sufficient residual power to pursue a hegemonic agenda unilaterally. Second, the possible interest of other regional states in the development of the organization as a means of balancing Russian power are outweighed by the fear that an effective Russian-dominated CIS would serve simply as a further useful instrument for the projection of Russian power at their expense.

On the surface, this would suggest that Western states should not only not take the CIS seriously, but should actively oppose its legitimation as a Chapter VIII organization or its possible consolidation. Such a conclusion would, I think, be too hasty.

As I understand it, Western states have several shared objectives in the former Soviet region. One is the defence of the sovereignty of the former Soviet republics as signatories of the UN Charter and as members of the OSCE. To the extent that Russia is permitted systematically to violate its commitments under the statutes of these organizations, this weakens regional and global norms. On the other hand, the Western states also share an interest in regional stability in the former Soviet Union. They are unwilling either unilaterally or multilaterally to make a contribution sufficient to attain this objective. Russia appears to have both the capacity and the will to enhance stability in the region, a stability that is arguably a prerequisite for economic and political development. Third, and despite the assertive quality of Russia's regional policy and the events in Chechnya, the West has a persistent interest in sustaining close and positive relations with the Russian Federation specifically. This is a product of the substantial political interdependence characterizing Russian-Western relations across a broad range of issues from European security architecture through nuclear arms control to the effectiveness of the UN Security Council on issues not related to Russia.

The bottom line is that Russia is asserting itself in the CIS region, that the West is unable and/or unwilling to supplant Russia in its exercise of power in pursuit of interest and stability, that this exercise reflects at least in part defensible Russian security interests, and that open resistance would jeopardize Russian-Western relations. The real question for Western policymakers should be what can be done to moderate Russian assertion, to redirect it in more benign and internationally respectable directions.

The CIS may have a role here. Making CIS peacekeeping activities genuinely multilateral could have a restraining effect on Russian behaviour. This would require Western contribution to cover the financial costs of non-Russian participants in such missions. Given the burden that Russian peacekeeping operations are placing on an already strained Russian defence budget, Western financial contributions could provide substantial leverage over Russian behaviour in the field and possibly over the development of the CIS in a more multilateral direction. Third, OSCE and/or UN observation of CIS activities in the field enhances transparency and moderates the behaviour of Russian units involved in peacekeeping operations.[29]

In short, although the CIS is hardly an impressive regional organization when it comes to the production of the public good of regional security, there is reason to work toward improving its performance rather than ignoring or abandoning it. Few tools are available to moderate Russian regional assertiveness. The CIS may be one of them.

Notes

The author is grateful to the following organizations and programmes for their support of his research: The Cooperative Security Competitive Program of the Department of Foreign Affairs and International Trade (Canada), The Military and Strategic Studies Program of the Department of National Defence (Canada), and the Humanitarian and War Project of Watson Institute for International Studies, Brown University (USA).

1.   I follow John Ruggie's definition of multilateralism:

> [M]ultilateralism is an institutional form which coordinates relations among three or more states on the basis of "generalized" principles of conduct - that is, principles which specify appropriate conduct for a class of actions, without regard to the particularistic interests of the parties or the strategic exigencies that may exist in any specific occurrence.

> John G. Ruggie, "Multilateralism: The Anatomy of an Institution," *International Organization,* 46:3 (Summer 1992): 571.

2.   The CIS also has a potentially important economic dimension. This lies beyond the purview of this analysis. Although at various times in its short history, the organization has had formal responsibilities across an array of issues related to security (e.g., joint command of former Soviet military forces and joint control of nuclear weapons), these also lie outside the frame of reference of this study. The basic focus here is on the role of the organization as a device for the management of local conflict.

3.   S. Neil MacFarlane and Thomas G. Weiss, "Regional Organizations and Regional Security," *Security Studies,* 2:1 (Autumn 1992): 6-37; and "The United Nations, Regional Organizations and Human Security: Building Theory in Central America," *Third World Quarterly,* 15:2 (1994): 277-93.

4.   MacFarlane and Weiss "Regional Organizations," p. 30.

5.   Ann Sheehy, "Seven States Sign Charter Strengthening CIIS," *RFE/RL Research Reports* 2:9, (26 February 1993): 10.

6.   For an English translation of the text, see *RFE/RL Research Report* 2:25, (18 June 1993): 4-5.

7.   For a similar assessment, see Suzanne Crow, "Russia Promotes the CIS as an International Organization," *RFE/RL Research Reports* 3:11, (18 March 1994): 33.

8. Elizabeth Teague, "The CIS: An Unpredictable Future," *RFE/RL Research Reports* 3:1, (7 January 1994): 9.

9. On this point, see the analysis of Erik Whitlock, "The CIS Economies: Divergent and Troubled Paths," *RFE/RL Research Reports* 3:1, (7 January 1994): 13-14. Whitlock notes the significance of the decision of the Russian Central Bank to end the flow of noncash rubles between Russia and the rest in July 1992, and the Russian currency reform in July 1993 in accounting for the collapse of monetary integration. Efforts to resurrect the ruble zone in the autumn of 1993 were stymied by Russian insistence that other former Soviet republics had to surrender control over monetary policy to Russia in return for membership. For a useful analysis of the CIS Interstate Bank project, see Daniel Gros, "The Genesis and Demise of the Interstate Bank Project," in *Trade in the Newly Independent States,* ed. Constantine Michalopoulos and David Tarr (Washington, DC: World Bank, 1994), pp. 229-35.

10. On this point, see Stephen Foye, "End of CIS Command Heralds New Russian Defense Policy," *RFE/RL Research Reports* 2:27, (2 July 1993): 46.

11. As cited in Stephen Foye, "The Armed Forces of the CIS: Legacies and Strategies, *RFE/RL Research Reports* 3:1, (7 January 1994): 20.

12. Parenthetically, the Osset peacekeeping force is an intriguing departure from standard practice, in that it explicitly includes units of the disputing parties. That the Russians were pressing for a removal of Georgian and Osset units and the confiscation of their heavy military equipment in early 1995 suggests that they do not judge the experiment to have been a success.

13. On this point, see Andrei Zagorsky, et al., "Die Gemeinschaft Unabhaengiger Staaten: Entwicklungen und Perspektiven," *Berichte des Bundesinstituts fur Ostwissenschaftliche ind Internationale Studien* 50 (1992).

14. See Robert Gilpon, *War and Change in World Politics* (Cambridge: Cambridge University Press, 1981), pp. 28-29, 35-36.

15. See S. Neil MacFarlane, "Russia, The West and European Security," *Survival,* 35, 3 (Autumn 1993):7-18; S. Neil MacFarlane "Russian Conceptions of Europe," *Post-Soviet Affairs,* 10:3 (July-September 1994): 241-44.

16. On this point, see Crow, "Russia Promotes the CIS," pp. 33-4.

17. The pact was originally watered down into a memorandum on principles of mutual relations and then disappeared altogether. Proposals for a joint air defence system also collapsed at this meeting. See the account in OMRI *Daily Digest,* no. 31, Part I, 13 February 1995.

18. It is noteworthy that the agreement was endorsed only by Kazakhstan, Kyrgyzstan, Russia, Tajikistan, and Uzbekistan. For texts of the agreements, see *Informatsionnyi Vestnik Soveta Glav Gosudarstv i Soveta Glav Pravitel'stv SNG,* (1992) and (1993).

19. Kreikemeyer and Zagorsky, "Die Gemeinschaft Unabhaengiger Staaten: Entwicklungen und Perpektiven, p. 13. The authors note, however, that despite the specific terms of reference of the agreement, it has come to be used as a precedent for subsequent decisions of the CIS on matters related to peacekeeping.

20. It is worth recalling in this context the definition of multilateralism proffered at the beginning of this chapter. It refers to an acceptance of generalized principles of cooperation, "without

regard to the particularistic interests of the parties or the strategic exigencies that may exist in any specific occurrence."

21. The agreement establishing the force envisaged the following proportions in troop contributions: Kazakhstan -- 15 percent, Kyrgyzstan -- 10 percent, Russia -- 50 percent, Tajikistan -- 10 percent, and Uzbekistan -- 15 percent.

22. I am not claiming that these groups were acting at the behest of the Russian government. They had reasons of their own. Nonetheless, bringing Georgia back into a close and dependent relationship with Russia was the objective, and destabilization was the means. Russian Federation volunteers served this purpose, whatever their own motivations. Moreover, had the Russian government sought to prevent their arrival, they could have attempted to control their frontier, which they did not do.

23. Vladimir Zaynetdinov and Sergey Chernykh, "Moscow-Tbilisi: Friendship Demands Sacrifices," *KOMSOMOLSKAYA PRAVDA*, 5 February 1994; translated in *FBIS-SOV-94-026*, 8 February 1994.

24. Interviews in Tbilisi, March 1995.

25. CIS peacekeeping operations relating to the Abkhaz question were acknowledged in UN Security Council Resolution 937 (21 July 1994). The resolution responded to Russian requests for financial assistance by establishing a voluntary fund into which contributions could be paid. See Anna Kriekemeyer and Andrei Zagorsky (eds.), "The Mechanisms and Capacity of the CIS in Peacekeeping," in *The Role of Russia in Eurasia,* ed. Lena Jonson (Boulder: Westview Press, 1996).

26. Armenian Defence Minister Serzh Sakisyan has been quoted as saying that Armenia wants the Russians to stay forever, in Pavel Felgenauer, *Segodnya,* 21 October, 1994, p. 2. See also "Moscow Rejects Secondary Role in Karabakh Peace Operation," *Interfax*, 29 November 1994, in *FBIS-SOV-94-230,* 30 November 1994.

27. Thomas Goltz, "Letter from Eurasia: The Hidden Russian Hand," *Foreign Policy,* 92 (Fall 1993): 92-116.

28. See *Nezavisimaya Gazeta,* 24 November 1993, and 19 January 1994.

29. In a recent visit to CIS and UNOMIG units in eastern Abkhazia, it was clear from interviews with Russian officers that they were very attentive to the presence of non-CIS observers. My own judgement of the situation was that as they became more accustomed to the UN presence, evidence of "partiality" in their activities diminished.

PART IV
Conclusion

Michel Fortmann
S. Neil MacFarlane
Stéphane Roussel

The Limits of Multilateralism in Regional Security

The Triumph of Pessimism

In the introduction to this volume, we mentioned several reasons why regional security institutions appeared indispensable in the fluid and uncertain environment of the current international system. But indispensability does not necessarily imply efficacy. What is the current state of mind in the community of scholars in international relations with respect to multilateralism and regional security institutions? Have these institutions fulfilled the tasks for which they were designed? Are they a preferred means for dealing with current regional security problems?

When we started on this project, we did not expect it to be an apology on the virtues of multilateralism, or an absolute corroboration of liberal institutionalism. But we did count on a general confirmation of the significance of multilateralism and cooperative security in world politics, somewhat along the lines of Keohane, Nye's and Hoffman's 1993 argument in their book *After the Cold War*. In their concluding remarks, Keohane et al. noted that international institutions profoundly conditioned the way governments reacted to the end of the Cold War:

> Europe was an institutionally dense environment in which the expectations of states' leaders were shaped by the rules and practices of institutions and in which they routinely responded to initiatives from international organizations as well as using these organizations for their own purposes.[1]

Likewise, in their account of the recent mutation of the inter-American system, some observers have also concluded that the hemisphere is currently characterized by "the emergence of a new paradigm of cooperation ... based on a commitment to partnership."[2] In short, we expected most of the panels to reach reasonably positive and optimistic conclusions in regard to international cooperation in the area of regional security.

This expectation was misplaced. As we prepared the various chapters for publication, we were rather surprised by their gloomy — and sometimes cynical — tone. The extent to which this pessimism has spread is striking. Most of the authors conclude that regional security institutions still face considerable difficulties. We should ask ourselves why the interest in multilateralism and regional security — so perceptible in 1993-94 — did not catch on, and seems, on the contrary, to have petered out. Was the trend toward greater multilateralism in the early 1990s only a mirage created by the turbulence associated with the end of the Cold War? What is left of the concept on the practical as well as the theoretical level? The sources of this deepening pessimism deserve to be systematically explored.

The Neorealist View

Not surprisingly, those authors in our group who are methodologically close to the neorealist school share the latter's scepticism on multilateralism. Multilateralism and international institutions are but reflections of power relations in the international system. Multilateral cooperation is short-circuited when it runs up against the interests of principal actors in the system. This type of analysis seems particularly effective in regions characterized by a marked asymmetry of power. Hence, those authors considering the inter-American system, such as David Mares or Harold Klepak, are far from sharing the optimism of Augusto Varas' remark cited above. They see the unequal distribution of power between the United States and Latin America as the principal obstacle to the establishment of a real security community. Such a pronounced asymmetry tempts the most powerful state to act unilaterally rather than to wrap itself up in a multilateral process involving actors less than enthusiastic about the course of action preferred by the dominant power.

A second critical element that can be drawn from these analyses is that common problems do not necessarily produce common interests. Numerous states find themselves faced by similar problems, but they can perceive them differently; their policy responses, consequently, may also differ. Moreover, the effect of "global" problems may be felt differently from one region to another, or even from one state to another. In other words, interdependence and common problems do not automatically result in conversion to the virtues of multilateralism. Even where multilateral institutions exist, they need time and energy to cross the barrier of differing perceptions and national experiences. The two interconnected dimensions of security examined here in the Latin American context — the struggle against drug trafficking, democratic development, and the defence of human rights — provide eloquent examples of this problem.

Beyond this, multilateral cooperation carries certain costs in time, energy, loss of control and compromise on objectives. International institutions tend to develop bureaucracies that are often neither prompt nor effective. Their decision processes are often complex and require consensus among members which is, in and of itself, difficult to obtain. In the face of a collective problem, states will generally weigh the pro's and con's of multilateral action and will take account of the costs that it implies. In this fashion, states will logically have a tendency to prefer unilateral or bilateral options to multilateral solutions, especially when, as Albrecht Schnabel points out, they consider the matter in question to be of vital interest.

The idea that international institutions are above all instruments in the hands of great powers is well represented in the analyses of Albrecht Schnabel and Neil MacFarlane. Institutions are a means of legitimizing actions and neutralization of possible criticism (as is evident in the case of Russian "peacekeeping operations in the near aborad"). Allen Sens, Zoltan Barany and, to a lesser extent, Brian Job show that the logic of interests, the desire to attenuate the security dilemma, and the recourse to institutions as instruments of state security policy are not limited to great powers, but are also present in the behaviour of small states.

These analyses return us to a number of core postulates of the neorealist literature. The cases examined here of cooperation observed since the end of the Cold War do not appear to call into question the fundamental logic of state behaviour dictated by the anarchic quality of international relations. Indeed, these examples may be explained to a large extent in Hobbesian terms.

These arguments seem convincing in many respects and do not seem to leave much space for institutionalist logic. However, the problems identified by these authors concern for the most part the costs associated with one or another multilateral project and the divergence of interest between actors. Even though these act as substantial obstacles to the practice of multilateralism, they do not fatally undermine the institutionalist approach to multilateralism.

The Institutionalist View

Authors closer to the liberal institutionalist tradition, nonetheless, evince a prudent tone and also admit that multilateral institutions face difficulties in fulfilling the tasks posed for them in the domain of security. One of the principal problems they face in this regard is linked to the lack of coherence among the rules and norms that constitute institutions or regimes, as is emphasized at different levels by both David Long and Albert Legault. A second cause of the lack of effectiveness of these institutions lies in a lack of leadership and in the reticence of states to engage in actions and processes of uncertain outcome as is evident, for example, in the work of Gordon Mace, Guy Gosselin, and Louis Bélanger. Finally, as Brian Job stresses, the more members an institution has, the more likely it is to run up against resistance when the time comes to assume serious obligations that may have significant consequences.[3] States consequently will seek to come together in smaller groups. This problem was significant, for example, in the attempts of the CSCE/OSCE to respond to the crisis in the former Yugoslavia, although in his chapter Albert Legault tends to play down the significance of this obstacle in this case.

In general, although the several institutionalists in the group remain critical of the achievements of regional security institutions, most of them reserve judgement, preferring a longer term evaluation of the viability and effectiveness of multilateral cooperation. Moreover, the somewhat pessimistic conclusions drawn from the bulk of our case studies are not necessarily generalizable to multilateralism as a whole. Looking at multilateralism more broadly, the terrain is more stable than it would appear from these studies.

Five propositions shared to varying degrees by this group of authors deserve to be summarized here. The first is linked to economic rationality. It is a truism that the world, and particularly the community of advanced industrial states, is increasingly economically interdependent. The impact of this phenomenon on the development of multilateral institutions and regimes is well known. In a global market where export-led growth is an imperative and where the risks of currency crisis or market failure are a constant danger, states have a common interest in creating general trading regimes where competition can take place in a stable and regulated environment. Collaboration and regulation are a matter of economic survival. In the economic realm, then, deepening multilateral cooperation seems not to be a question of if, but of when.

The impact of these developments in the international economy on security is insufficiently addressed in the literature.[4] Robert Cox, however, reminds us that political multilateralism — of which security regimes are an element — is a natural extension of economic multilateralism and in turn reinforces the economic dimension.[5] In other words, the enlargement of NATO to the East may be perceived as a logical follow-up to the extension of a free trade area to the East.

The second argument is security-related. Large-scale warfare between industrialized countries is economically and politically less and less viable, and, therefore, increasingly unattractive as a policy option. Moreover, with the end of the Cold War many countries are considering the upkeep of armies as a net drain on their economy, and entire continents are likely to turn into vast *monitored security zones* as a result of the conclusion of multiple arms control treaties since the 1980s. This evolution favours the creation and maintenance of interlocking security and arms control regimes like the Partnership for Peace and the Conventional Forces in Europe (CFE) Treaty. On the global scene, the very recent indefinite extension of the Non-Proliferation Treaty (NPT) suggests that similar considerations may stimulate global security cooperation in specific areas.

The third argument, again, is also well known: the growth of transnational problems and challenges, among them environmental degradation, the population explosion, and the management of nonrenewable resources, is a fact of life, which in turn creates unavoidable pressures for regional and global cooperation. Again in the words of Robert Cox, and referring to the environment "the ecosystem is no longer to be thought as an inert, passive limit to human activity. It has to be thought as a non-human, active force capable of dramatic interventions affecting human conditions and survival."[6] In other words, the ecosystem, like the global economy, requires some form of multilateral regulatory regime in order to be stabilized.

Fourth, multilateral institutions offer state and nonstate actors a number of advantages and perform a number of functions in their efforts to cope with these global problems:

- they facilitate the circulation of information and the socialization of elites;

- they enhance transparency and predication in interstate interactions;

- they furnish channels permitting smaller states and nongovernmental entities to exercise influence in international relations;

- they contribute to the structuring of state priorities and to determining the way in which problems are approached. They also sometimes oblige states to take a position on subjects that might otherwise be neglected, as was the case in the former Yugoslav conflict.

- they participate in the surveillance of state activities, and provide a forum for denouncing activities that do not conform to norms or rules.

- they can serve as a means of pressuring particular states. For example, Neil MacFarlane suggests that the process of cooperation in which Russia has engaged itself to maintain peace in the "near abroad" itself constitutes a constraint on Russian policy to the extent that this process becomes a means that the West can use to pressure Russia to respect international norms.[7]

In a nutshell, from the point of view of the state, regimes/multilateral institutions are useful instruments.

Fifth is the issue of values evident, for example, in the chapter by Andy Knight. Recourse to rationalist arguments is only one way to look at multilateralism. Beyond the state level of analysis, there exists a set of values, beliefs, and ideas that transcend frontiers and are communicated between societies often before being accepted by individual states. They are, in this respect, social products that serve as reference points not only for individuals, but also for groups and their representatives, and serve to shape their comportment while providing standards for evaluating that of others. As Knight notes, international institutions in the past were often produced by civil society before being a matter for state interaction. He argues that the conditions for this kind of bottom-up multilateralism may be reappearing. States ignore at their peril ideas and values that have resonance not only within the societies that they govern, but to an increasing degree in entire regions if not in the international system as a whole. Whether states like it or not, there exists an entire sphere of multilateralism that escapes their control and that cannot be easily manipulated. The establishment of these values and ideas is a long-term process fraught with difficulties as the analyses in this volume suggest, but the gradual emergence of an *international society* cannot be ignored. From this point of view, the emergence of regional communities, such as that of the Euro-Atlantic area, could be an important signal.

These five considerations permit us to retain a certain optimism regarding the viability and utility of multilateral institutions in the longer term. It is noteworthy, however, that, with the examination of the study by Legault the case studies examined here indicate that the evolving record of multilateral cooperation is weakest in the realm of security, broadly defined. They remind us strongly of the many and profound obstacles to effective multilateralism in the realm of regional security. The weakness of the empirical record of multilateralism in security since the end of the Cold War reflects several factors, at both the level of the state and of organizations. Although states may face similar problems, their perceptions and interpretations of these problems are rooted in domestic political culture and hence may vary considerably. Shared problems, moreover, may have differential impacts on particular states, inhibiting the development of cooperative responses. While the gains from multilateral cooperation are likely to be long term and general, the focus of policy processes within states is generally short term and particular. Asymmetries of power supplement differing definitions of state interest in dictating differential approaches to the issue of multilateral cooperation.

At the level of organizations, multilateral bureaucracies are notoriously inefficient and inflexible. As such, they are poor vehicles for the articulation and implementation of shared state interests. The rules of decisionmaking of such organizations, and notably the emphasis in many on consensus, constrain action on security issues. The effectiveness of such organizations is often limited by the exclusive quality of their membership. Paradoxically, as organizations become more inclusive, this complicates effective decisionmaking even further.

More basically, the sceptical conclusions of the case studies included here serve as a confirmation of Charles Lipson's conclusion that regimes in the realm of security are much rarer than they are in, say, economics, since "the immediate and potentially grave losses to a player who attempts to cooperate without reciprocation" and the "risks associated with inadequate monitoring of others' decisions and actions" are much higher. Cooperation in this area is inhibited particularly by the strong incentives to defect from the regime and the considerable perils of defection for those remaining in the system.[8]

Conclusion

The end of the Cold War gave birth to a collective expectation that global issues would be tackled differently in a world unshackled from its bipolar chains. In other words, there was a diffuse but real hope that Western political and economic doctrines could inspire a new kind of international politics predicated on a global perspective and a more equitable world view. To paraphrase Stanley Hoffman "Marxism was discredited. Realism promised only the perpetuation of the same old game ... international liberalism, thus was elevated as the only hopeful vision of world affairs."[9] Indeed, as Thomas Risse-Kappen reminds us, "the norms of multilateralism ... originated in the West as part of the liberal internationalist world view."[10]

But, if liberal internationalism offers a promising vision, it is far from being a program of action. In fact, it is woolly and wracked by contradictions. It lacks a set of clear principles on the basis of which to set goals. It is in dire need of a thread that would allow the development of a strategy. It is also in disarray over methods for defending or promoting its vision. It is no wonder, in that perspective that the promise of a new world order or the notion of "regional security architectures" were quickly revealed for what they were, namely "empty promises." To a large extent, the practical difficulties of multilateralism were compounded by the fact that its doctrinal road map was in existent. In other words, in the area of politics, actors are facing persistent uncertainties about their environment, their interests, and the ways to maximize them. Thus, they need a simple, straightforward, and practical world view as a guide for action and as a normative reference to legitimize their policies.

Pure realism, however factually compelling, is no answer here,

for realism, though logically overwhelming, does not provide us with the springs of action which are necessary even to the pursuit of thought.... Consistent realism excludes four things which appear essential ingredients of all effective political thinking: a finite goal, an emotional appeal, a right of moral judgment, and a ground for action.[11]

The need — as yet unfulfilled — is for a body of theory in international relations that provides normative guidance while taking fuller account of the structural constraints on cooperation in contemporary world politics. These studies suggest that, as yet, security studies, in particular, is a long distance short of this goal.

Notes

1. Robert Keohane and Stanley Hoffmann, "Conclusions: Structure, Strategy, and Institutional Roles," in After the Cold War, International Institutions and State Strategies in Europe, 1989-1991, ed. Robert Koehane, Joseph Nye and Stanley Hoffmann (Cambridge: Harvard University Press, 1993), p. 381.

2. Augusto Varas, "From Coercion to Partnership: A New Paradigm for Security Cooperation in the Western Hemisphere," in The United States and Latin America in the 1990s: Beyond the Cold War, ed. Jonathan Hartlyn, Lars Schoultz and Augusto Varas (Chapel Hill, NC: University of North Carolina Press, 1992), p. 53.

3. Note, however, that Miles Kahler questions the point that institutions with greater numbers of members are less efficient. See "Multilateralism with Small and Large Numbers," International Organization, 46:3 (Summer 1992): 681-708.

4. For a notable initial analysis, see Andrew Hurrell, "Triggers, Nests and Path Dependence: Understanding the Links between Economic and Security Regionalism," paper presented at the annual meetings of the International Studies Association, San Diego, 21-25 April 1996.

5. Robert Cox, "Multilateralism and World Order," Review of International Studies, 18 (1992): 162.

6. Cox, "Multilateralism and World Order," p. 178.

7. This list is based in part on Margaret P. Karns and Karen A. Mingst, " Multilateral Institutions and International Security," in World Security, Trends and Challenges at Century's End, ed. Michael Klare and D.C. Thomas (New York: St. Martin's Press, 1991), pp. 267-69.

8. See David Lipson, "International Cooperation in Economic and Security Affairs," in *Neorealism and Neoliberalism,* ed. David Baldwin (New York: Columbia University Press, 1993), pp. 71-2.

9. Stanley Hoffmann, "The Crisis of Liberal Internationalism," *Foreign Policy*, 98 (Spring 1995): 177.

10. Thomas Risse-Kappen, "Between a New World Order and None: Explaining the Re-Emergence of the United Nations in World Politics," Occasional Paper no. 29 (Toronto: Centre for International and Strategic Studies, York University, 1995), p. 17.

11. E. H. Carr, *The Twenty Years Crisis, 1919-1939* (New-York: MacMillan 1939), p. 89, quoted in Mark Zacher and Richard A. Mathew, "Liberal International Theory: Common Threads, Divergent Strands," paper presented at the annual meeting of the APSA, Chicago, 3-6 September 1992, p. 46.

Contributors

Zoltan Barany   Department of Government, University of Texas at Austin.

Louis Bélanger   Département de science politique, Université Laval.

Michel Fortmann   Département de science politique, Université de Montréal.

Guy Gosselin   Département de science politique, Université Laval.

Brian L. Job   Department of Political Science, University of British Columbia.

Harold P. Klepak   Department of History, Royal Military College, Kingston.

W. Andy Knight   Political Studies Department, Bishop's University, Montreal.

Albert Legault   Département de science politique, Université Laval.

David Long   Norman Paterson School of International Affairs, Carleton University, Ottawa.

Gordon Mace   Département de science politique, Université Laval.

David R. Mares   Department of Political Science, University of California, San Diego.

S. Neil MacFarlane St. Anne's College, Oxford University.

Stéphane Roussel Département de science politique, Université de Montréal.

Albrecht Schnabel International Relations and European Studies Programme, Central European University, Budapest.

Allen G. Sens   Department of Political Science, University of British Columbia.

Glossary

ACDA	Arms Control and Disarmament Agency
ASEAN	Association of South East Asian Nations
CBM	Confidence Building Measures
CEE	Central and Eastern Europe
CEI	Central European Initiative
CFE	Conventional Force in Europe Treaty
CFSP	Common Foreign and Security Policy
CICAD	Inter-American Drug Abuse Control Commission
CIDI	Inter-American Council of Integral Development
CIECC	Inter-American Council for Education, Science and Culture
CIES	Inter-American Economic and Social Council
CIS	Commonwealth of Independent States
CLADDE	Latin American Center for Defense and Disarmament
CMEA	Council of Mutual Economic Assistance
CSCE	Conference on Security and Cooperation in Europe
ECSC	European Coal and Steel Community
EEC	European Economic Community
EP	European Parliament
EPC	European Political Cooperation
EU	European Union
GATT	General Agreement on Tariffs and Trade
HDI	Human Development Index
IEO	International Economic Order
IISS	International Institute for Strategic Studies
IR	International Relations
NACC	North Atlantic Cooperation Council
NAFTA	North American Free Trade Agreement
NATO	North Atlantic Treaty Organization
NGO	Non-Governmental Organization
NPT	Non-Proliferation Treaty
NSWP	Non-Soviet Warsaw Pact
OAS	Organization of American States
OAU	Organization of African Unity
OSCE	Organization on Security and Cooperation in Europe

PAU	Pan-American Union
PfP	Partnership for Peace
RIO TREATY	Inter-American Treaty of Reciprocal Assistance
SEA	Single European Act
UN	United Nations
UNDP	United Nations Development Programme
UNPROFOR	UN Protection Force in the Former Yugoslavia
WTO	Warsaw Treaty Organization
ZNLA	Zapatista National Liberation Army

THE PEARSON PEACEKEEPING CENTRE AND THE NEW PEACEKEEPING PARTNERSHIP

The mission of the Lester B. Pearson Canadian International Peacekeeping Training Centre is to provide national and international participants with the opportunity to examine specific peacekeeping issues and to update their knowledge of the latest peacekeeping practices. To guide its activities, the PPC has developed the concept of the **New Peacekeeping Partnership**, the term applied to those organizations and individuals that work together to improve the effectiveness of modern peacekeeping operations. It includes: the military; civil police; government, and non-government agencies dealing with human rights and humanitarian assistance; diplomats; the media; and organizations sponsoring development and democratization programmes.

The Pearson Peacekeeping Centre offers a multifaceted curriculum of special interest to all the stakeholders associated with peacekeeping operations, through an extensive schedule of conferences, seminars, workshops, training and educational courses. Off-campus activities are conducted by mobile training teams or through electronic distant-learning technology.

The Centre also sponsors field research with deployed peacekeeping missions and a Visiting Scholar Programme. Researchers in any peacekeeping-related discipline can arrange for access to the Centre's archives. In addition to its scheduled functions, the Centre has the ability to respond quickly to requests for specialized research or customized training packages. It also functions as an information clearing house and research centre and its multidisciplinary approach reflects the changes in the international environment and "The Changing Face of Peacekeeping". The Centre also conducts a sizeable and active internship programme which allows students to gain valuable working experience while learning more about peacekeeping.

For more information on the Pearson Peacekeeping Centre's programmes, activities and publications, please contact:

Alex Morrison, President, The Pearson Peacekeeping Centre
Cornwallis Park, PO Box 100, Clementsport, NS B0S 1E0 CANADA
Tel: (902) 638-8041 Fax: (902) 638-3344
Email: amorriso@ppc.cdnpeacekeeping.ns.ca
Website: http://www.cdnpeacekeeping.ns.ca

The Pearson Peacekeeping Centre is named in honour of Lester B. Pearson, former Prime Minister of Canada. In 1956, at the time of the Suez Crisis, he invented peacekeeping for which he was awarded the 1957 Nobel Peace Prize.

The Centre (a division of the Canadian Institute of Strategic Studies), established by the Government of Canada in 1994, is funded, in part, by the Department of Foreign Affairs and International Trade and the Department of National Defence of Canada.
Le Centre (une division de l'Institut canadien d'études stratégiques) a été établi par le Gouvernement du Canada en 1994. Le soutien financier du Centre provient, en partie, des ministères des Affaires étrangères et du commerce international et de la défense nationale.

The Lester B. Pearson
Canadian International Peacekeeping
Training Centre

Le centre canadien international
Lester B. Pearson pour la formation
en maintien de la paix

THE CANADIAN PEACEKEEPING PRESS

The Canadian Peacekeeping Press, the publishing arm of the Pearson Peacekeeping Centre, has a number of publications of interest. These include: *UN Peace Operations and the Role of Japan* (edited by Alex Morrison and James Kiras, softcover, 123 pp., $20 + taxes and shipping); *UN Rapid Reaction Capabilities <<Les capacités de réaction rapide de l'ONU>>*, (edited by David Cox and Albert Legault, softcover, 219 pp., $25 + GST and shipping); and *Peacekeeping and the Coming Anarchy,* (the first title in the Pearson Paper series, the content of which was derived from a roundtable held at the Pearson Peacekeeping Centre in March 1995, edited by Alex Morrison and Dale Anderson, softcover, 72 pp., $15 + taxes and shipping).

Recent publications of the Canadian Peacekeeping Press include: *Theory, Doctrine and Practice of Conflict De-escalation in Peacekeeping Operations* (by David Last, softcover, 152 pp., $23.50 + taxes and shipping); *Facing the Future: Proceedings of the 1996 Canada-Japan Conference on Modern Peacekeeping* (edited by Alex Morrison, Ken Eyre and Roger Chiasson, softcover, 222 pp., $20 + GST and shipping); and *Seeds of Freedom: Personal Reflections on the Dawning of Democracy* (by Senator Al Graham, softcover, 288 pp., $30 + taxes and shipping).

To obtain a Publications Catalogue or for more information on the Canadian Peacekeeping Press, please contact:

James Kiras
Publications Manager
Pearson Peacekeeping Centre
Cornwallis Park, PO Box 100
Clementsport, NS B0S 1E0
Tel: (902) 638-8611 x 161
Fax: (902) 638-8576
Email: jkiras@ppc.cdnpeacekeeping.ns.ca
Website: http://www.cdnpeacekeeping.ns.ca

The Centre (a division of the Canadian Institute of Strategic Studies), established by the Government of Canada in 1994, is funded, in part, by the Department of Foreign Affairs and International Trade and the Department of National Defence of Canada.
Le Centre (une division de l'Institut canadien d'études stratégiques) a été établi par le Gouvernement du Canada en 1994. Le soutien financier du Centre provient, en partie, des ministères des Affaires étrangères et du commerce international et de la défense nationale.

THE CANADIAN INSTITUTE OF STRATEGIC STUDIES

President, Don Macnamara, OMM, CD, MA
Executive Director, Alex Morrison, MSC, CD, MA

The Canadian Institute of Strategic Studies (CISS) provides the forum and is the vehicle to stimulate the research, study, analysis and discussion of the strategic implications of major national and international issues, events and trends as they affect Canada and Canadians.

The CISS is currently working independently or in conjunction with related organizations in a number of fields, including Canadian security and sovereignty; arms control and disarmament; Canada-US security cooperation; Maritime and Arctic security; Asia-Pacific security studies; social issues such as drugs, poverty and justice; national and international environmental issues; and regional and global trade issues.

CISS publications include:

Free with membership:

The Canadian Strategic Forecast
Seminar Proceedings
Strategic Datalinks
Strategic Profile Canada
The CISS Bulletin
Peacekeeping and International
 Relations (6 issues per year)
Canadian Defence Quarterly
(4 issues per year)

By Subscription:

The McNaughton Papers (The Canadian Journal of Strategic Studies — 2 issues per year)

The CISS is a non-profit, non-partisan voluntary organization which maintains an independent posture and does not advocate any particular interest.

For membership, seminar and publications information, please contact:

The Canadian Institute of Strategic Studies
Box 2321
2300 Yonge Street, Suite 402
Toronto, ON M4P 1E4
Tel: (416) 322-8128 Fax: (416) 322-8129
Email: ciss@inforamp.net
Internet: http://www.ciss.ca